The

Norton Scores

An Anthology for Listening

Fifth Edition

VOLUME II

The Norton Scores

An Anthology for Listening

❑

Fifth Edition
in Two Volumes

VOLUME II:
Schubert to the Present

Edited by
Roger Kamien
Professor of Music,
Hebrew University, Jerusalem, Israel

W · W · NORTON & COMPANY
New York   London

Acknowledgments

The texts for items 1, 10, and 18 are from *The Ring of Words* by Philip L. Miller. Reprinted by permission of Doubleday & Company, Inc., and Philip L. Miller.
Item 13: Translation of the libretto © 1967 by William Mann. Reprinted by kind permission of Deutsche Grammophon GmbH, Hamburg.
Libretto for items 20 and 22 reprinted through the courtesy of Decca International.
The text translation for item 34 is by Sarah E. Soulsby, London, 1981. Reprinted through the courtesy of London Records, a Division of PolyGram Classics, Inc.
The text translation for item 35 is by Steven Ledbetter.
The text translation for item 48 is from Federico García Lorca, *Selected Poems*. Copyright 1955 by New Directions Publishing Corporation. Reprinted by permission of New Directions Publishing Corporation.

ISBN 0-393-95747-0

W. W. Norton & Company, Inc., 500 Fifth Avenue, New York, N.Y. 10110
W. W. Norton & Company, Ltd., 10 Coptic Street, London WC1A 1PU

6 7 8 9 0

Contents

◻

Preface

◻

This anthology is designed for use in introductory music courses, where the ability to read music is not a prerequisite. The unique system of highlighting employed in this book enables students to follow full orchestral scores after about one hour of instruction. This system also has the advantage of permitting students who *can* read music to perceive every aspect of the score. It is felt that our system of highlighting will be of greater pedagogical value than artificially condensed scores, which restrict the student's vision to pre-selected elements of the music. The use of scores in introductory courses makes the student's listening experience more intense and meaningful, and permits the instructor to discuss music in greater depth.

The works included in this Fifth Edition have been chosen from among those most frequently studied in introductory courses. The selections range from Gregorian chant to the present day, and represent a wide variety of forms, genres, and performing media. To make this Fifth Edition reflect today's concert repertory more closely, increased emphasis has been placed on instrumental and secular music of earlier periods and on music of the present century. A majority of the pieces are given in their entirety, while the others are represented by complete movements or sections particularly suitable for classroom study. Scenes from operas and some choral works are presented in vocal score, while all others are reprinted in their full original form. In the case of a few recent works, obstacles of copyright or practicality prevented inclusion of a complete score. This anthology may be used independently, or along with any introductory text. The publishers have prepared a set of recordings to accompany *The Norton Scores*.

A few words about the highlighting system employed in the full scores: Each system of score is covered with a light gray screen, and the most prominent line in the music at any given point is spotlighted by a white band (see No. 1 in sample on page *x*). In cases where two or more simultaneous lines are equally prominent, they are each highlighted. Cohen a musical line continues from one system or page to the next, the white highlighting band ends with a wedge shape at the right-hand margin, and its continuation begins with a reverse wedge shape (see No. 2 in sample). By following these white bands in sequence through the score, the listener will perceive the notes corresponding to the most audible lines. Naturally, the highlighting will not *always* correspond with the most prominent instruments in a specific recording, for performances differ in their emphasis of particular lines. In such cases, we have highlighted those parts that, in our opinion, *should* emerge most clearly. (There are occasional passages in complex twentieth-century works where no single line represents the musical continuity. In such passages we have drawn the listener's attention to the most audible musical events while endeavoring to keep the highlighting as simple as possible.) To facilitate the following of highlighted scores, a narrow white band running the full width of the page has been placed between systems when there is more than one on a page.

It must be emphasized that we do not seek here to *analyze* melodic structure, contrapuntal texture, or any other aspect of the music. The highlighting may break off before the end of a phrase when the entrance of another part is more audible, and during long-held notes the attention will usually be drawn to more rhythmically active parts. The highlighting technique has been used primarily for instrumental music; in vocal works, the text printed under the music provides a firm guideline for the novice score-reader.

A few suggestions for the use of this anthology may be found useful:

1. The rudiments of musical notation should be introduced with a view to preparing the student to associate audible melodic contours with their written equivalents. It is more important for beginning students to recognize rising and falling lines, and long and short notes, than to identify specific pitches or rhythms. It is helpful to explain the function of a tie, and the layout of a full score.

2. Before listening to a work, it is best for students to familiarize themselves with the names and abbreviations for instruments used in that particular score (a glossary of instrumental names and abbreviations will be found at the conclusion of the book). We have retained the Italian, German, French, and English names used in the scores reproduced in this anthology. This exposure to a wide range of terminology will prepare students for later encounters with scores.

3. Students should be careful to notice whether there is more than one system on a page of score. They should be alerted for tempo changes, repeat signs, and *da capo* indications. Since performances often differ, it is helpful for the instructor to forewarn the class about the specific repeats made or not made in the recordings used for listening.

4. When a piece is very fast or difficult, it is helpful to listen once without a score.

5. It is best to begin with music that is relatively simple to follow: e.g. (in approximate order of difficulty) Handel, "Comfort ye" from *Messiah;* the first and third movements of Mozart's *Eine kleine Nachtmusik;* and the second movement of Haydn's Symphony No. 104 in D major (*London*).

6. Important thematic material and passages that are difficult to follow should be pointed out in advance and played either on the recording or at the piano. (We have found that rapid sections featuring two simultaneously highlighted instruments sometimes present difficulties for the students—e.g. Beethoven, Symphony No. 5, first movement, m. 65 ff.)

We have attempted to keep the highlighted bands simple in shape while showing as much of the essential slurs and dynamic indication as possible. Occasionally, because of the layout of the original score, stray stems and slurs will intrude upon the white area and instrumental directions will be excluded from the highlighting. (Naturally, the beginning of a highlighted area will not always carry a dynamic or similar indication, as the indication may have occurred measures earlier when the instrument in question was not the most prominent.) As students become more experienced in following the scores, they can be encouraged to direct their attention outside the highlighted areas, and with practice should eventually develop the skill to read conventional scores.

I should like to record here my great debt to the late Nathan Broder, who originated the system of highlighting employed here and whose advice and counsel were invaluable. My thanks go also to Mr. David Hamilton, and to Claire Brook and Juli Goldfein of W. W. Norton, for many helpful suggestions. I am most grateful to my wife, Anita, who worked with me on every aspect of the book. She is truly the co-editor of this anthology.

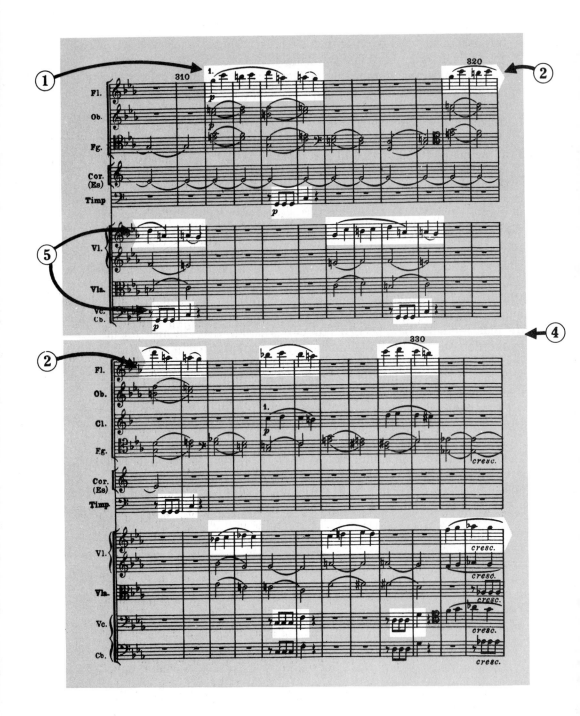

HOW TO FOLLOW THE
HIGHLIGHTED SCORES

1. The most prominent line in the music at any given time is highlighted by a white band.
2. When a musical line continues from one system (group of staffs) or page to the next, the white highlighted band ends with a wedge shape, and its continuation begins with a reverse wedge shape.
3. By following the highlighted bands in sequence through the score, the listener will perceive the notes corresponding to the most audible lines.
4. A narrow white band running the full width of the page separates one system from another when there is more than one on a page. It is very important to be alert for these separating bands.
5. When two or more lines are equally prominent, they are each highlighted. When encountering such passages for the first time, it is sometimes best to focus on only one of the lines.

The

Norton Scores

An Anthology for Listening

Fifth Edition

Volume II

I. Franz Schubert (1797-1828),

Erlkönig, D. 328 (1815)    5A/1   II/1/1

Translation

Wer reitet so spät durch Nacht
  und Wind?
Es ist der Vater mit seinem Kind;
er hat den Knaben wohl in dem Arm,
er fasst ihn sicher, er hält ihn warm.

"Mein Sohn, was birgst du so bang dein
  Gesicht?"
"Siehst, Vater, du den Erlkönig nicht?
den Erlenkönig mit Kron' und Schweif?"
"Mein Sohn, es ist ein Nebelstreif."

"Du liebes Kind, komm, geh' mit mir!
gar schöne Spiele spiel' ich mit dir;
manch' bunte Blumen sind an dem Strand;
meine Mutter hat manch' gülden Gewand."

"Mein Vater, mein Vater, und hörest du
  nicht,
was Erlenkönig mir leise verspricht?"
"Sei ruhig, bleibe ruhig, mein Kind;
in dürren Blättern säuselt der Wind."

"Willst, feiner Knage, du mit mir geh'n?
meine Töchter sollen dich warten schön;
meine Töchter führen den nächtlichen
  Reih'n
und wiegen und tanzen und singen dich ein."

"Mein Vater, mein Vater, und siehst du nicht
  dort
Erlkönigs Töchter am düstern Ort?"
"Mein Sohn, mein Sohn, ich seh' es genau,
es scheinen die alten Weiden so grau."

"Ich liebe dich, mich reizt deine schöne
  Gestalt,
und bist du nicht willig, so brauch' ich
  Gewalt."
"Mein Vater, mein Vater, jetzt fasst er
  mich an!
Erlkönig hat mir ein Leid's gethan!"

Dem Vater grauset's, er reitet geschwind,
er hält in Armen das ächzende Kind,
erreicht den Hof mit Müh' und Noth:
in seinem Armen das Kind war todt!

  JOHANN WOLFGANG VON GOETHE

Who rides so late through the night
  and the wind?
It is the father with his child;
he folds the boy close in his arms,
he clasps him securely, he holds him warmly.

'My son, who do you hide your face so
  anxiously?"
"Father, don't you see the Erlking?
The Erlking with his crown and his train?"
"My son, it is a streak of mist."

"Dear child, come, go with me!
I'll play the prettiest games with you.
Many colored flowers grow along the shore;
my mother has many golden garments."

"My father, my father, and don't you
  hear
the Erlking whispering promises to me?"
"Be quiet, stay quiet, my child;
the wind is rustling in the dead leaves."

"My handsome boy, will you come with me?
My daughters shall wait upon you;
my daughters lead off in the dance every
  night,
and cradle and dance and sing you to sleep."

"My father, my father, and don't you
  see there
the Erlking's daughters in the shadows?"
"My son, my son, I see it clearly;
the old willows look so gray."

"I love you, your beautiful figure
  delights me!
And if you are not willing, then I
  shall use force!"
"My father, my father, now he is taking
  hold of me!
The Erlking has hurt me!"

The father shudders, he rides swiftly on;
he holds in his arms the groaning child,
he reaches the courtyard weary and anxious:
in his arms the child was dead.

  PHILIP L. MILLER

2. Schubert

Symphony No. 8 in B minor, D. 759, (*Unfinished*), First movement (1822) S2B/2 S2/34

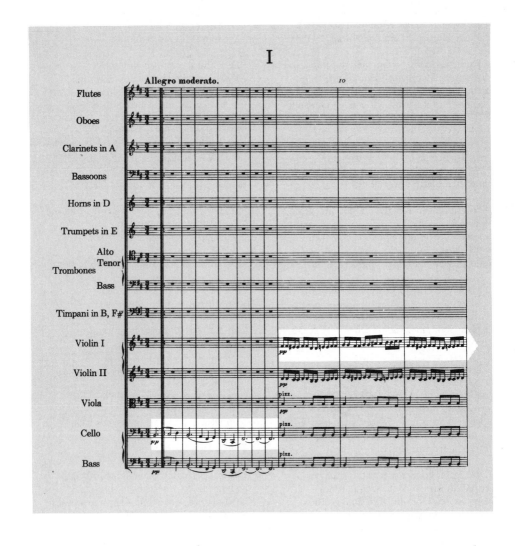

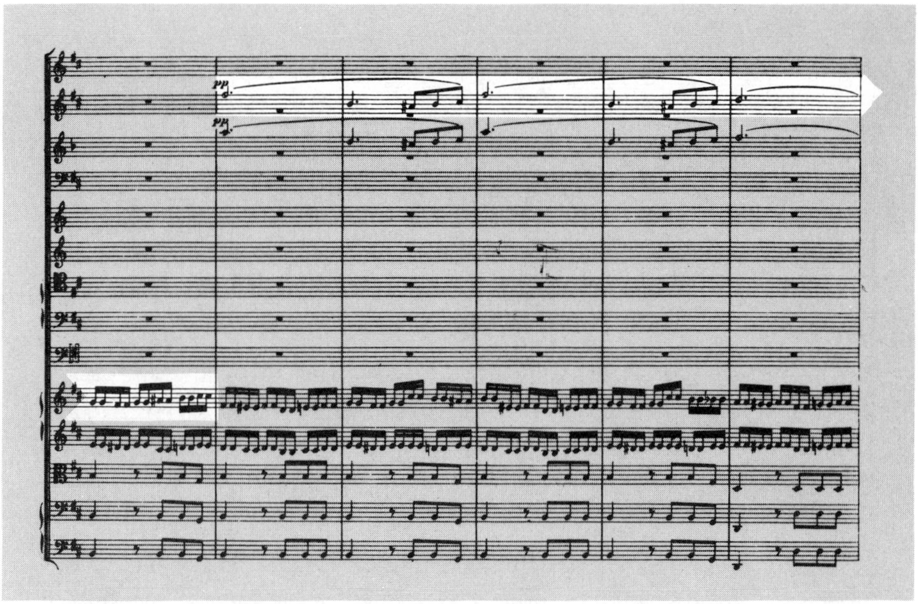
pp
pp

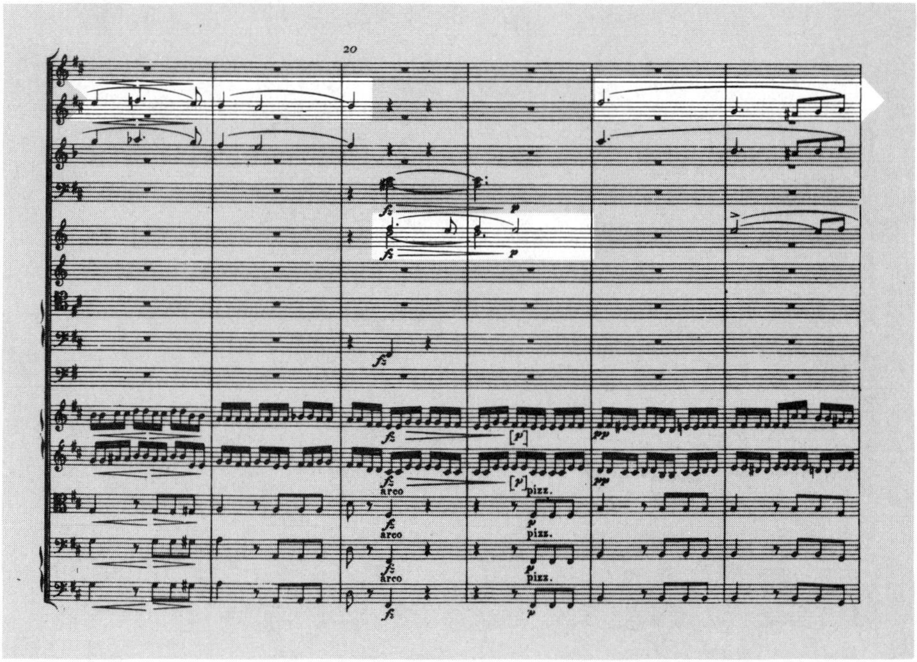
20
fz
p
[p]
pp
arco
pizz.

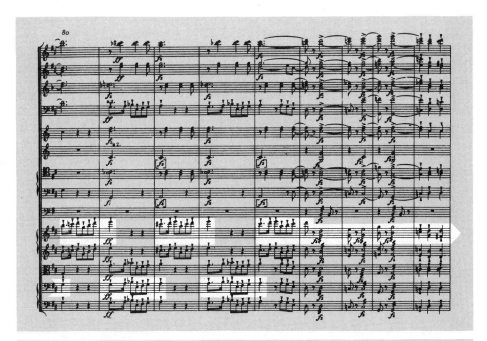

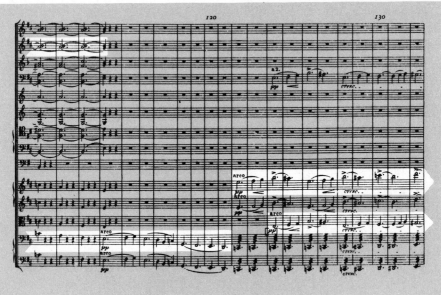

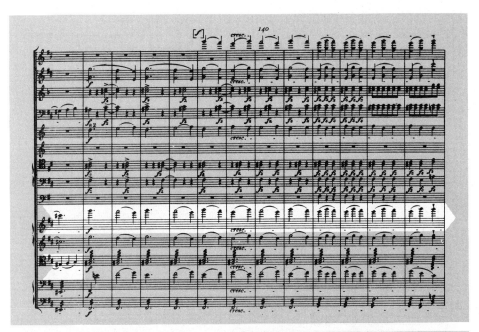

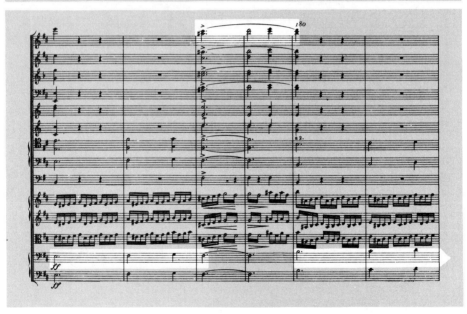

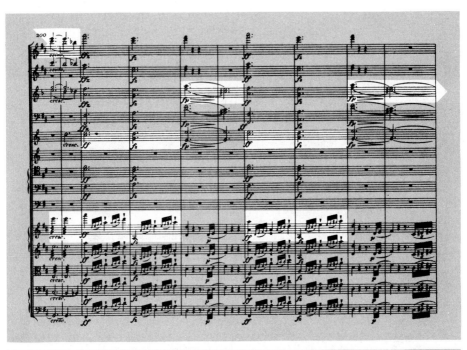

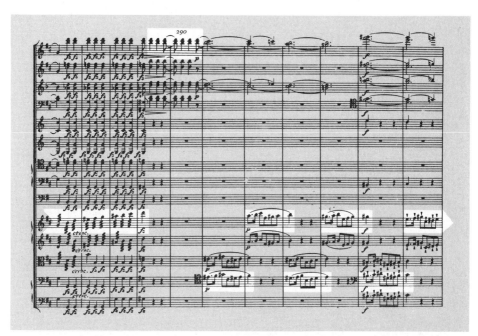

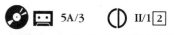

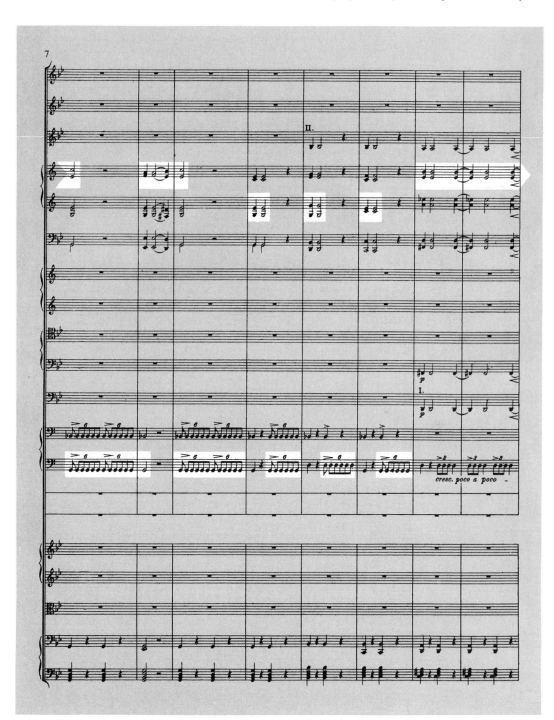

15
50
Clar.
Corni
Fag.
unis.
Soli
Ctti
Tr.
Tromb.
Oph. I.
Timp.
cresc.
cresc. molto
pizz.
Viol.
arco
unis.
dim.
50

26
Cor. III. IV.
Fag.
cresc
Timp.
Soli
Viol.
Vello. e C.B.
unis.
dim.

75

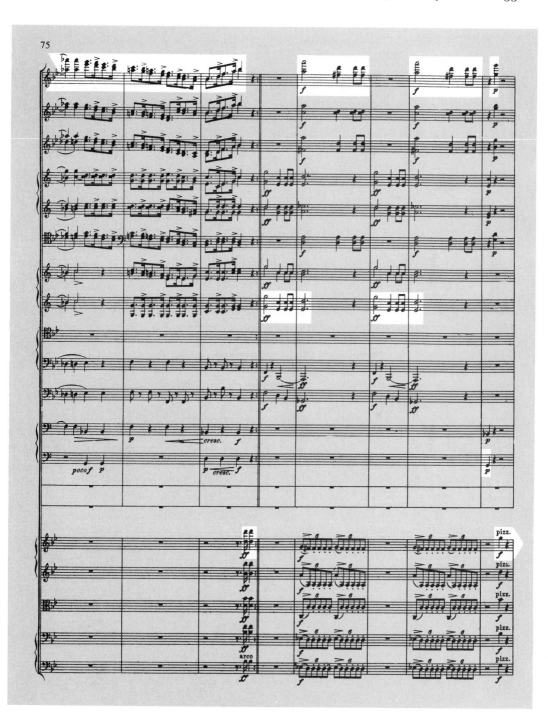

83
54
I.
Soli
Soli
(>)
II.
Oph. I.
Soli
Soli
poco f
f cresc.
cresc.
Cinelli
Solo
Gr. Tamb.
Solo
arco
pizz.
cresc.
54

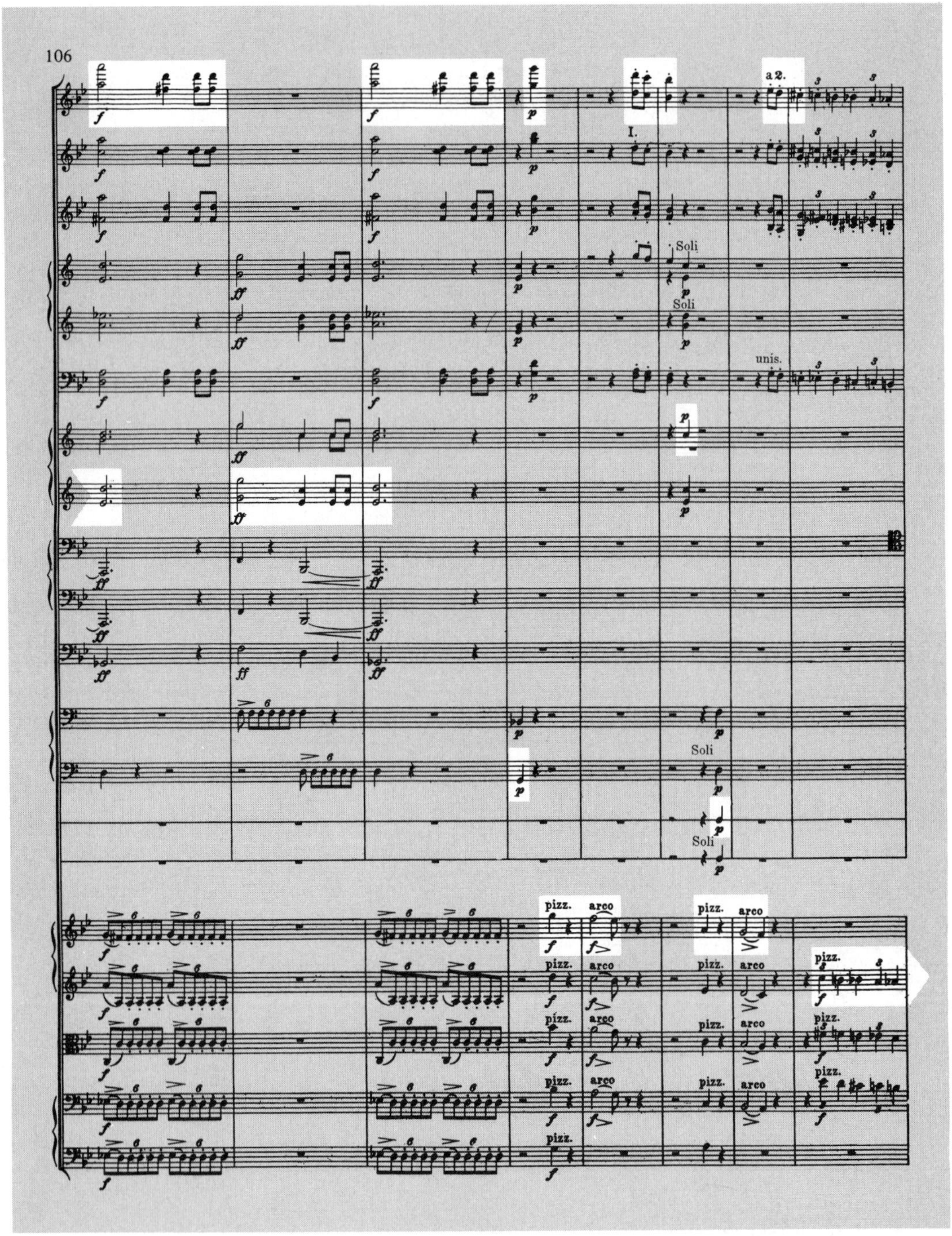
106
a 2.
I.
Soli
Soli
unis.
Soli
Soli
pizz.
arco
pizz.
arco
pizz.

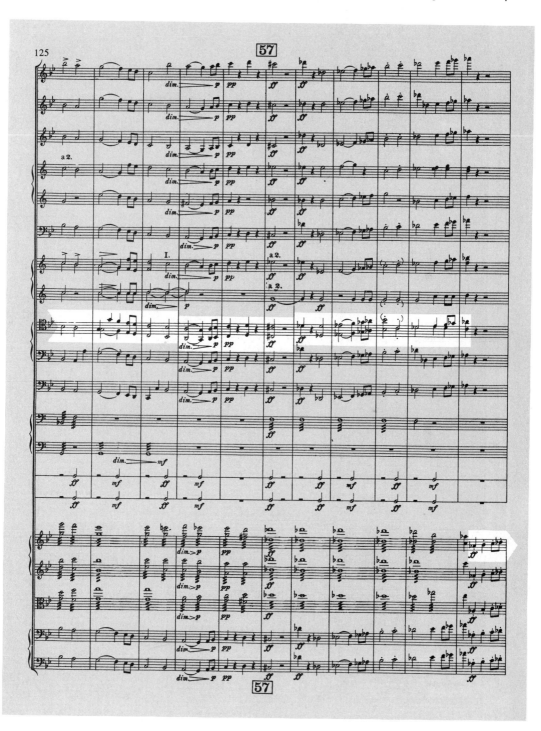

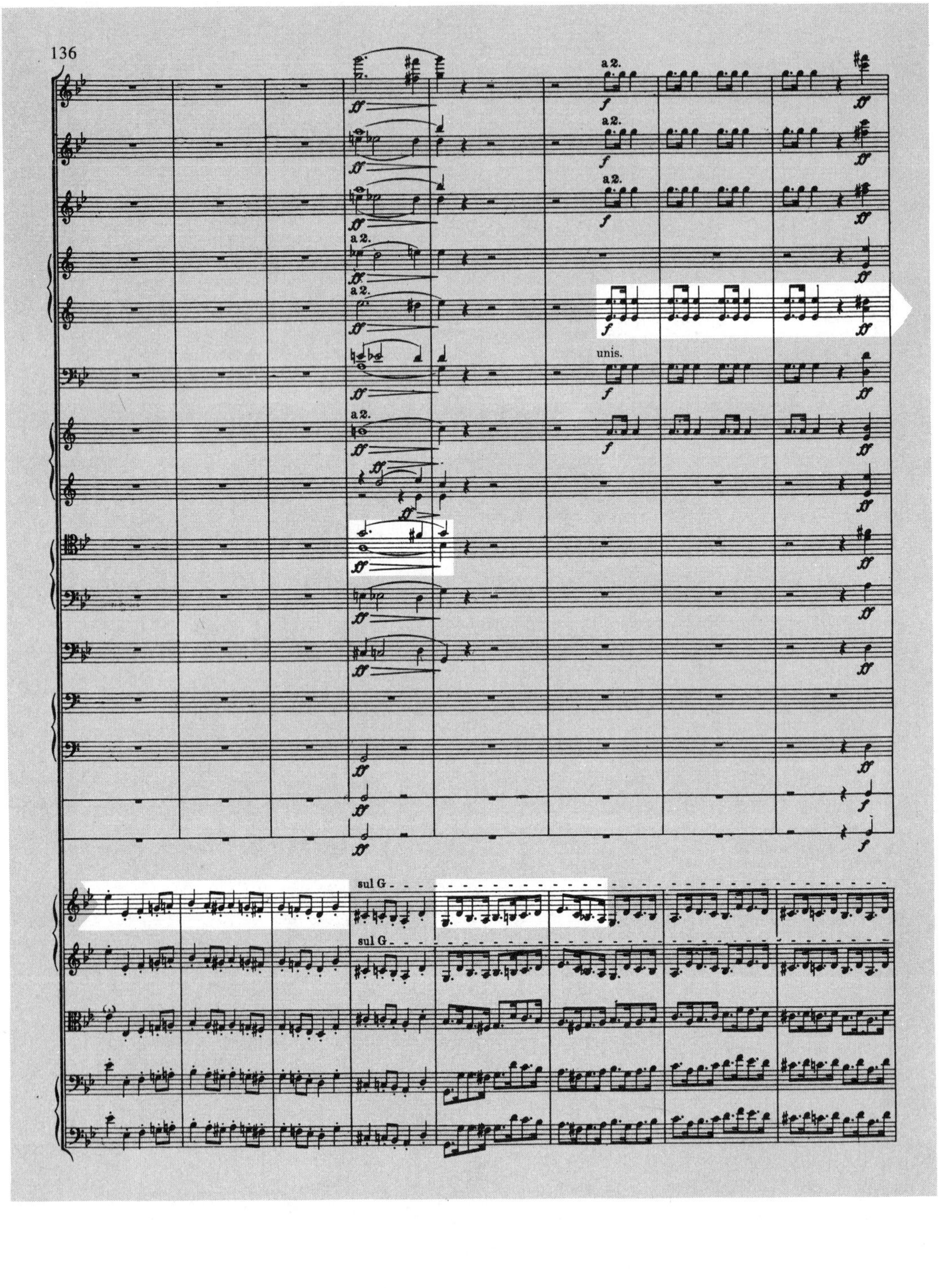
136
a 2.
unis.
sul G

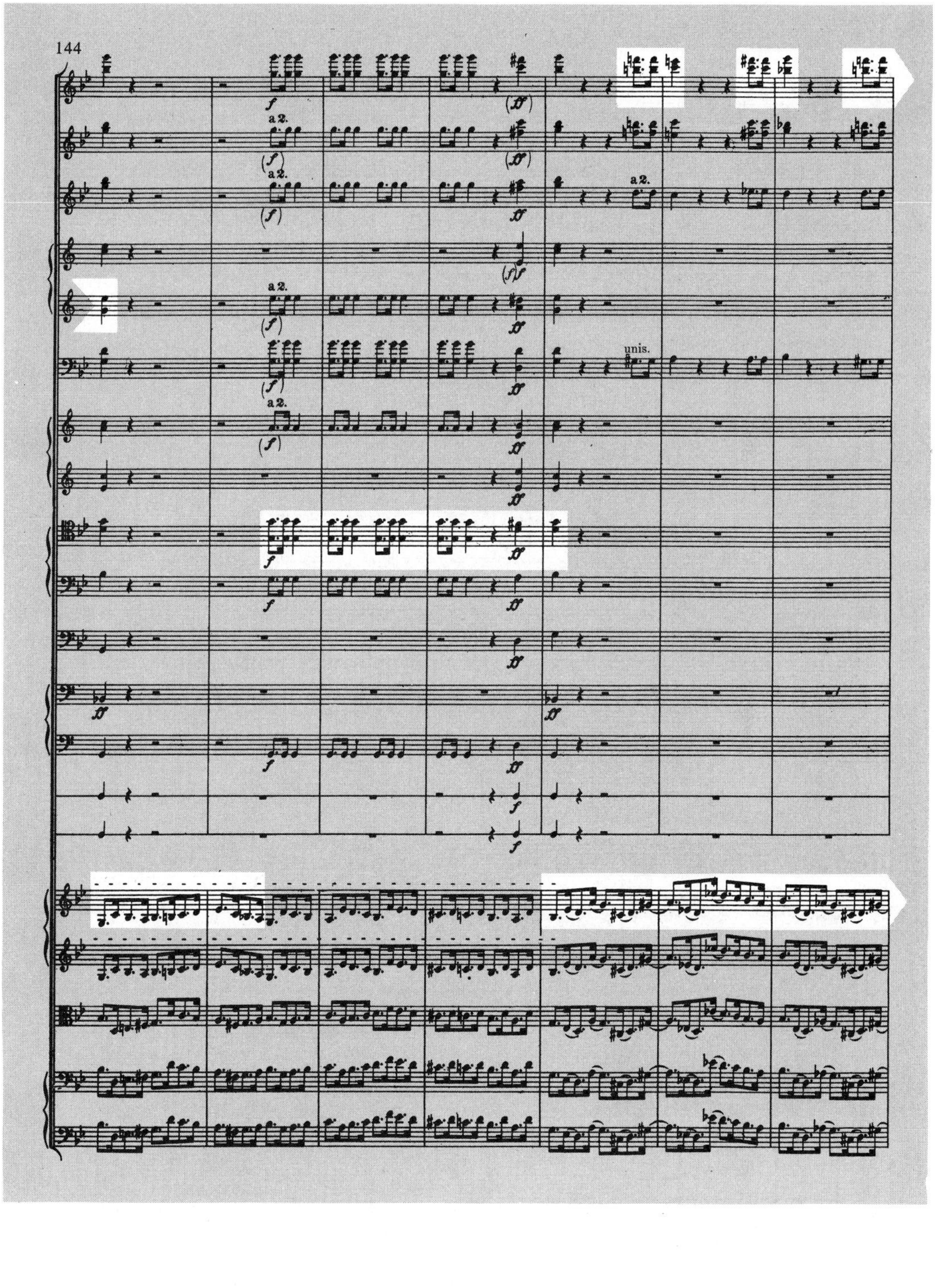
144
a 2.
a 2.
a 2.
a 2.
unis.
a 2.

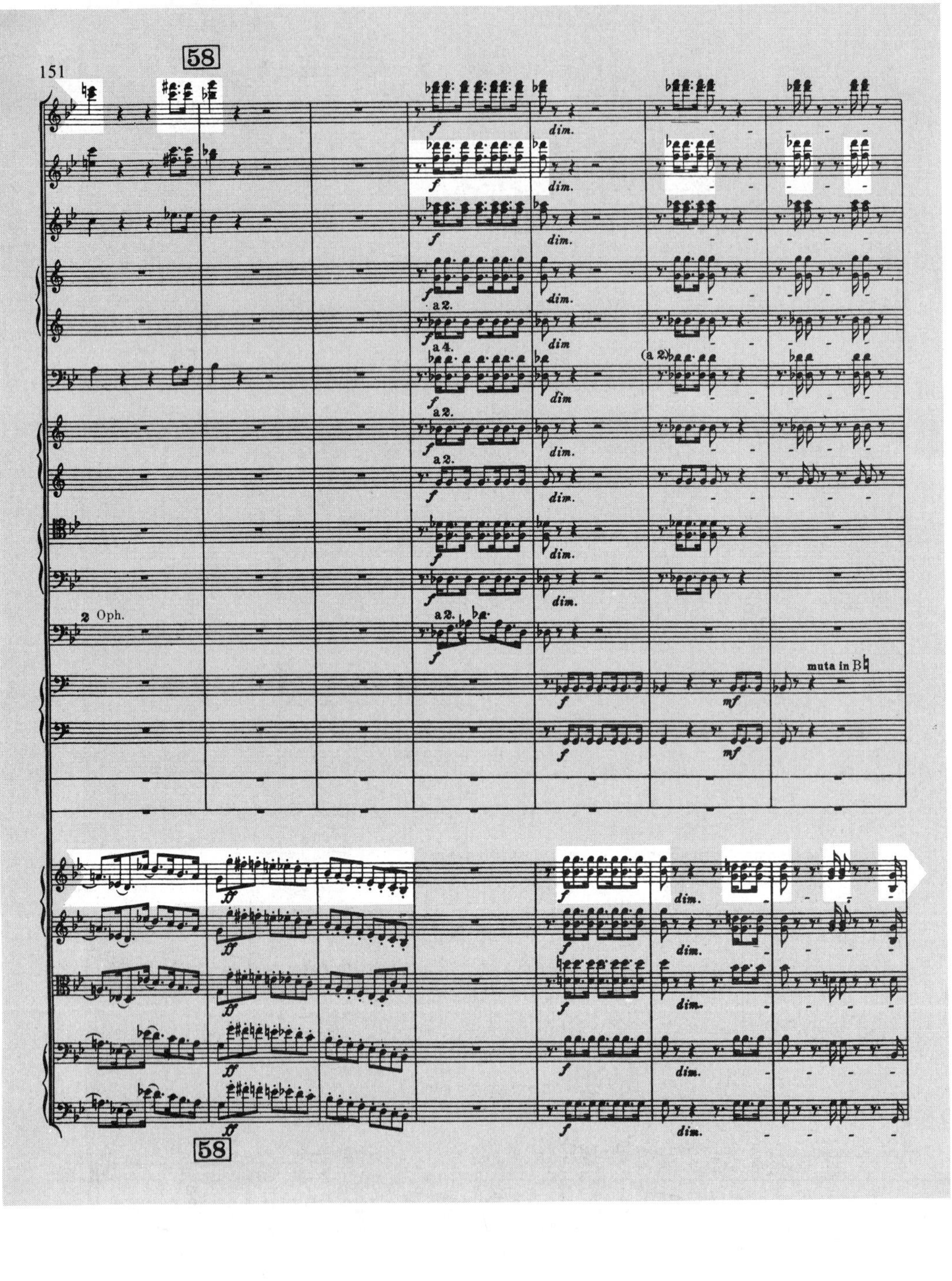
151
58
f
dim.
a 2.
a 4.
(a 2)
2 Oph.
muta in B♮
mf
ff
58

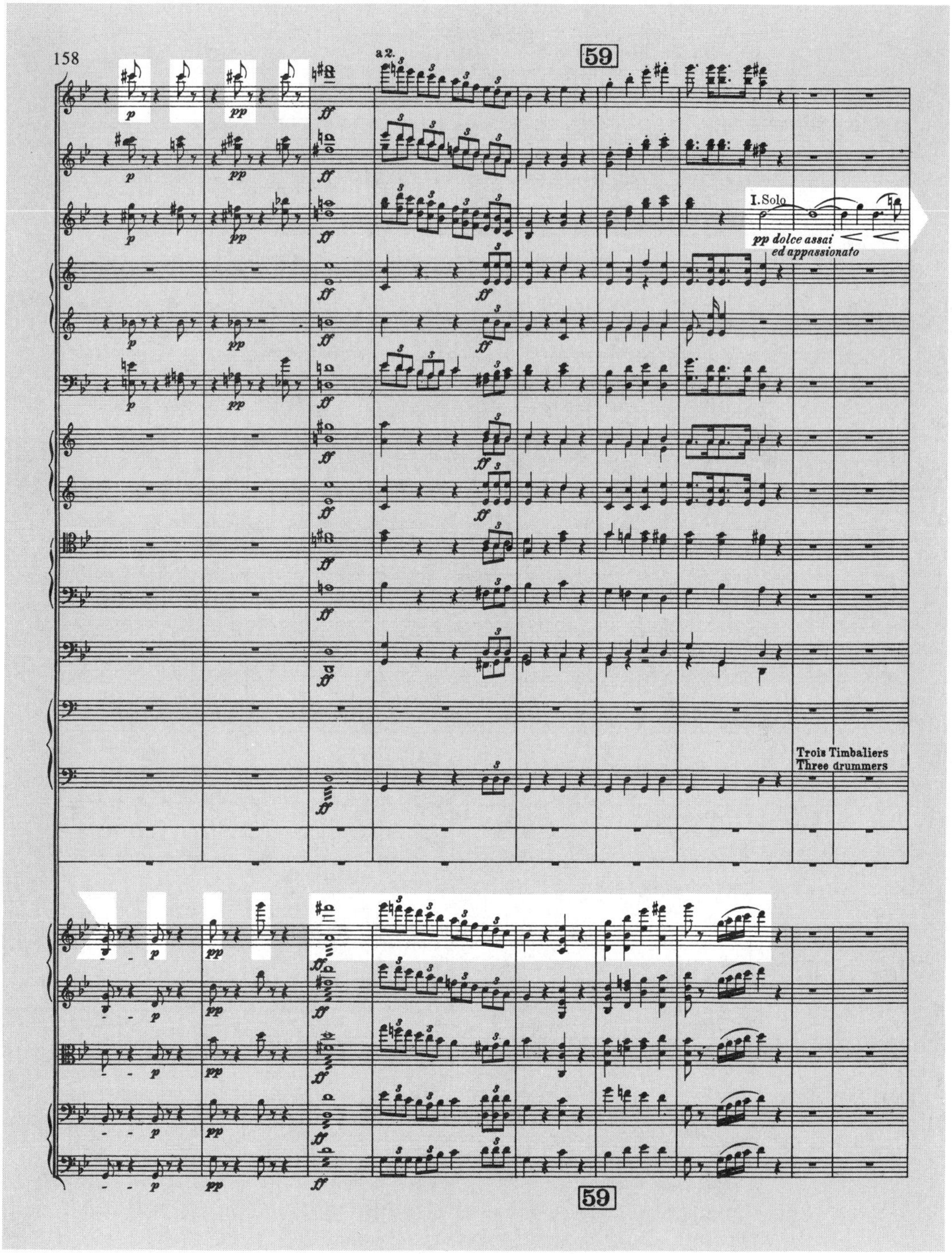
158
a 2.
59
I. Solo
pp dolce assai
ed appassionato
Trois Timbaliers
Three drummers
59

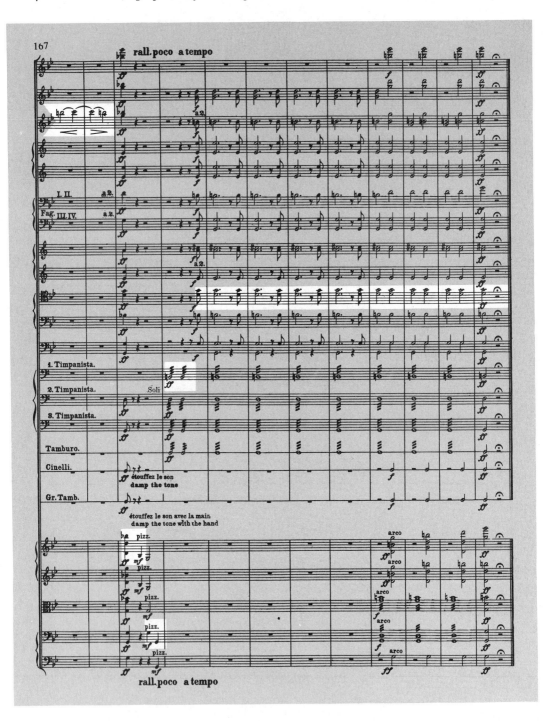

V

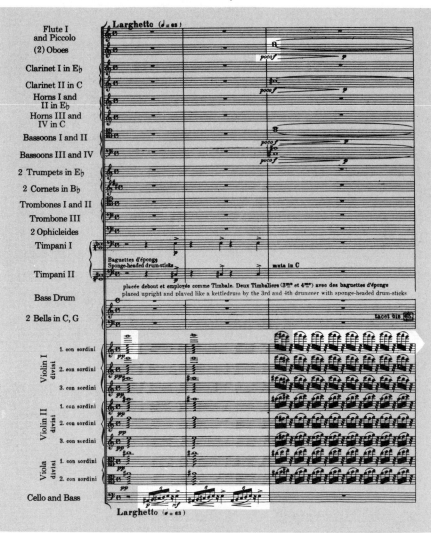

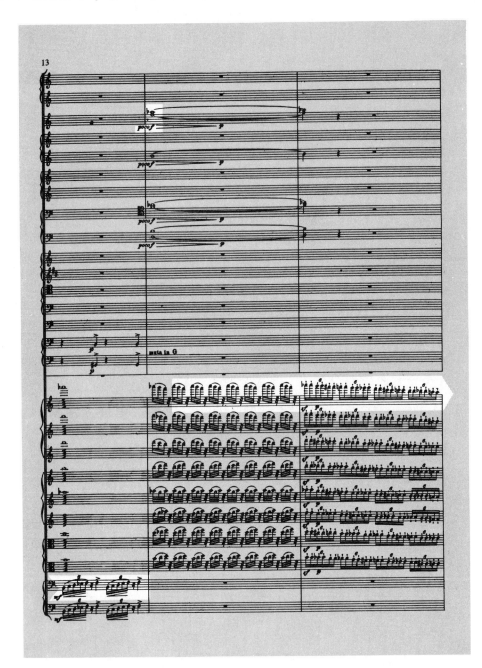

21
Allegro (♩. = 112)
Allegro assai (𝅝 = 76)
Solo lointain
distant
ppp
cresc.
a 2.
ouvert avec les cylindres
open, with valves
1.
p cresc. poco a poco
Sur les deux timbales
cresc. poco a poco
sans sourdine
sans sourdine
Allegro (♩. = 112)
Allegro assai (𝅝 = 76)

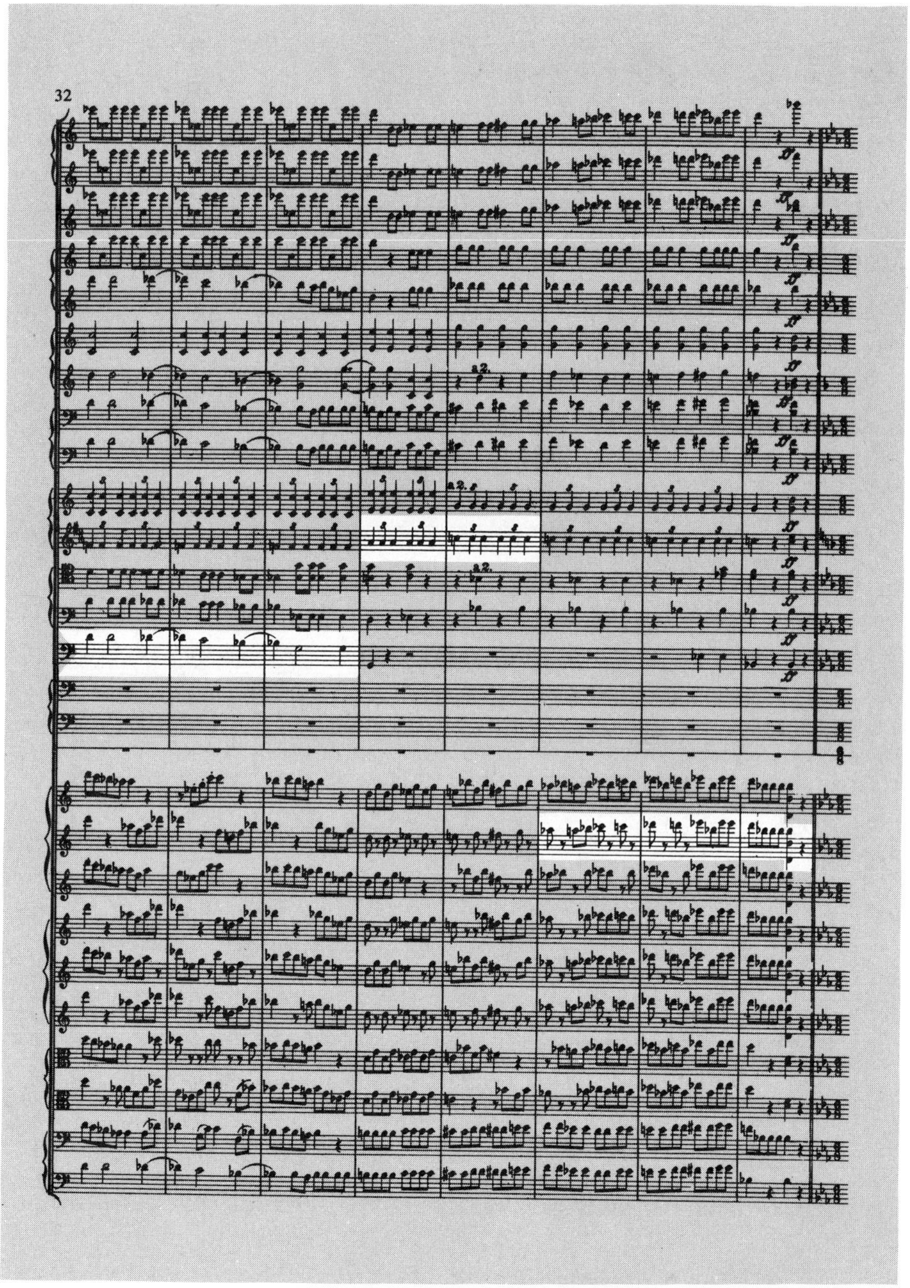
32
a2.
a2.

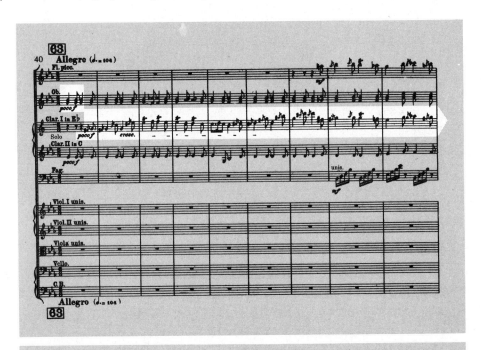

67
Fl.
Fl. picc.
Ob.
Clar.
a 2.
Cor.
unis.
Fag.
Tr.
C^tti
Tromb.
Oph.
Timp.
Viol.

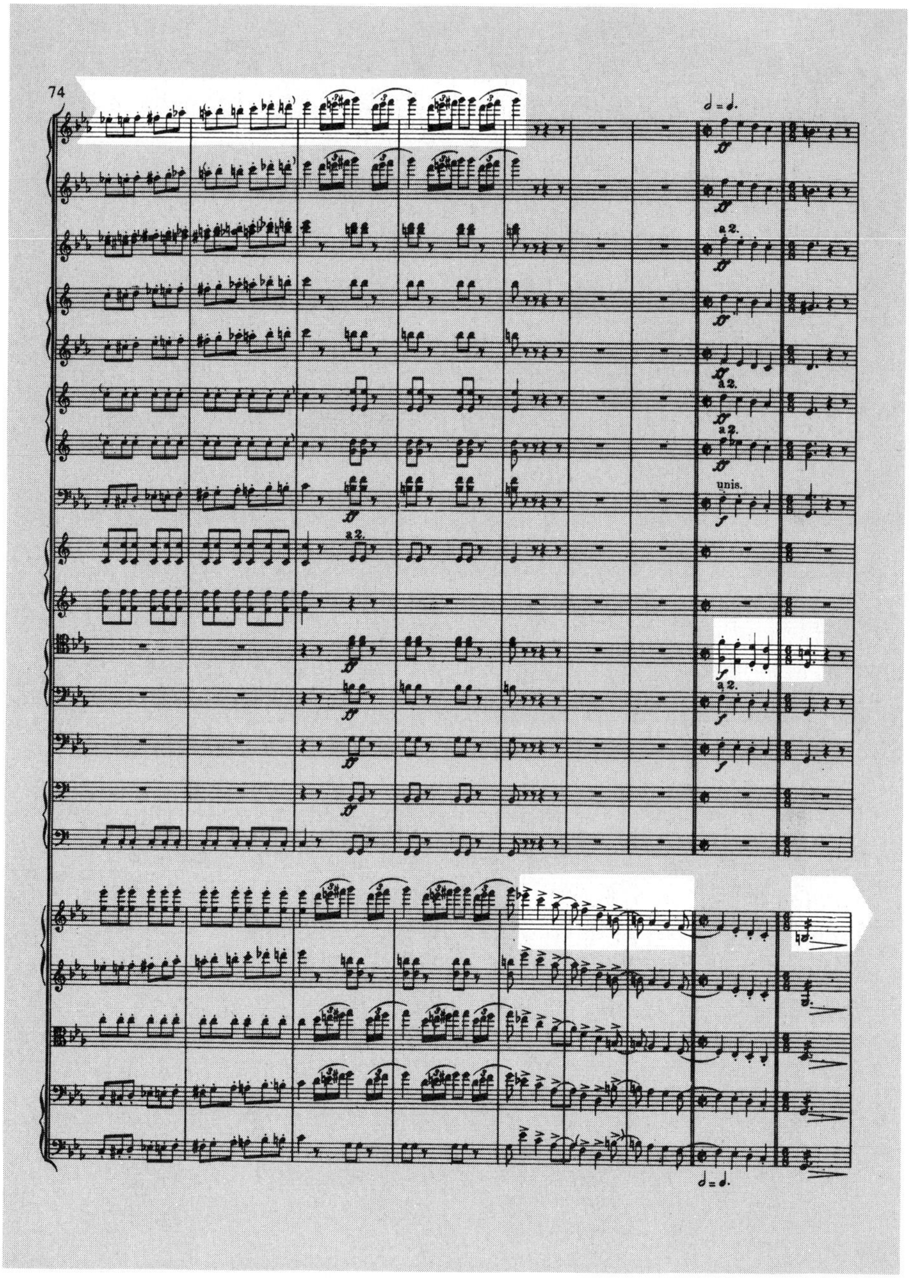
74
𝅗𝅥 = 𝅗𝅥.
a 2.
a 2.
a 2.
unis.
a 2.
a 2.
𝅗𝅥 = 𝅗𝅥.

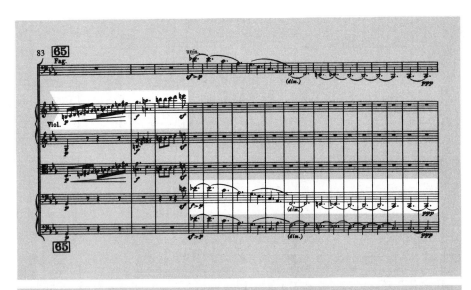

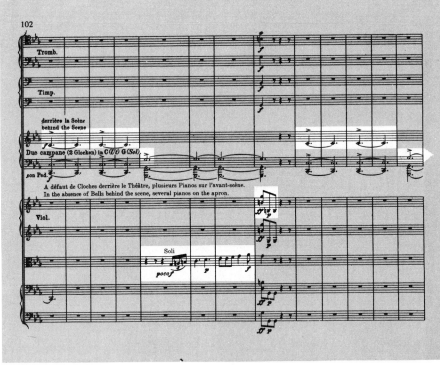

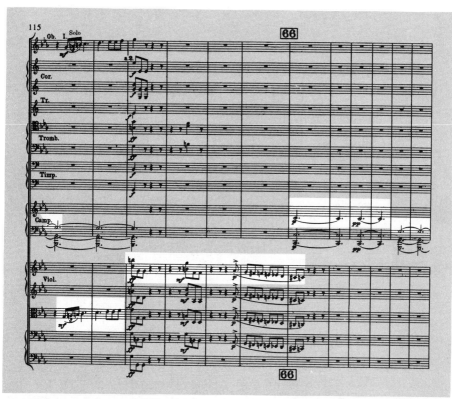

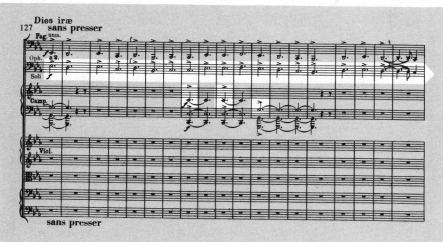

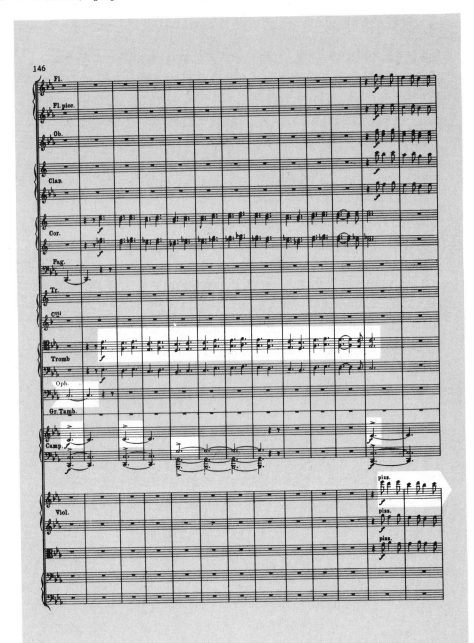

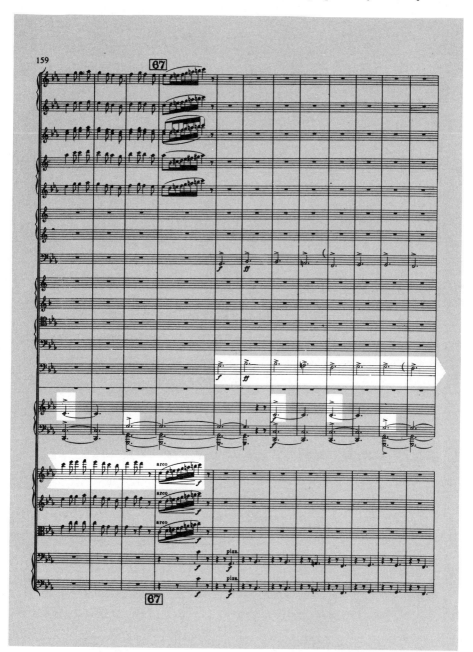

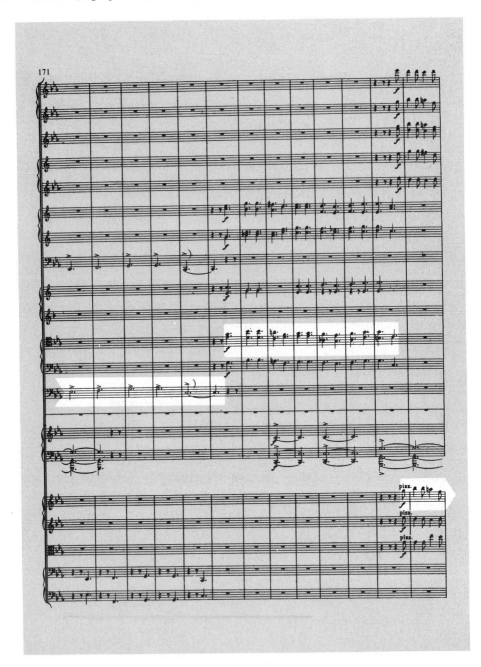

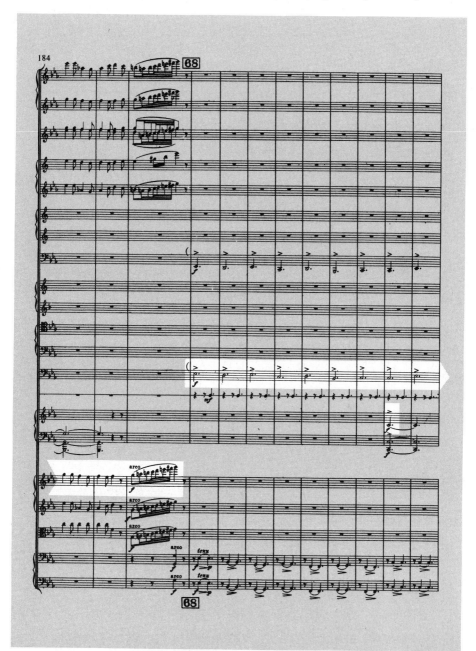

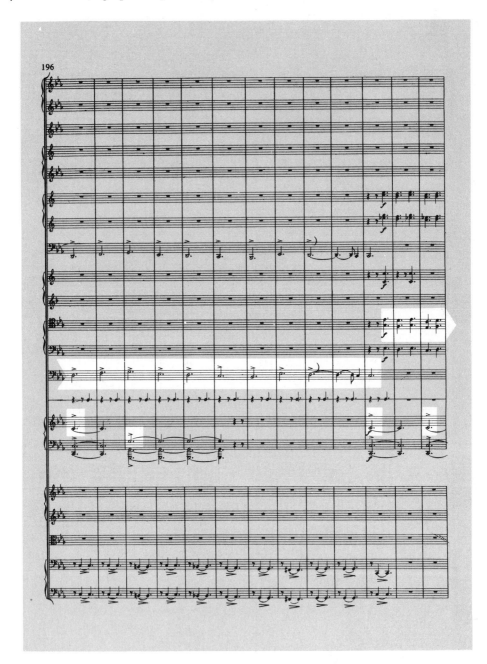

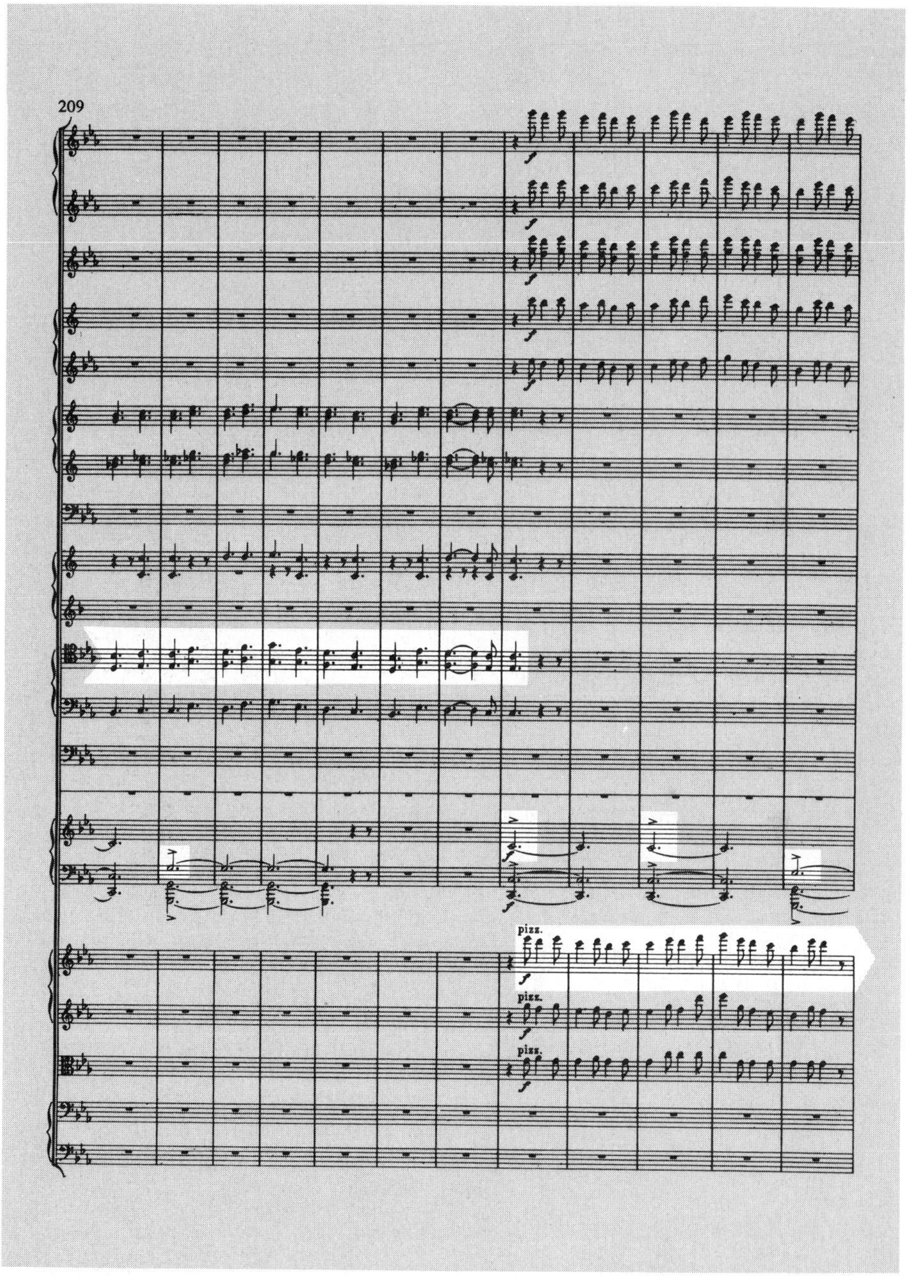
209
pizz.
pizz.
pizz.

Ronde du Sabbat
Witches' round dance
Un peu retenu

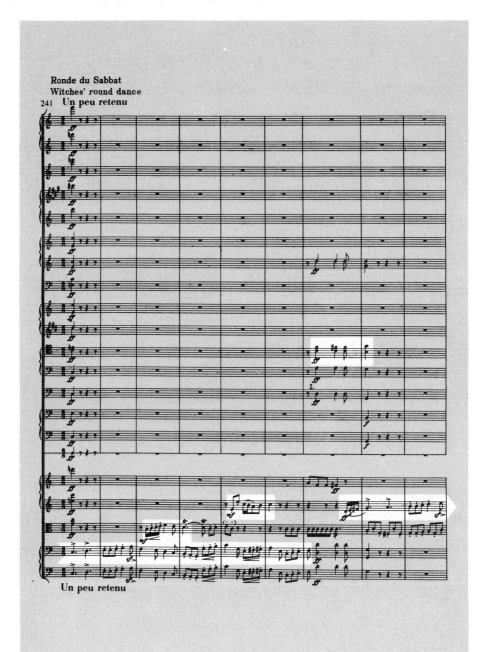

Un peu retenu

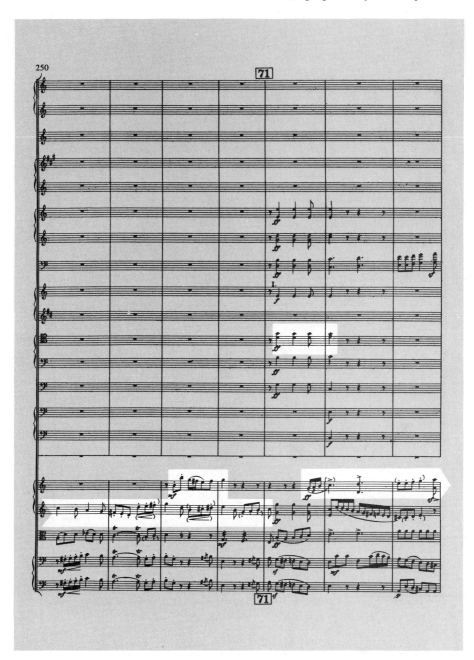

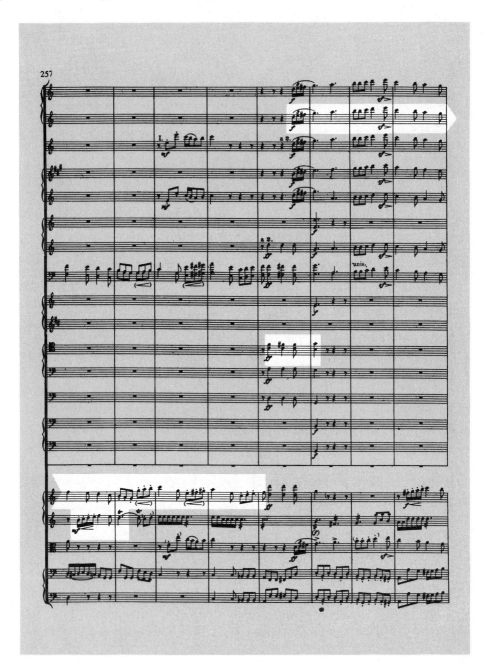

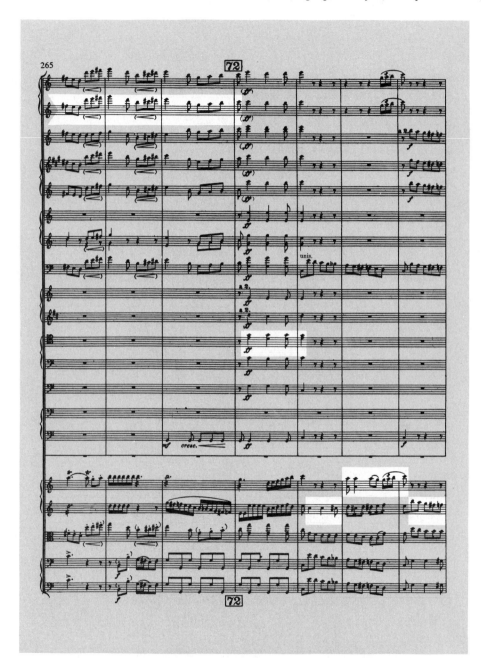

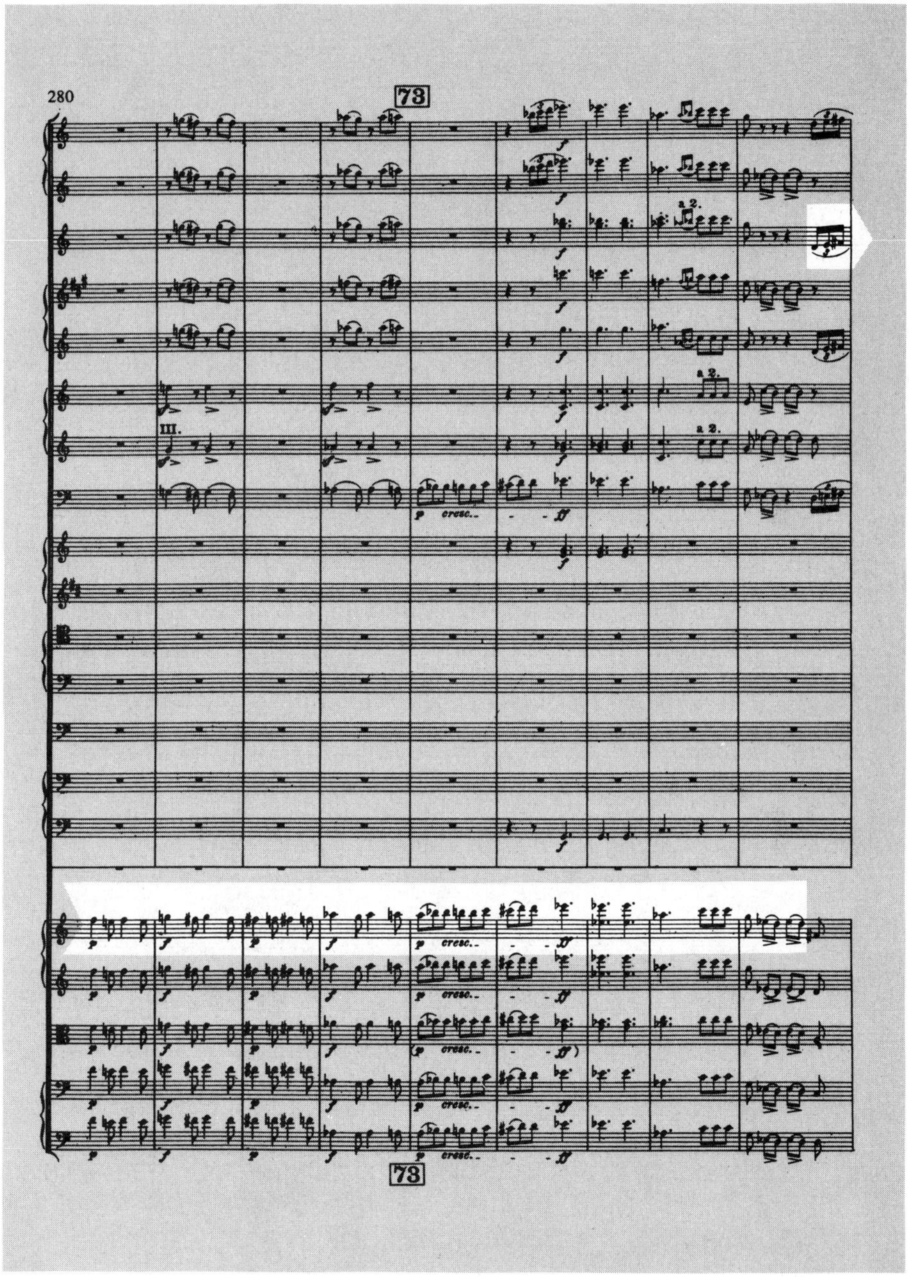
280
73
III.
a 2.
a 2.
a 2.
cresc.
cresc.
cresc.
cresc.
cresc.
cresc.
73

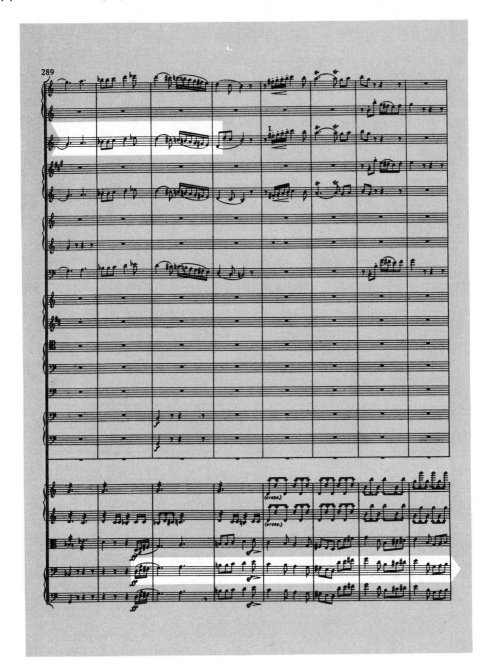

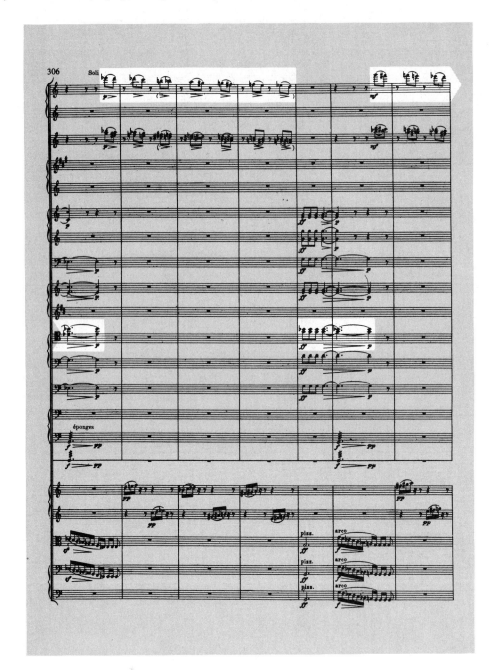

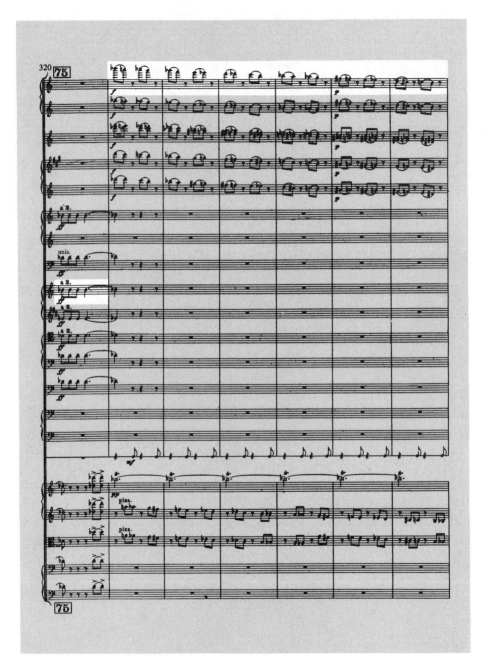

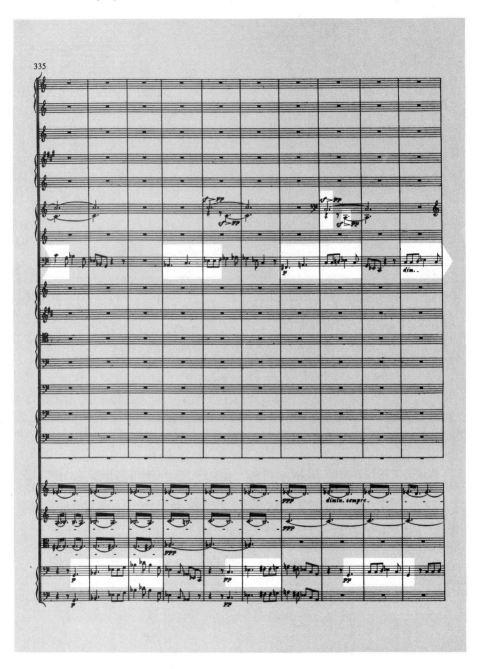

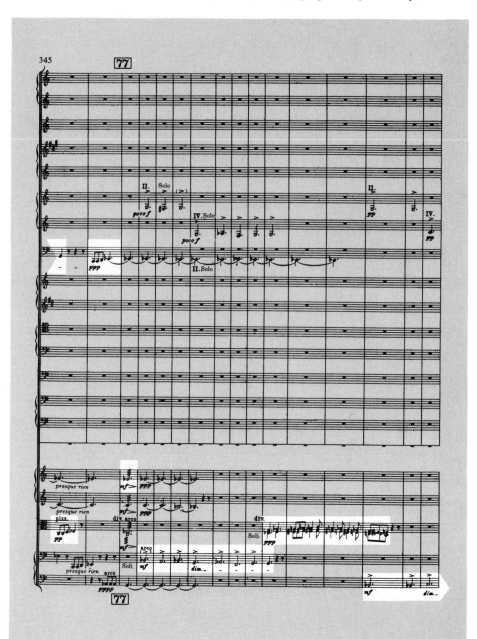

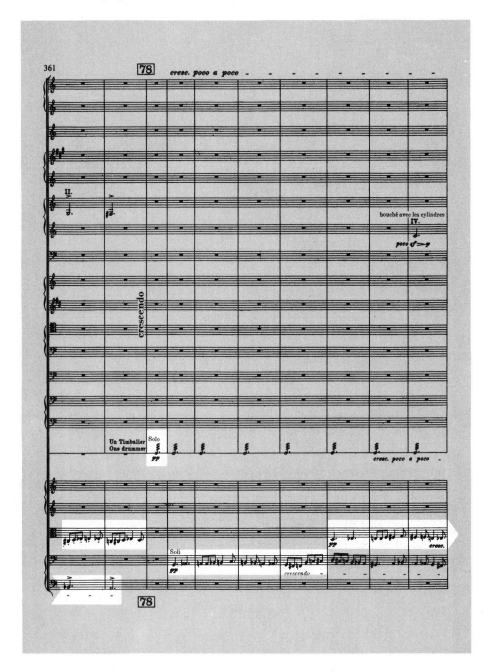

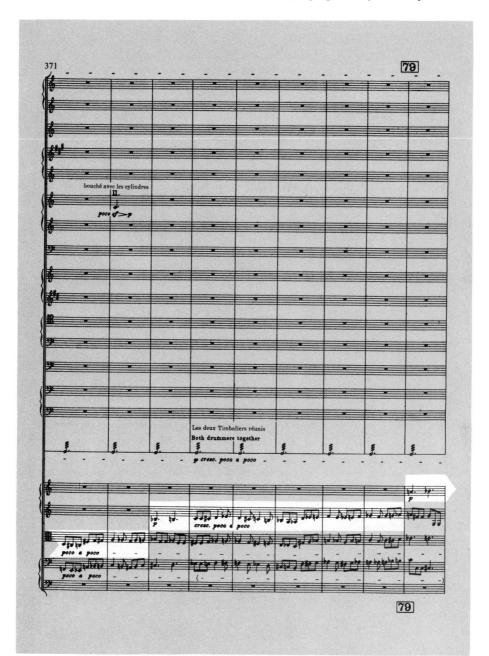

380
cresc.
cresc. sempre
cresc. poco a poco
mf
cresc sempre
cresc. (poco a poco)
f cresc. sempre
(cresc. poco a poco)
cresc. sempre

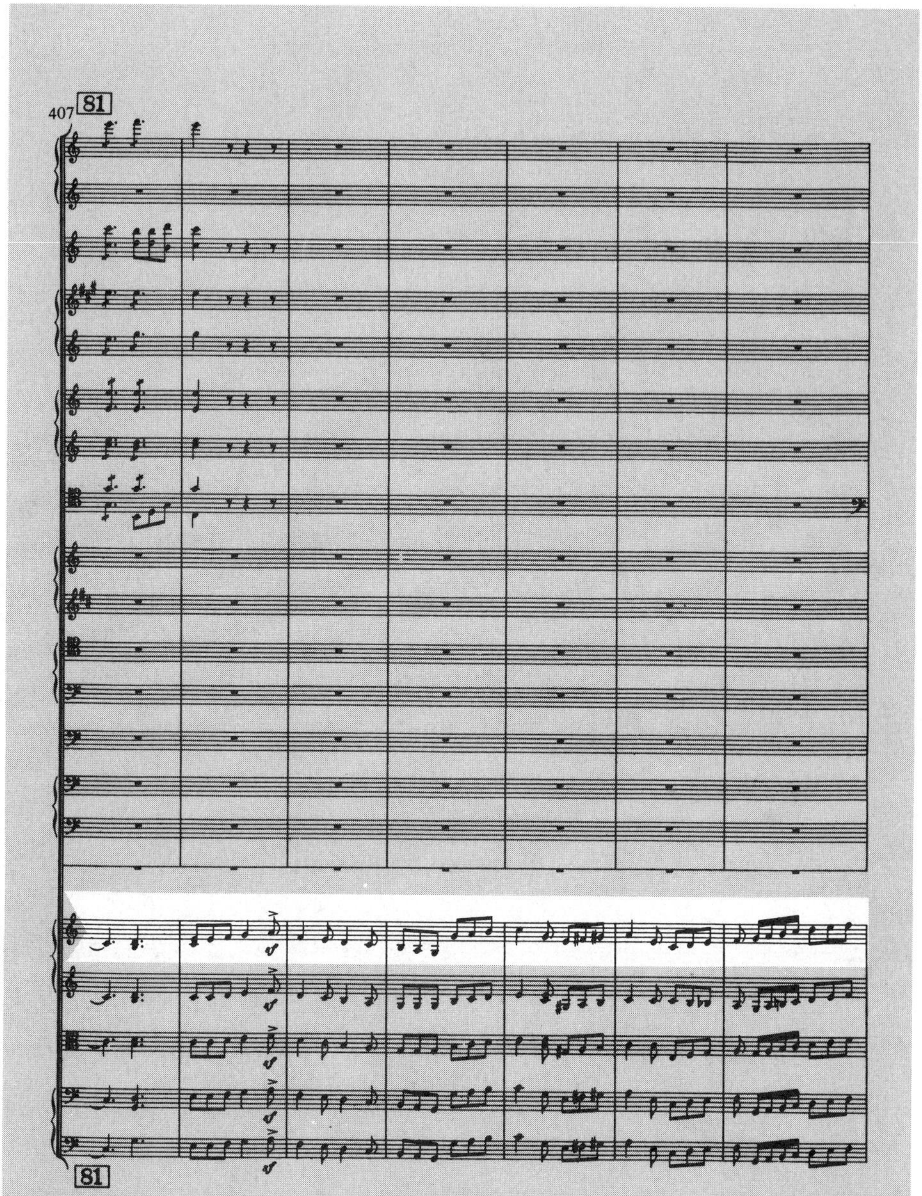
407
81
81

Dies irae et Ronde du Sabbat ensemble
Dies irae and witches' round dance together

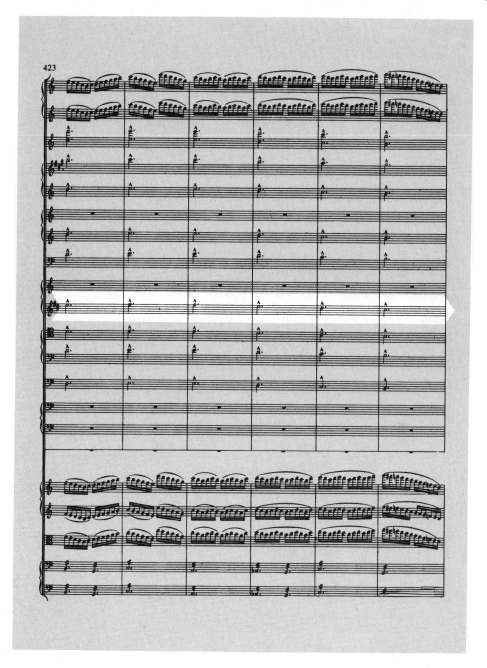

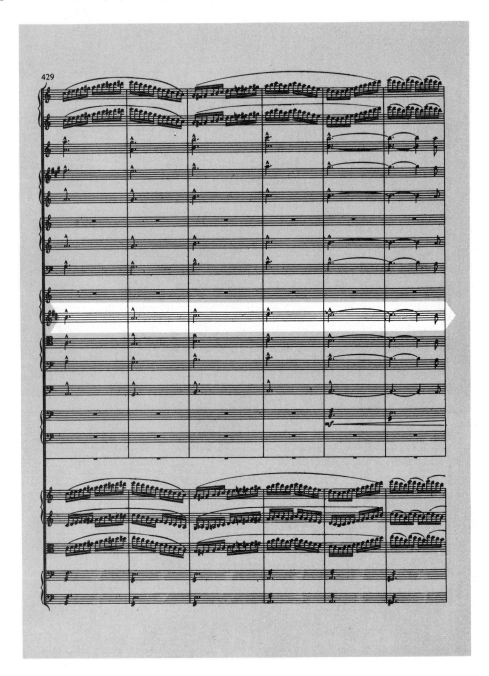

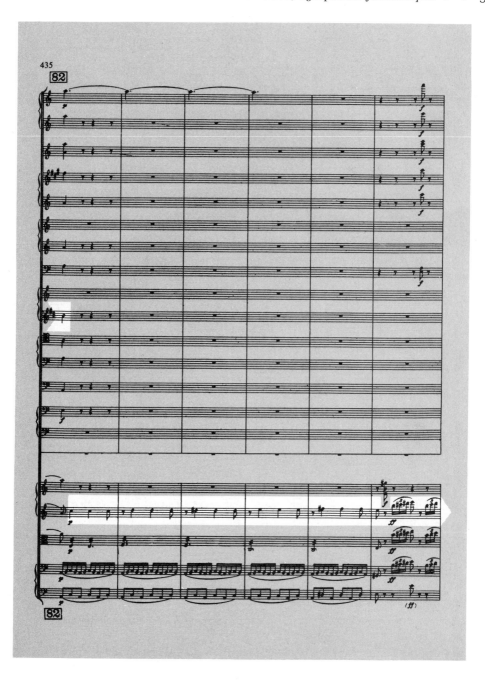

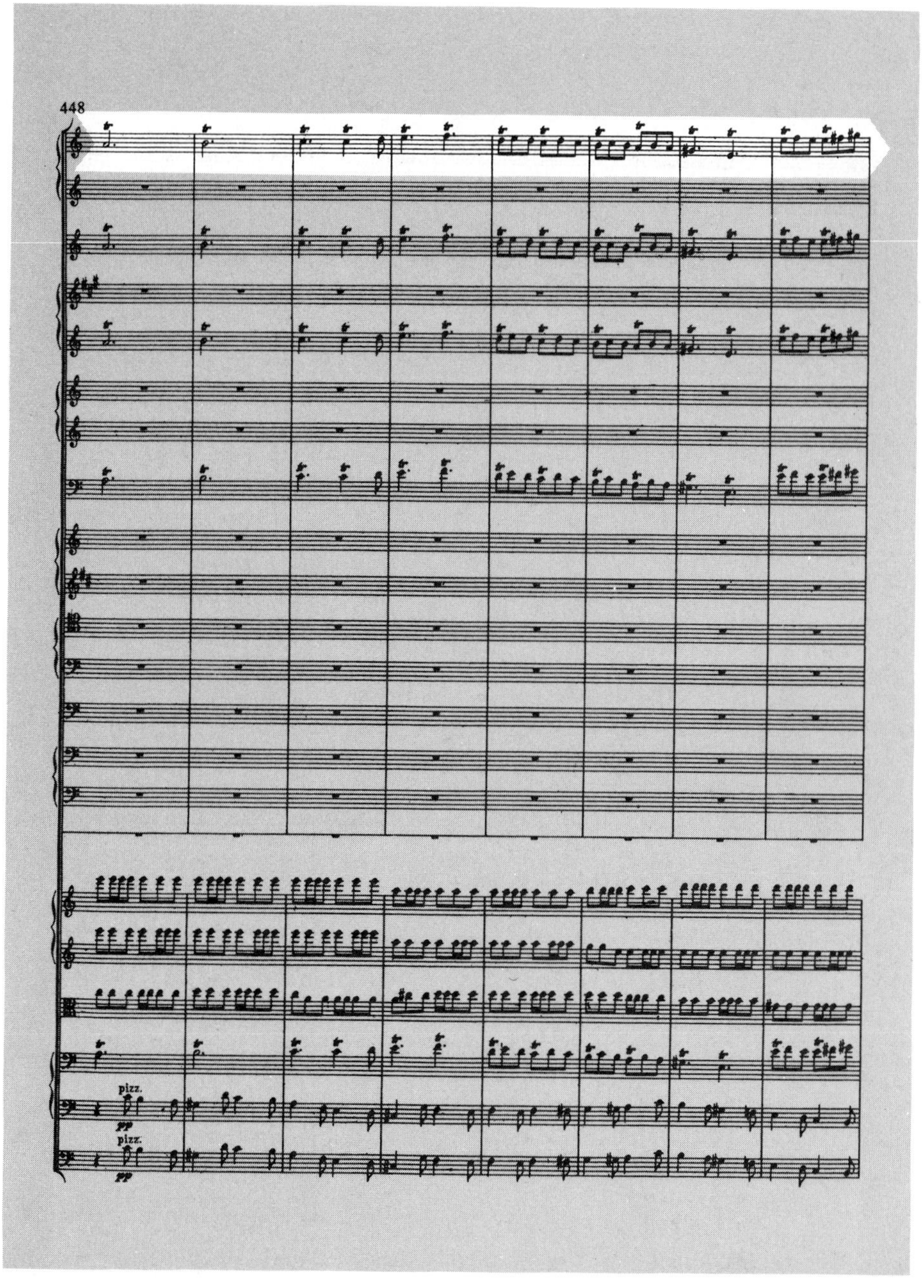
448
pizz.
pp
pizz.
pp

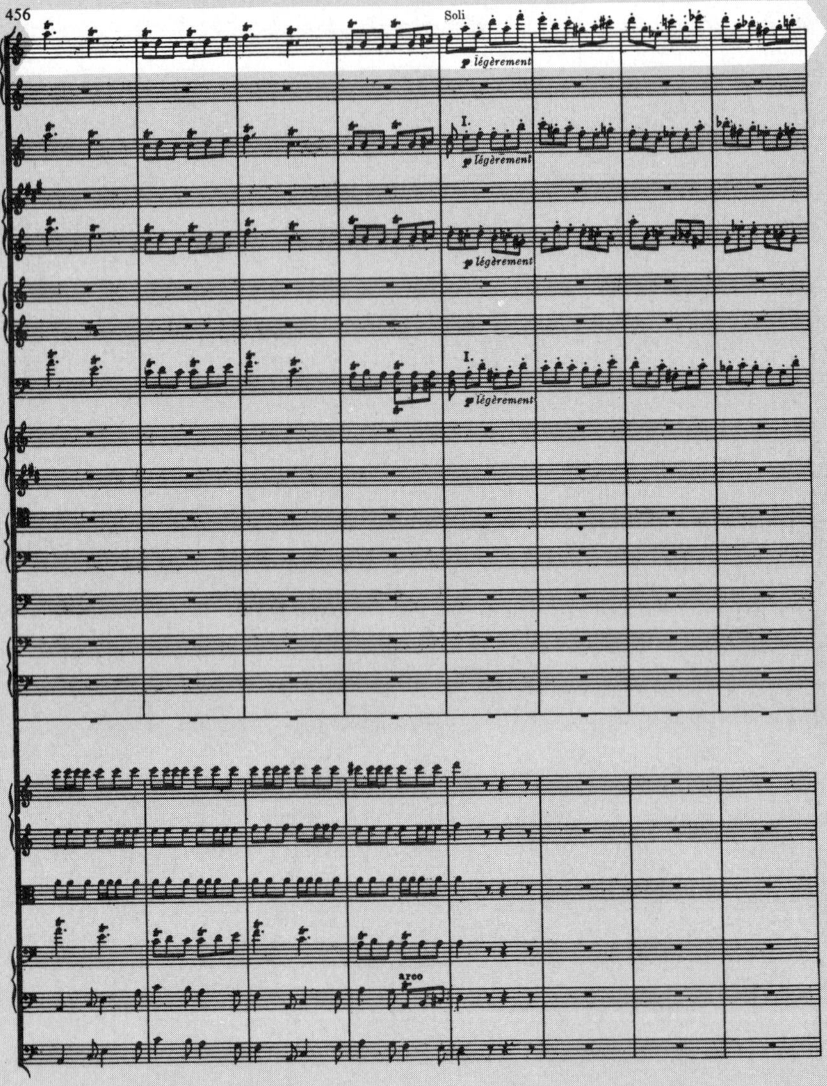
456
Soli
p légèrement
I.
p légèrement
p légèrement
I.
p légèrement
arco

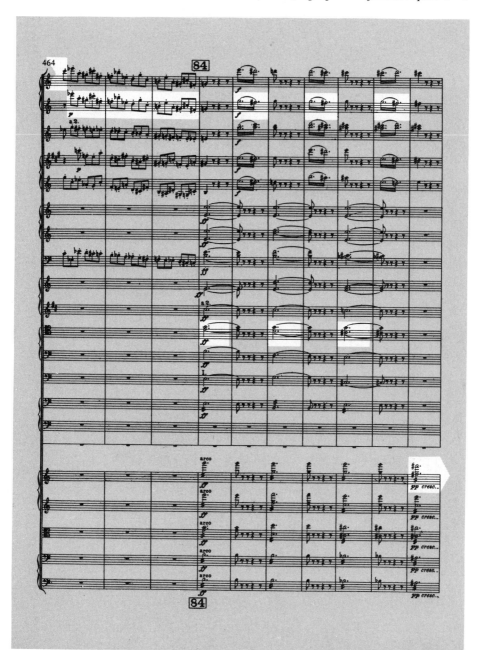

515
tenu
unis.
Coup frappé sur une Cymbale avec une baguette couverte d'éponge ou un tampon
Struck on a cymbal with a sponge-headed drum-stick or a padded stick
Cinelli.

4. Berlioz

L'enfance du Christ, "Adieu des bergers"
(1854) S3A/1 S3/1

TRANSLATION

Il s'en va loin de la terre
Ou dans l'étable il vit le jour,

De son père et de sa mère
Qu'il reste le constant amour!
Qu'il grandisse, qu'il prospère
Et qu'il soit père a son tour.

Oncques si chez l'idolâtre,
Il vient à sentir le malheur,
Fuyant la terre ma marâtre,
Chez nous qu'il revienne au bonheur!
Que la pauvreté du pâtre
Reste toujours chère a son coeur!

Cher enfant, Dieu te bénisse!
Dieu vous bénisse, heureux époux!
Que jamais de l'injustice
Vous ne puissiez sentir les coups!
Qu'un bon ange vous avertisse
Des dangers planant sur vous!

He goes forth far from the land
Where in the stable he first saw the light of
  day.
May he long enjoy the steadfast love
  of his father and his mother.
May he grow and prosper
  and may he be a good father in his turn.

If, surrounded by idolatry,
He should ever feel troubled,
Fleeing the hostile land
Let him return to us in happiness!
May we humble shepherds
Remain dear to his heart!

Dear child, God bless you!
God be with you, happy pair!
May you never feel the
  blows of injustice!
May an angel warn you
  of the dangers surrounding you!

5. Felix Mendelssohn (1809-1847),

A Midsummer Night's Dream, .
Overture (1826) and Nocturne (1843)   5A/4   II/1/[12]

Overture

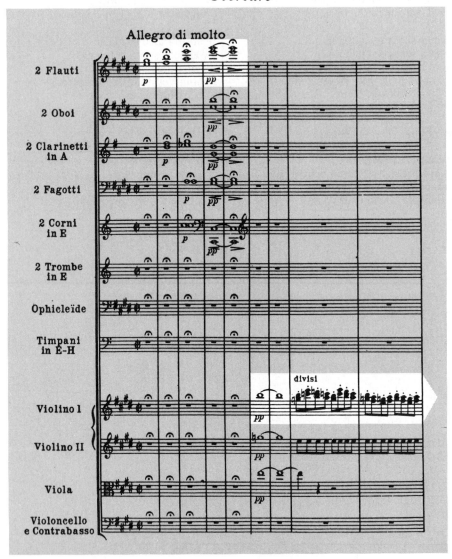

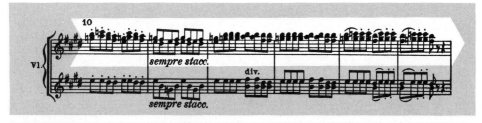

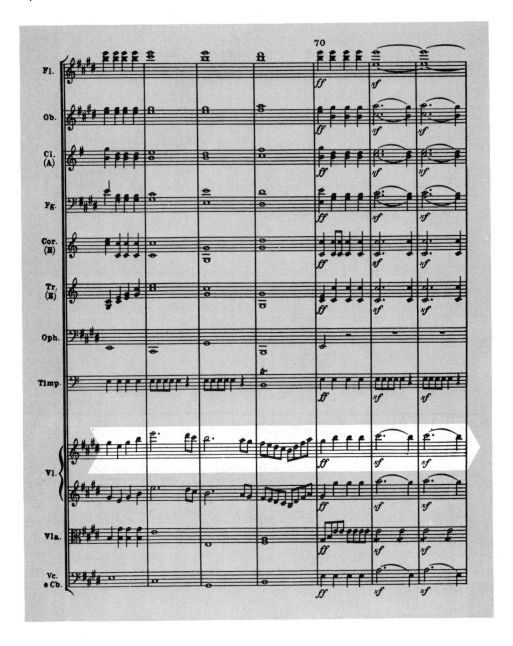

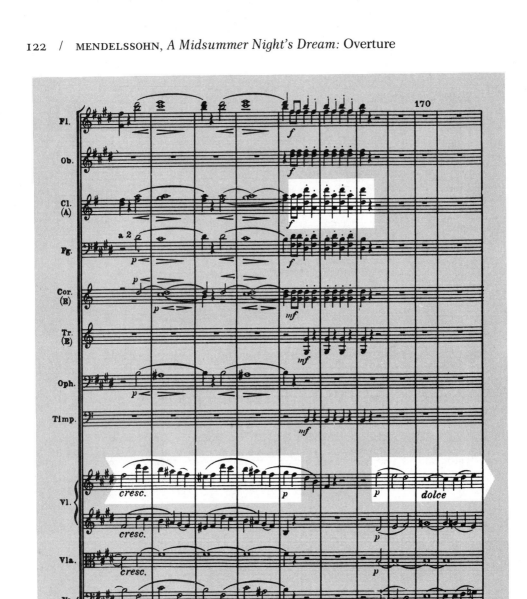

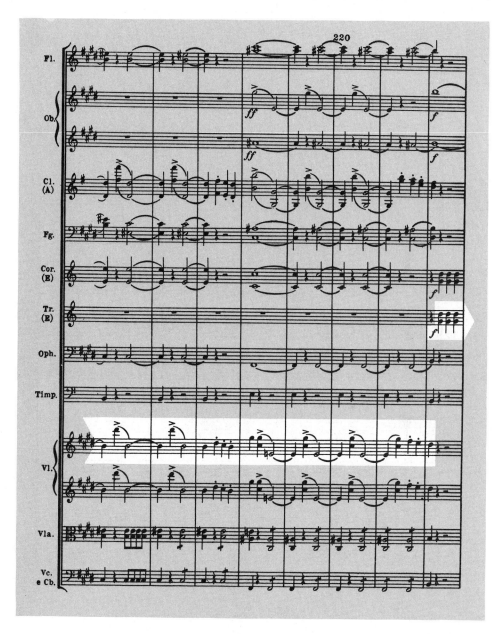

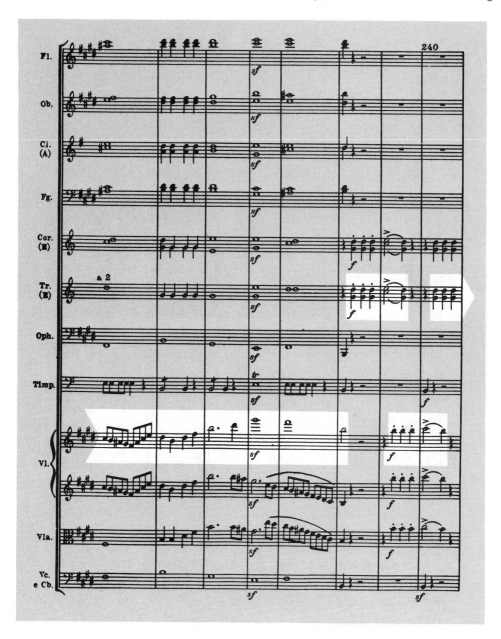

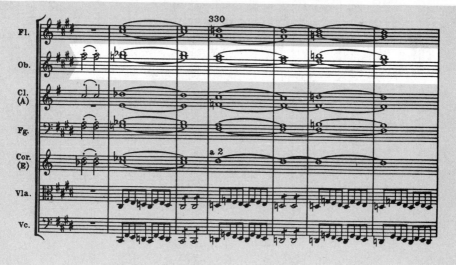

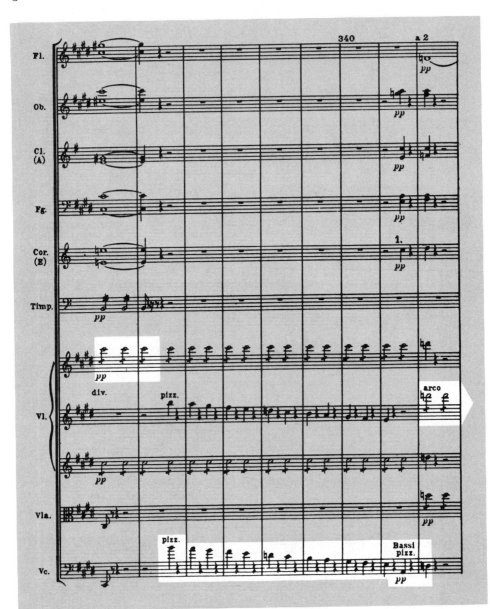

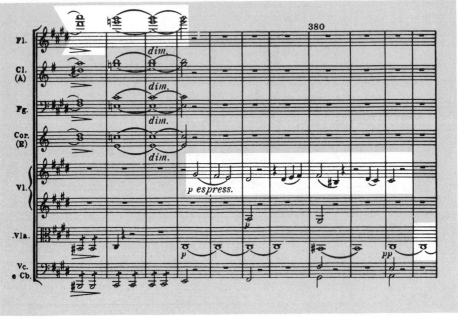

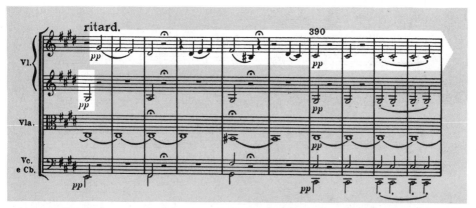

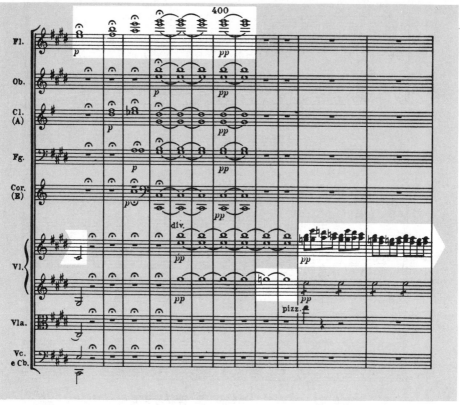

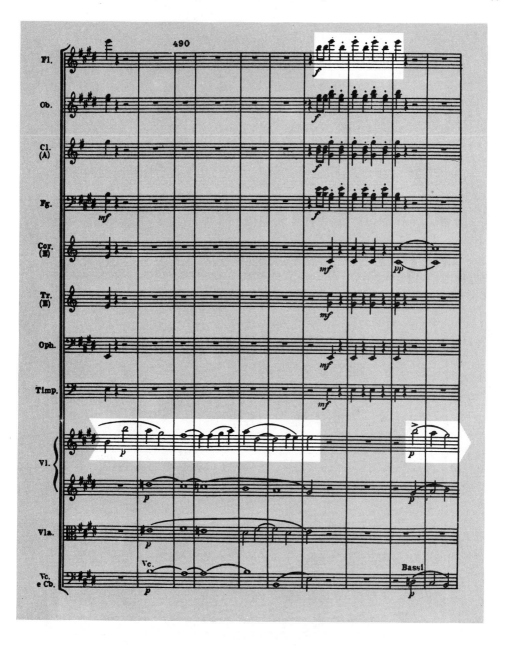

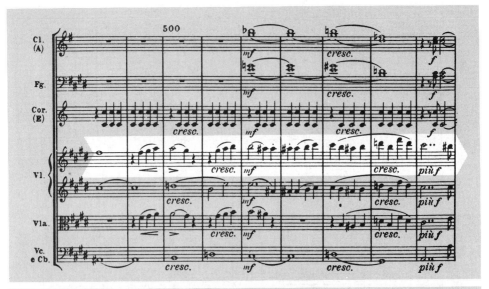

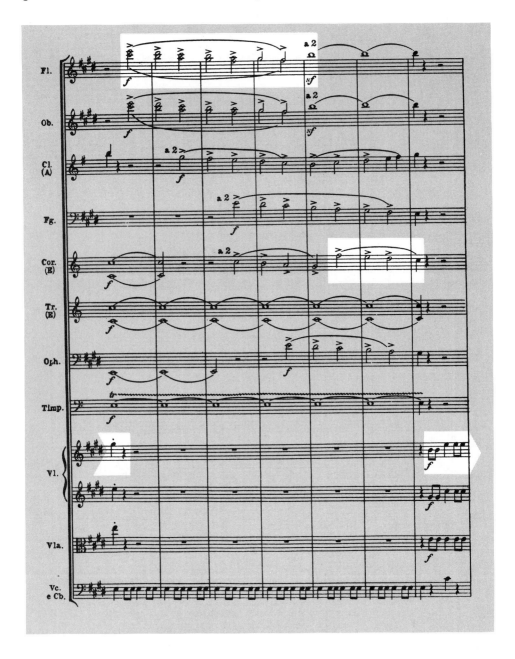

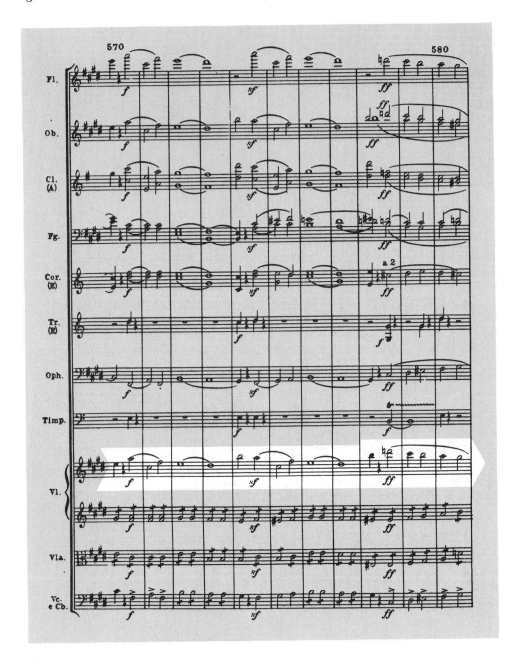

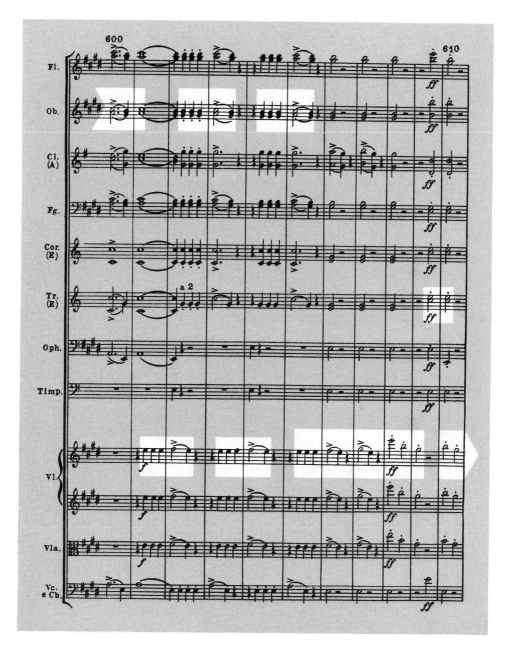

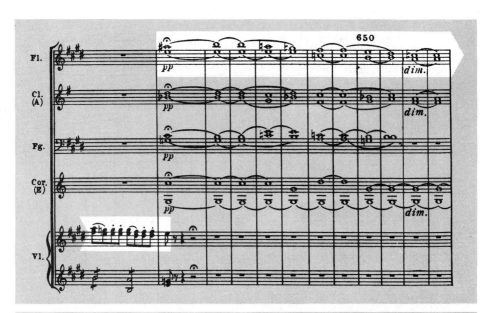

Nocturne

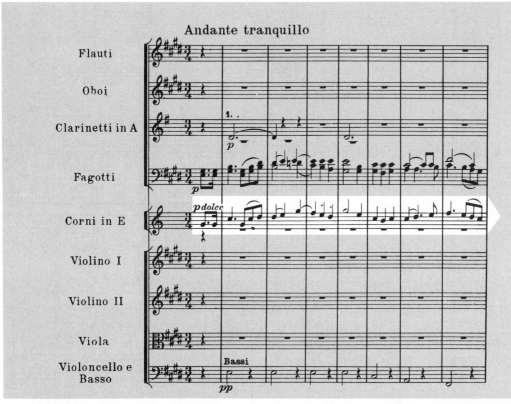

6. Mendelssohn

Symphony No. 4 in A major, *(Italian)* (1833)

  5B/2 II/1/17

I

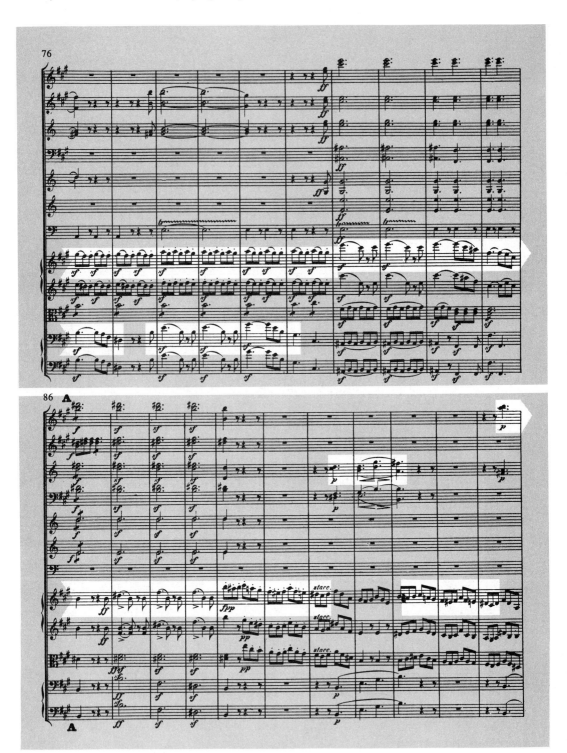

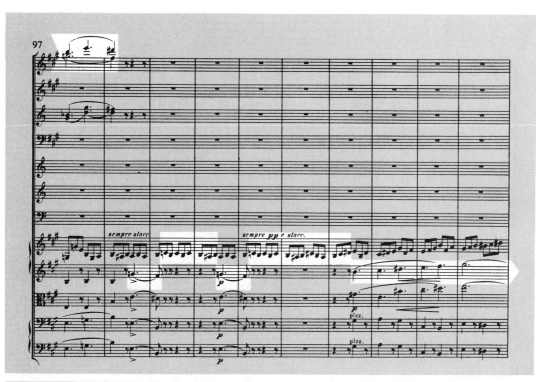

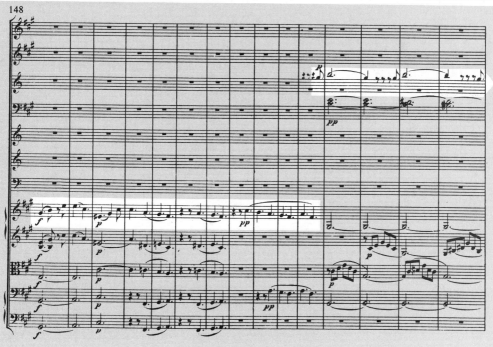

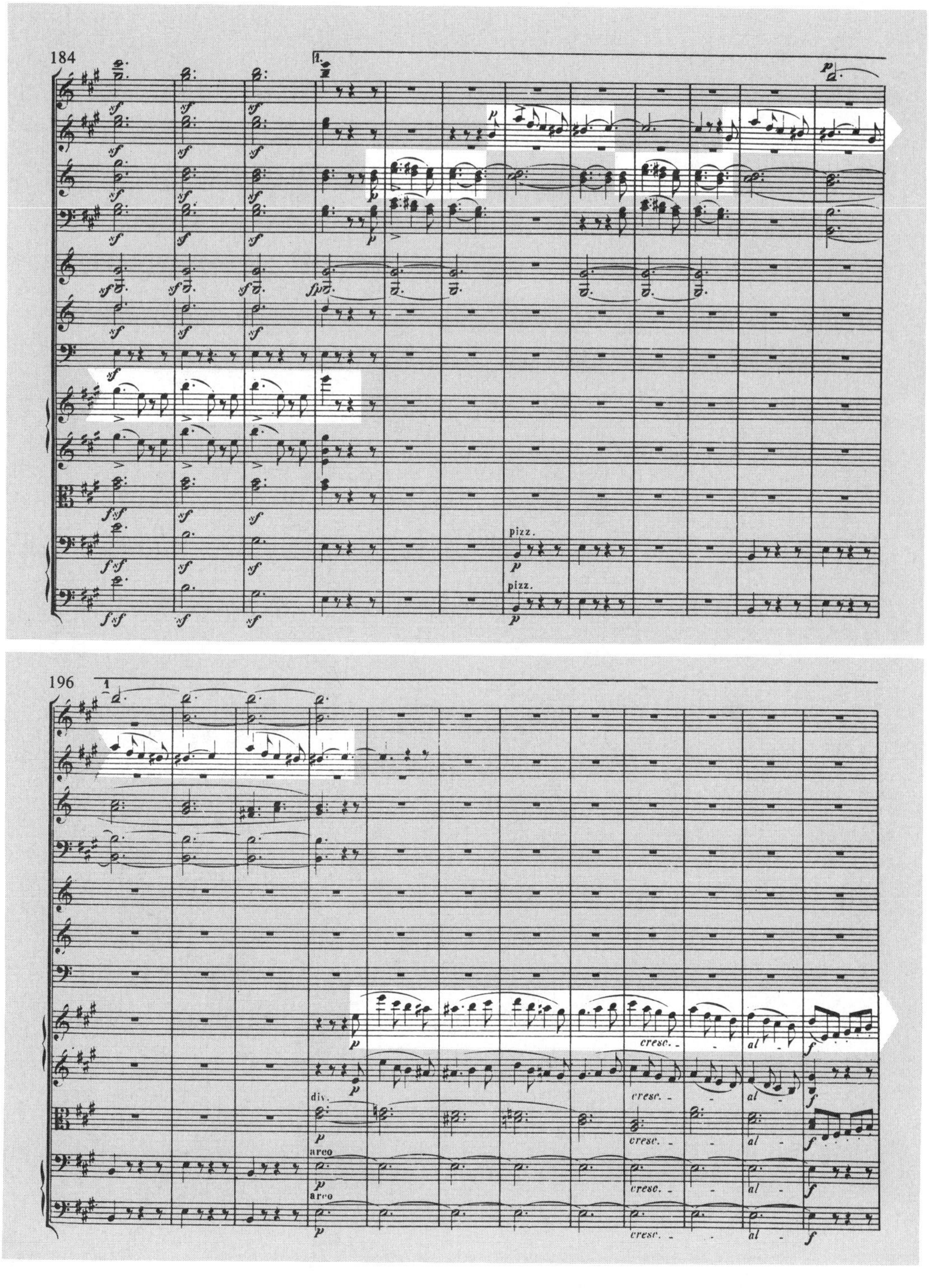
184
pizz.
pizz.
196
div.
arco
arco
cresc.
al

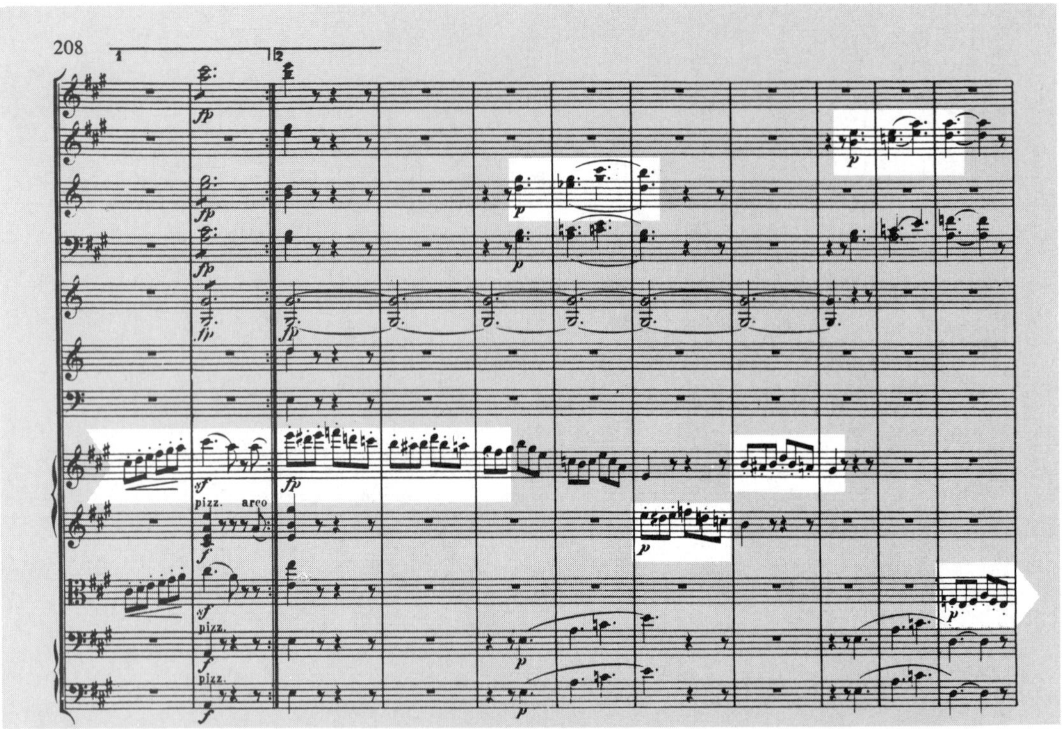
208
fp
pizz.
arco
sf
f
p

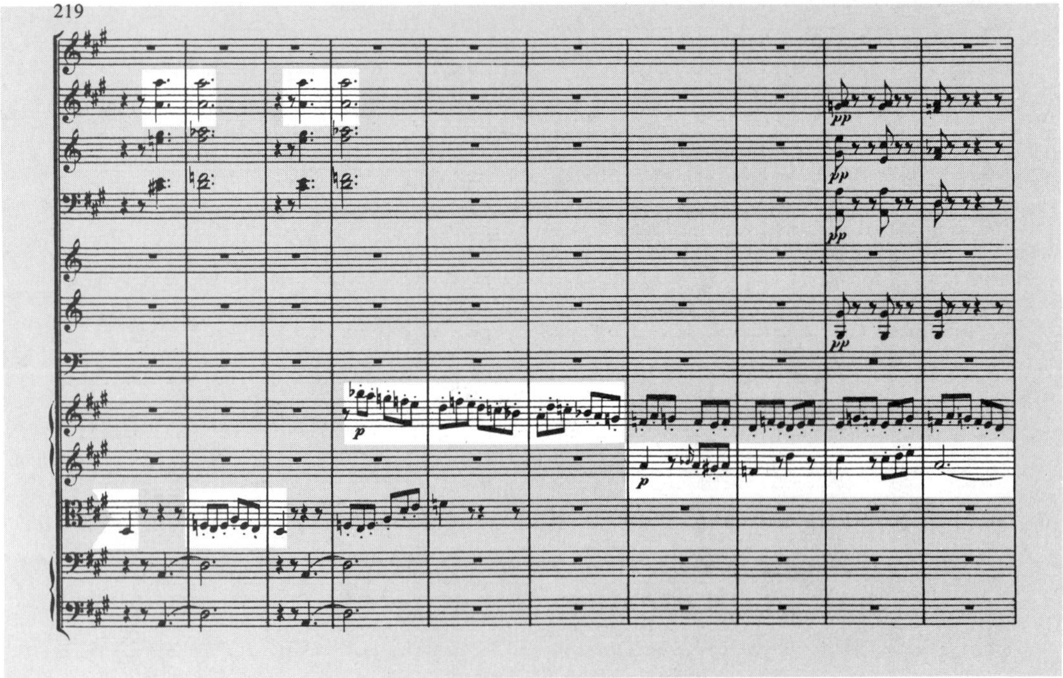
219
pp
p

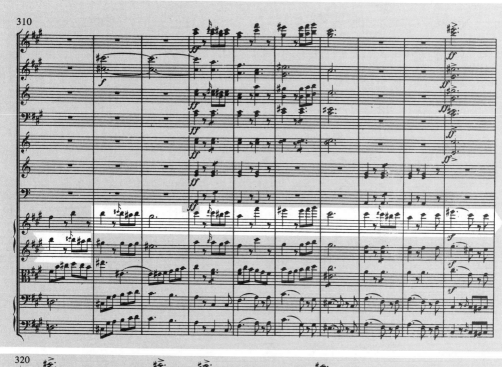

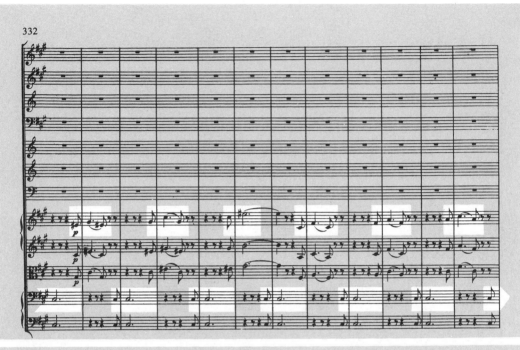

357
cresc.
mf
cresc.
sf
f
sf
poco a poco cresc.
mf
cresc.
p cresc.
poco a poco cresc.
cresc.
mf
cresc.
poco a poco cresc.
mf
cresc.
f
poco a poco cresc.
mf
cresc.
f

367
D
f
sf
f
sf
f
f
sf
sf
sf
sf
p
D

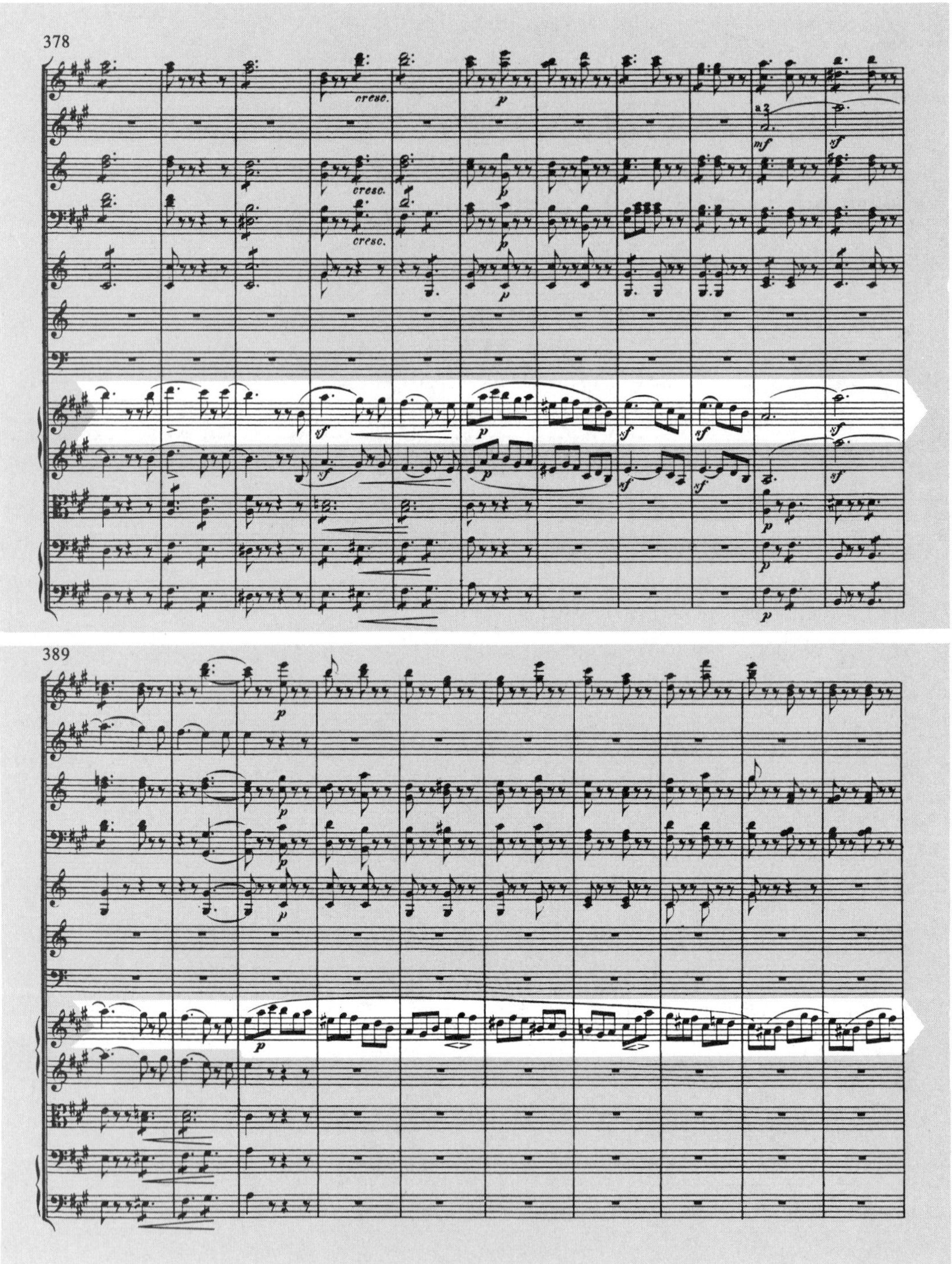
378
cresc.
p
a 2
mf
sf
389
p

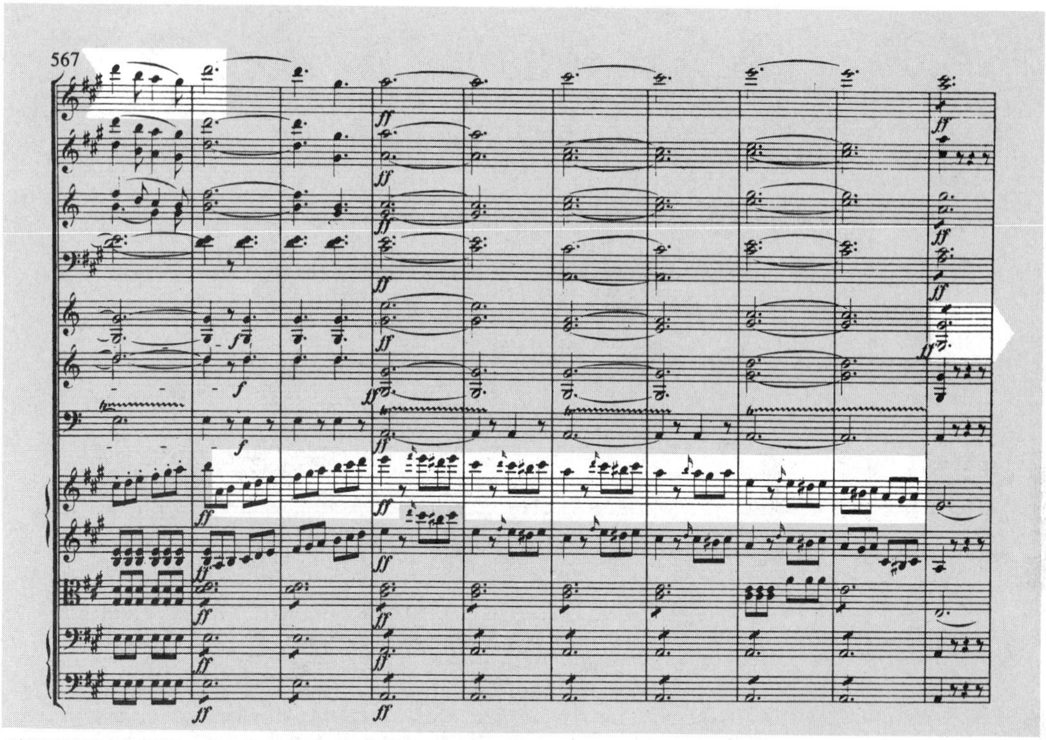
567
ff

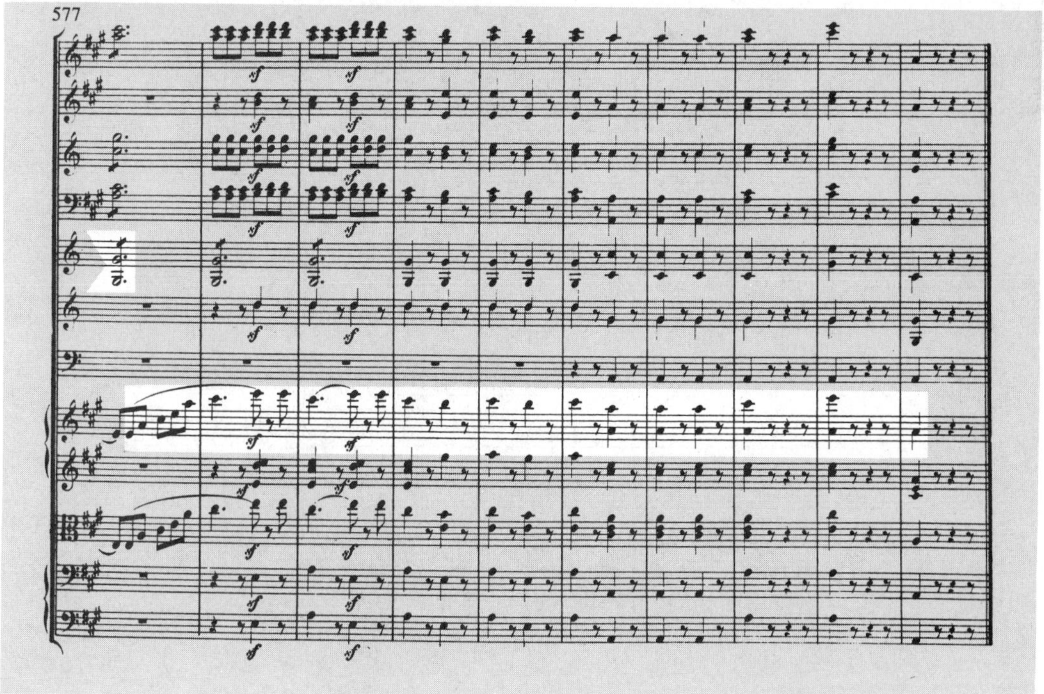
577
sf

III

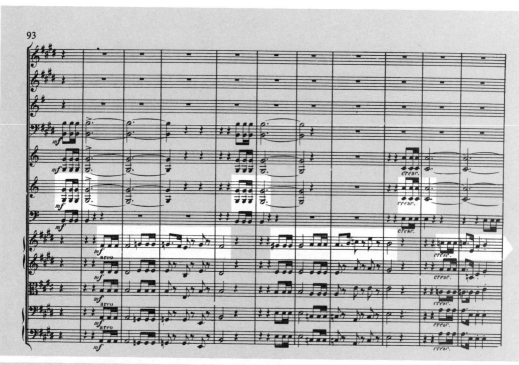

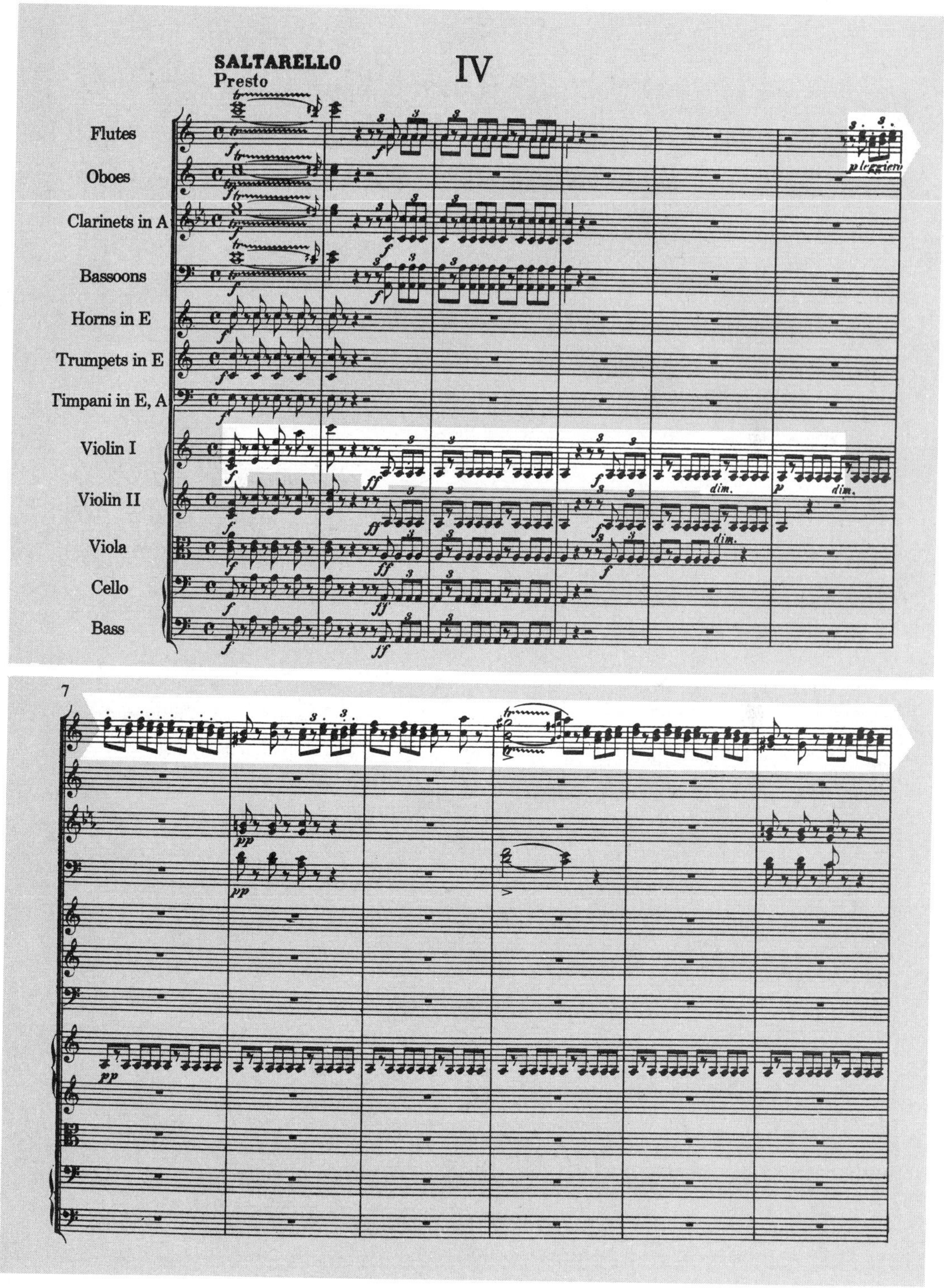
SALTARELLO
Presto
IV
Flutes
Oboes
Clarinets in A
Bassoons
Horns in E
Trumpets in E
Timpani in E, A
Violin I
Violin II
Viola
Cello
Bass
dim.
dim.
dim.
p leggiero
7

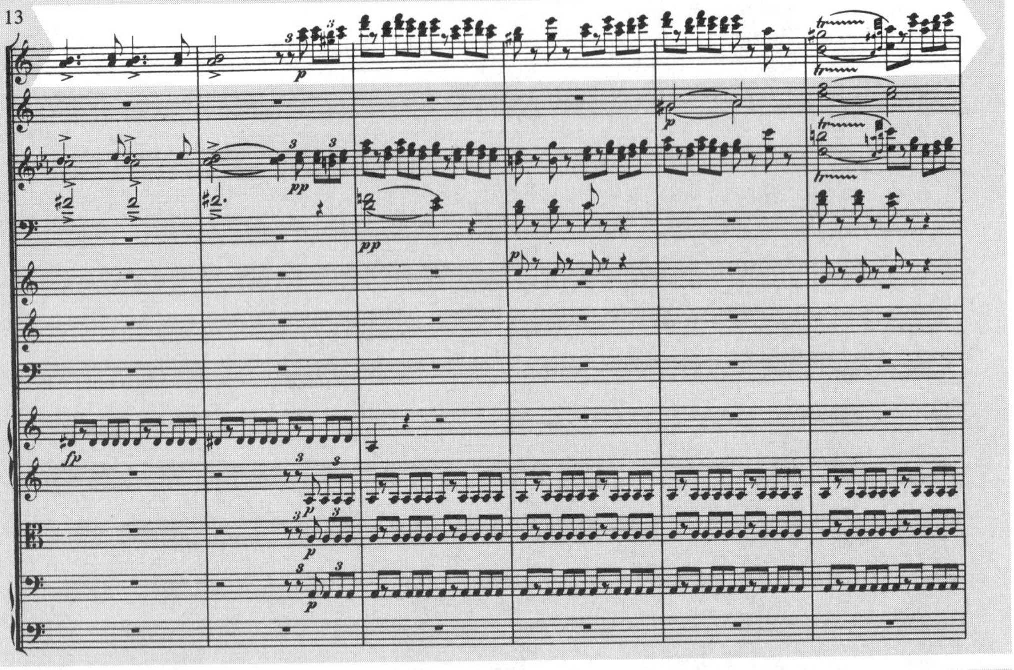
13
p
pp
pp
p
fp
p
p
p

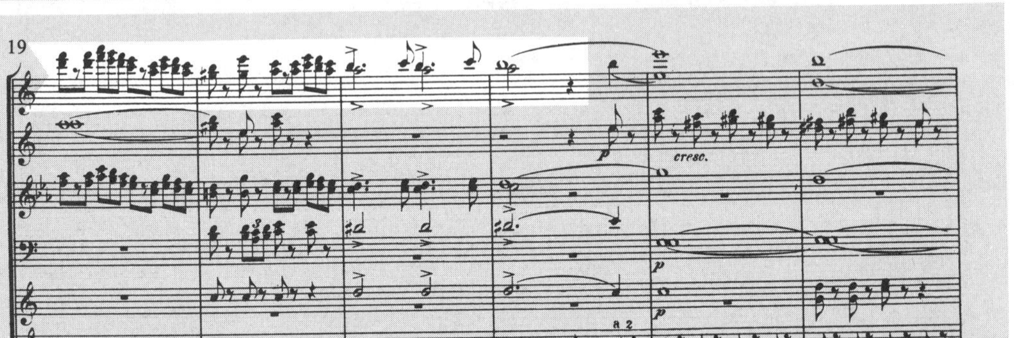
19
p
cresc.
p
p
a 2
pp
pp
p
sf
sf
sf

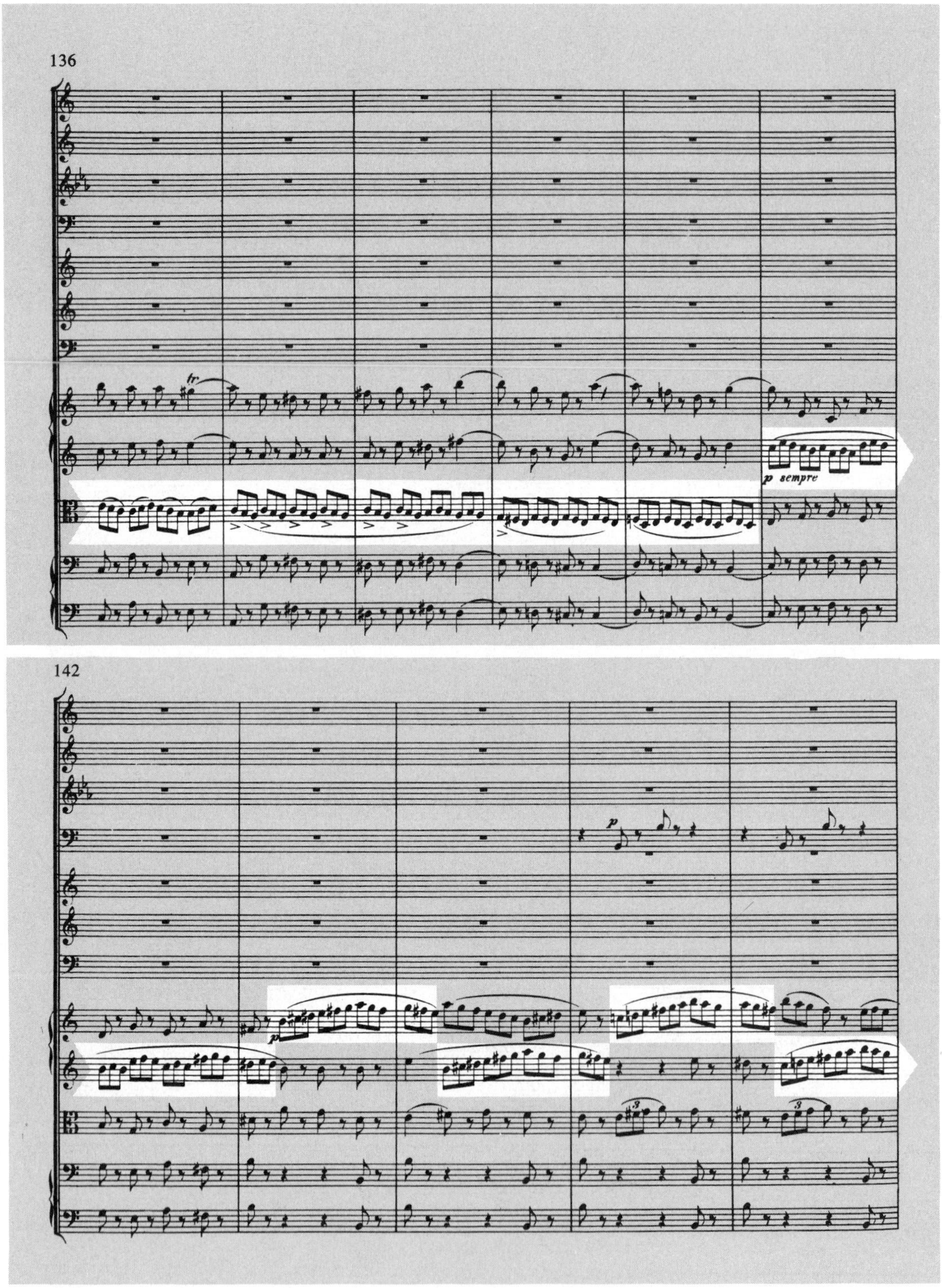
136
tr
p sempre
142
p

7. Frédéric François Chopin (1810-1849),

Prelude in E minor, Op. 28, No. 4
(publ. 1839)

8. Chopin

Polonaise in A-flat major, Op. 53
(1842)

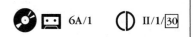 6A/1   II/1/30

9. Robert Schumann (1810-1856),

Carnaval, Op. 9, "Eusebius" and "Florestan" (1835) S3A/3 S3/8

Eusebius

Florestan

10. Schumann

Dichterliebe, Op. 48, "Ich grolle nicht"
(1840)

  5B/1   II/2/1

Nicht zu schnell.

Ich grolle nicht und wenn das Herz _____ auch bricht.

E _ wig verlor' _ nes Lieb, e _ wig verlor' _ nes Lieb, _____ ich grol _ _ le

nicht, ich grol _ _ le nicht. Wie du auch strahlst in Di _ a _ man _ ten pracht, es fällt kein

Strahl in dei _ nes Herzens Nacht. Das weiss ich längst.

Ich grolle nicht und wenn das Herz _____ auch bricht. Ich sah dich ja im

Translation

Ich grolle nicht und wenn das Herz
    auch bricht.
Ewig verlor'nes Lieb, ich grolle nicht.
Wie du auch strahlst in
    Diamantenpracht,
Es fällt kein Strahl in deines
    Herzens Nacht.

Das weiss ich längst. Ich sah dich ja im
    Traume,
Und sah die Nacht in deines Herzens
    Raume,
Und sah die Schlang', die dir am
    Herzen frisst,
Ich sah, mein Lieb, wie sehr du elend
    bist.

HEINRICH HEINE

I bear no grudge, even though my
    heart may break,
eternally lost love! I bear no grudge.
However you may shine in the
    splendor of your diamonds,
no ray of light falls in the darkness
    of your heart.

I have long known this. I saw you in
    a dream,
and saw the night within the void of
    your heart,
and saw the serpent that is eating
    your heart—
I saw, my love, how very miserable
    you are.

PHILIP L. MILLER

II. Schumann

Piano Concerto in A minor, Op. 54
(1841/45)

 6A/3 II/2/ 2

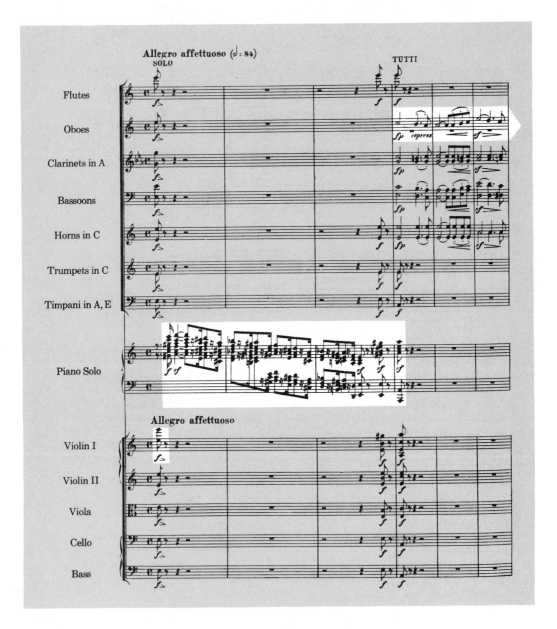

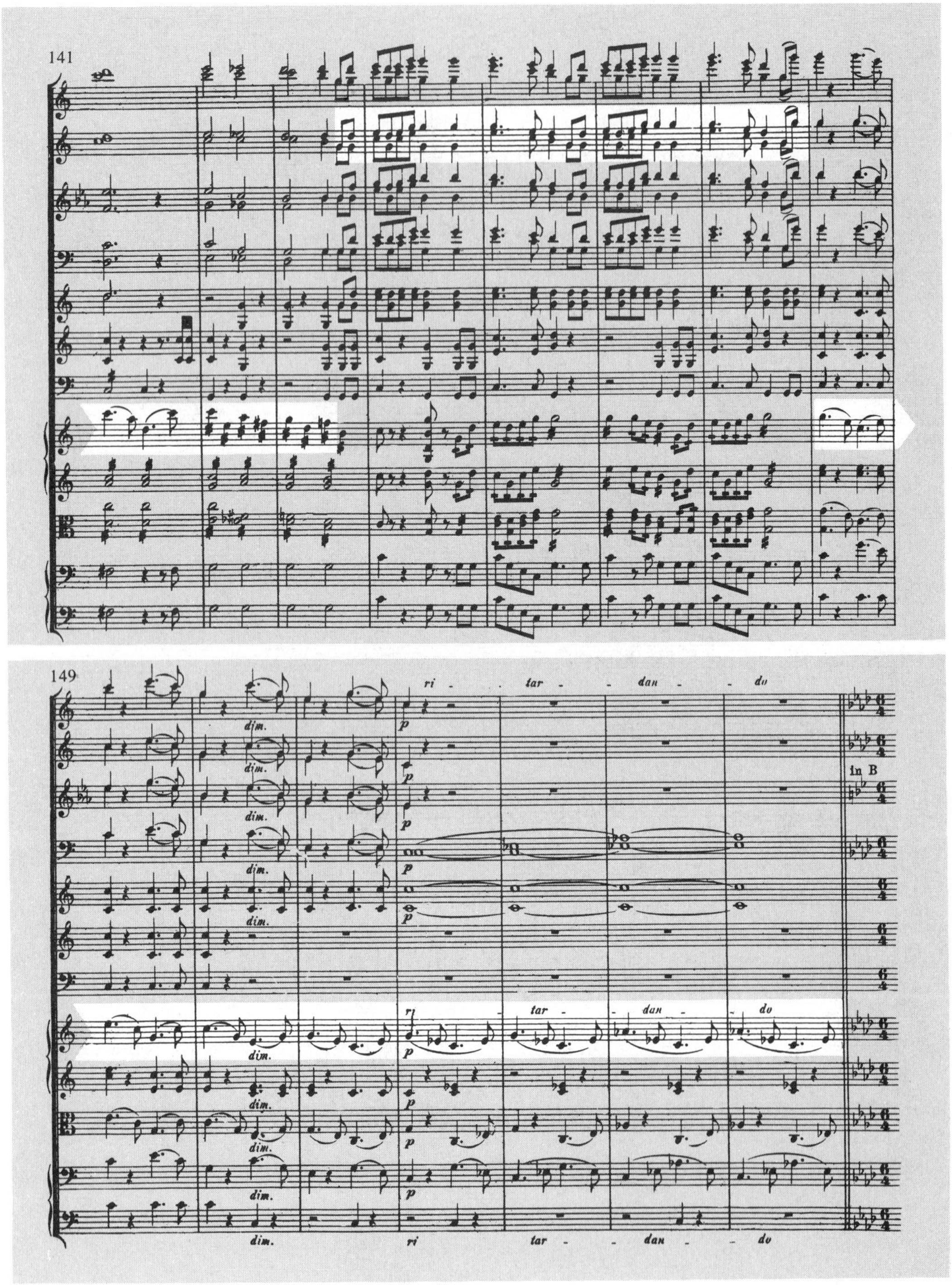
141
149
ri - tar - dan - do
dim.
p
in B

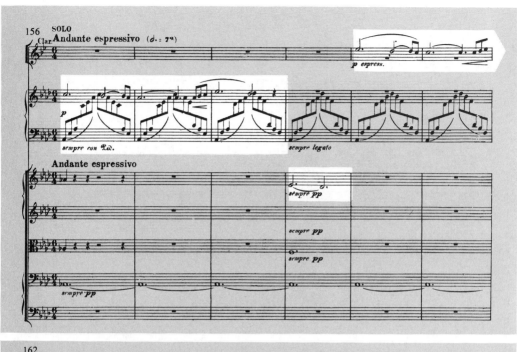

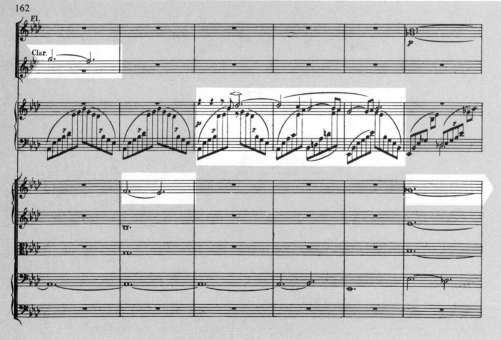

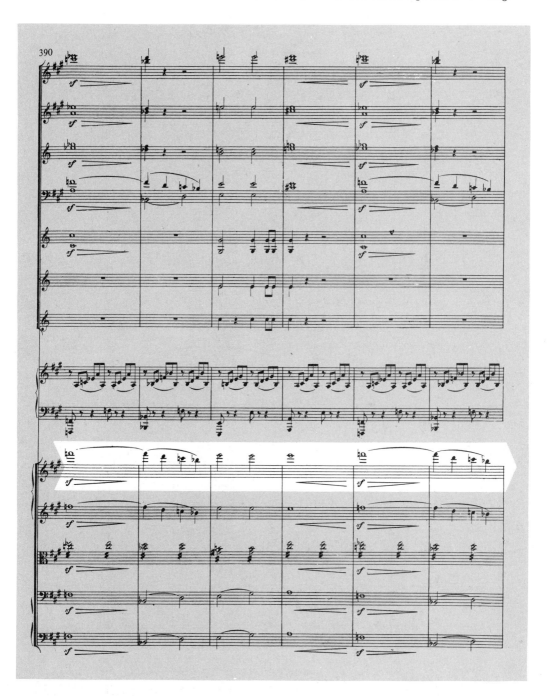

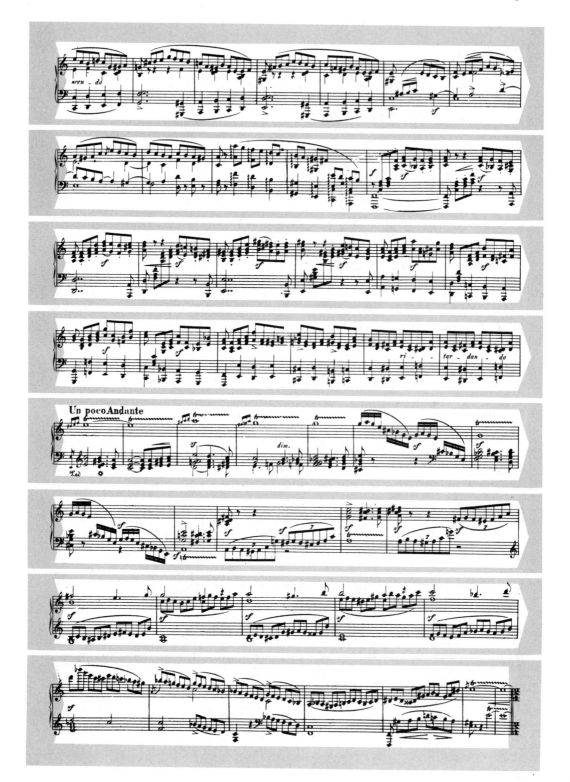

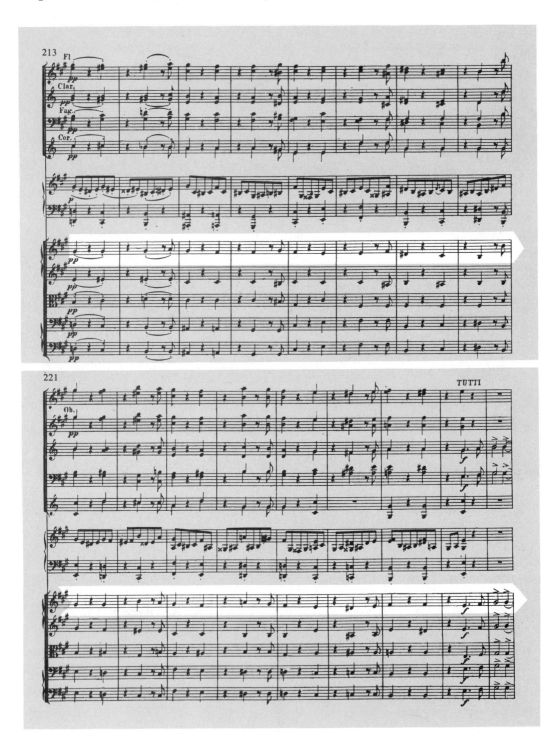

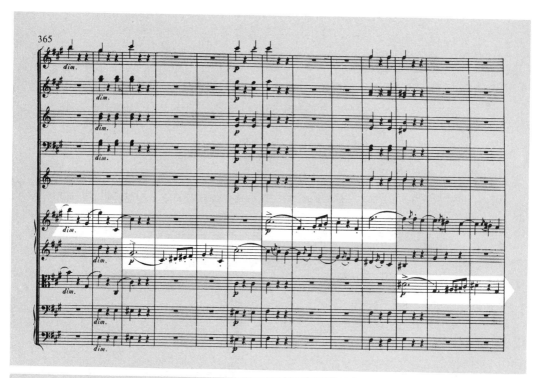

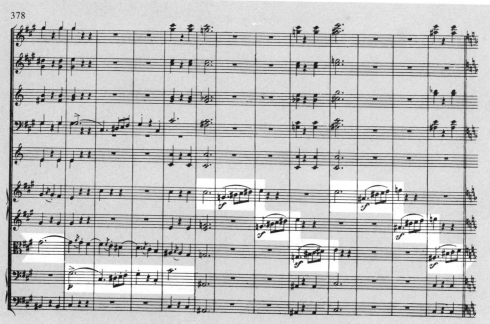

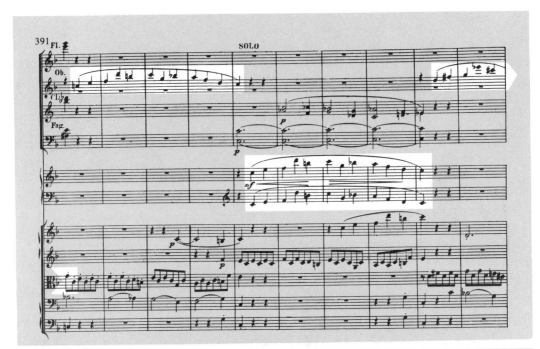

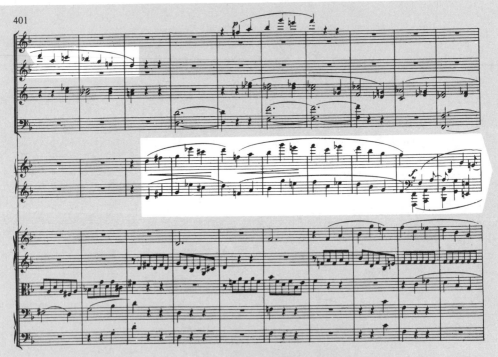

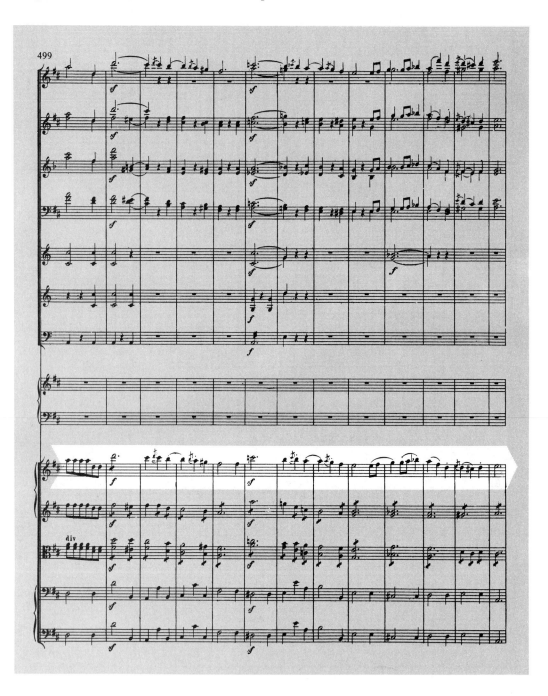

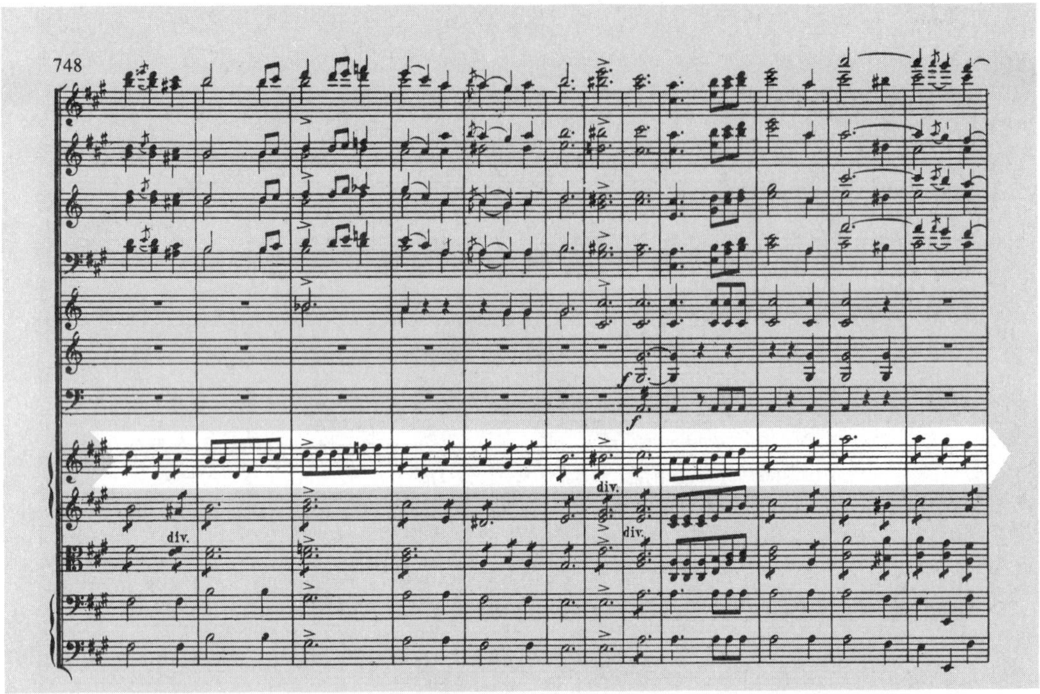
748
f
div.
div.
div.

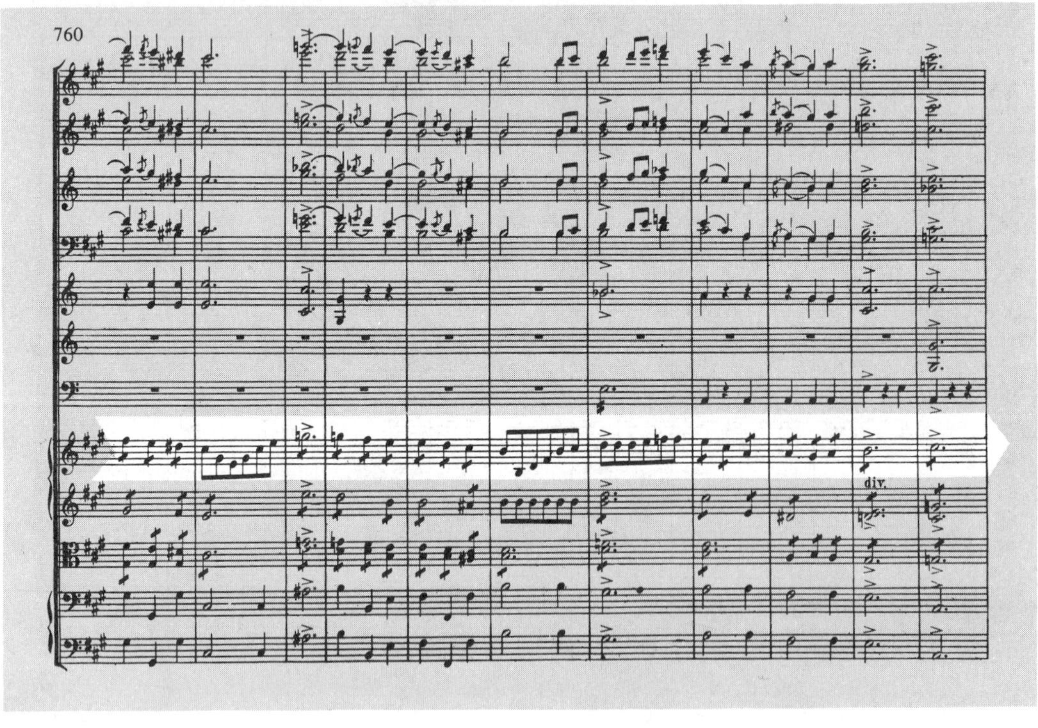
760
div.

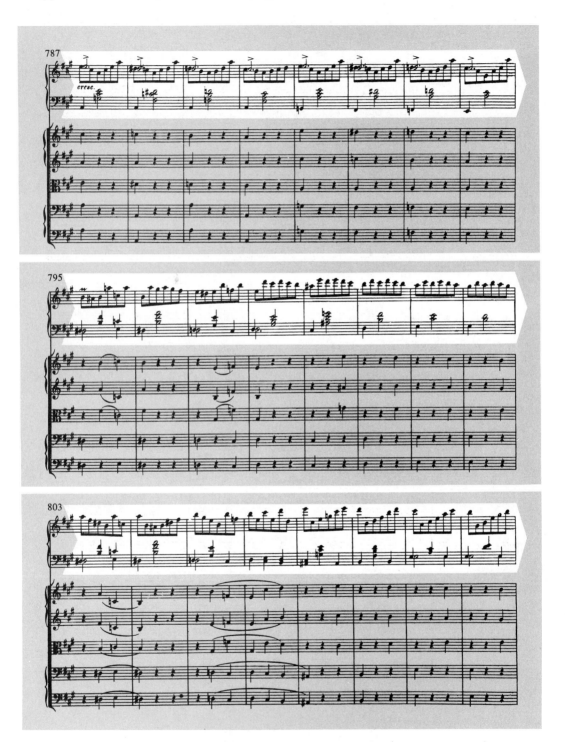

943

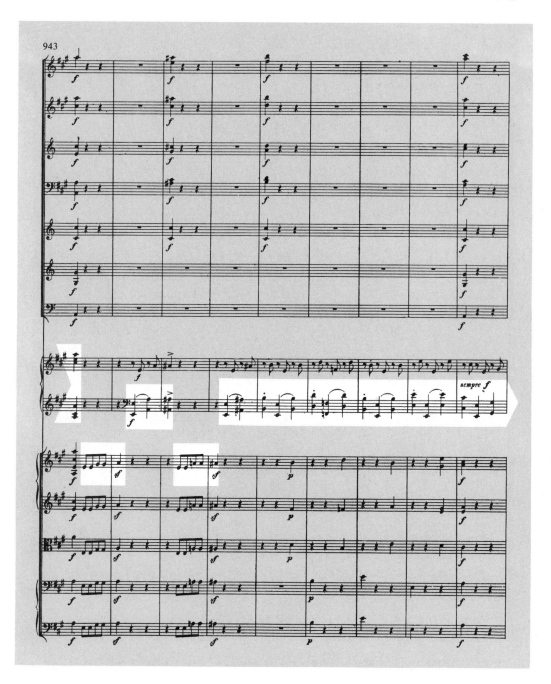

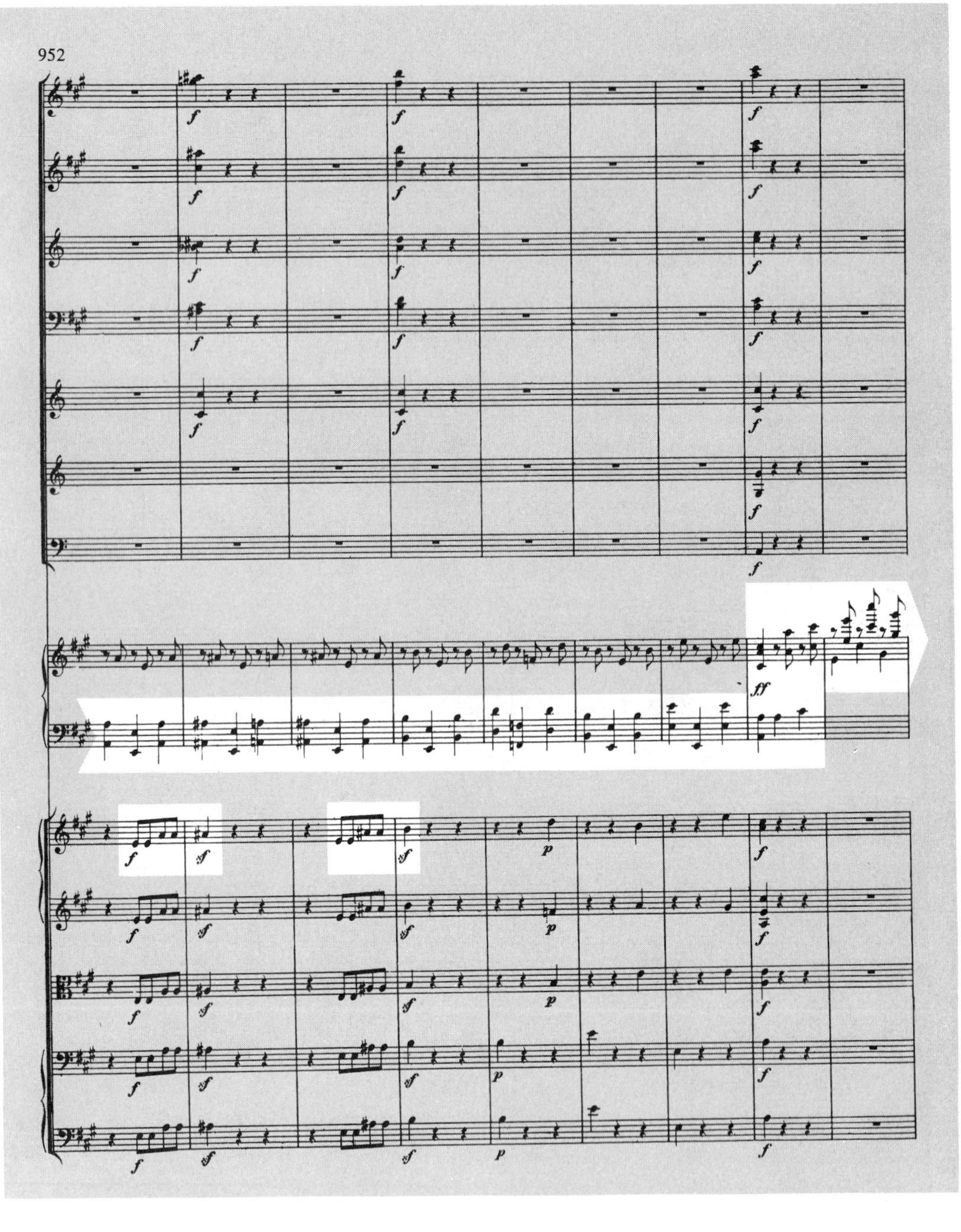
952

961

12. Franz Liszt (1811-1886),

Transcendental Etude No. 8,
Wilde Jagd (1851)

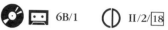 6B/1   II/2/18

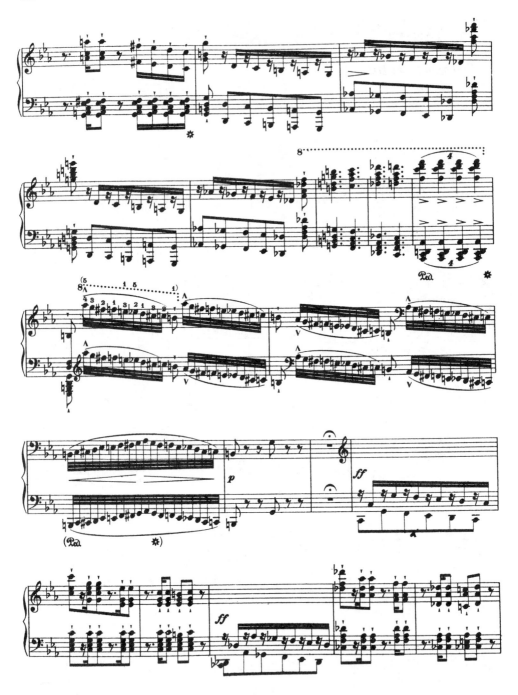

13. Richard Wagner (1813-1883),

Die Walküre, Act III, Scene 3, excerpt (1856)

  6B/2 II/2/21

(Sie sinkt mit geschlossenen Augen, sanft ermattend, in seine Arme zurück. Er geleitet sie zart auf einen niedrigen Mooshügel
(She sinks back with closed eyes, unconscious, in his arms. He gently bears her to a low mossy mound, which is overshadowed

zu liegen, über den sich eine breitästige Tanne ausstreckt.)
by a wide-spreading fir tree, and lays her upon it.)

(Er betrachtet sie und schliesst
(He looks upon her and closes

ihr den Helm: sein Auge weilt dann auf der Gestalt der Schlafenden, die er nun mit dem grossen Stahlschilde der Walküren ganz
her helmet: his eyes then rest on the form of the sleeper, which he now completely covers with the great steel shield of the

zudeckt. _ Langsam kehrt er sich ab, mit einem schmerzlichen Blicke wendet er sich noch einmal um.)
Valkyrie. _ He turns slowly away, then again turns round with a sorrowful look.)

WOTAN.

bann' ich dich heut'!
stir I thee now!

Her - auf,
Ap - pear!

wa - bern - de
come, wav - ing

Lo - he,
fire__

um - lod' - re mir
and wind thee in

feu - rig den
flames round the

(Er stösst mit dem Folgenden dreimal mit dem Speer auf den Stein.)
(During the following he strikes the rock thrice with his spear.)

(Erster (First
Stoss.) stroke.)

Fels!
fell!

Lo - ge!
Lo - ge!

(Zweiter.)
(Second.)

(Dritter.)
(Third.)

(Dem Stein entfährt ein Feuerstrahl.
(A flash of flame issues from

Lo - ge!
Lo - ge!

hie - her!
ap - pear!

der zur allmälich immer helleren Flammenglut anschwillt.)
the rock, which swells to an ever-brightening fiery glow.)

(Hier bricht die lichte Flackerlohe aus.)
(Here flickering flames break forth.)

Lichte Brunst umgiebt Wotan mit wildem Flackern. Er weis't mit dem Speere gebie-
Bright shooting flames surround Wotan. With his spear he directs the sea of fire

terisch dem Feuermeere den Umkreis des Felsenrandes zur Strömung an; alsbald zieht es sich nach dem Hintergrunde,wo es nun
to encircle the rocks; it presently spreads toward the background where it encloses the mountain in flames.)

(Er wendet sich langsam zum Gehen.)
(Slowly he turns to depart.)

p dolce

più p

sempre più p

(Er wendet sich nochmals mit dem Haupt und blickt zurück.)
(He turns his head again and locks back.)

mp

pp

(Er verschwindet durch das Feuer.)
He disappears through the fire.

mp

pp

P

pp

(Vorhang fällt.)
Curtain falls.

più pp

ppp

Stich u. Druck von B. Schott's Söhne in Mainz

14. Giuseppe Verdi (1813-1901),

La traviata, Finale of Act II
(1853)

 6B/3 II/2/26

rò, ma giu- ra in- nan- te che do- vun- que se- gui- ra- i, se- gui-
go; but not un - til You prom-ise on your word of hon-or To re-

Violetta.

Ah no, giam-ma - i. / Va, sciagu-
Ah no, I can-not! / You must be-

rai i pas- si mie - i. / No, giam-ma- i?
turn__ to the coun-try. / So you can not?

ra- to! scorda un no-me ch'è in-fa-ma- to, va, mi la- scia sul mo-
lieve me and for- get me. Go and leave me at this mo-ment. I im-

men- to__ di fug- gir- ti un giu- ra- men- to sa- cro io
plore you, for I gave my sol - emn word That I will

Allegro sostenuto.

Alfred.

O- gni suo aver tal fem-mi-na per a-mor mio sper-de - a, io
All she pos-sessed, this wom-an here Squan-dered on me, un-spar-ing. And

cie-co, vi - le, mi - sero, tut-to accettar po-te - a.
blind ly, vile ly, reck - less ly, I took it all, un-car - ing.

Ma è tempo anco - ra! ter - ger-mi da tan-ta mac - chia bra - mo,
But there is time to clear my-self, Time to re-pay such kind - ness.

qui ___ te - sti-mon vi chiamo, or te-stimon vi chia - mo,
I ___ call you all to wit-ness, I call you all to wit - ness,

or te-sti-mon vi chia - mo che qui, che qui pa - ga ta jo
I call you all to tes ti-fy That I have paid her back in

№ 15. "Di sprezzo degno se stesso rende.„
Continuation of Finale

(*Germont draws Alfred with him. The Baron follows him. Violetta is led by Flora into another room. The others disperse.*)

End of the Second Act.

15. Clara Schumann (1819-1896),

Quatre pièces fugitives, Op. 15, No. 3
(publ. 1845)

  6B/4

16. Bedřich Smetana (1824-1884),

Vlatava (The Moldau) from *Má Vlast (My Country)* (1874–79)

 7A/1   II/3/ 1

The Two Sources of the Moldau

Allegro (a 2 batt.) commodo non agitato

Kleine Flöte

2 Flöten

2 Oboen

2 Klarinetten in C

2 Fagotte

4 Hörner in C I II III IV

2 Trompeten in C

2 Posaunen

3. Posaune und Tuba

Pauken in E, H

Triangel

Große Trommel und Becken

Harfe (oder Klavier)

1. Violine

2. Violine

Bratsche

Violoncell

Kontrabaß

*Smaller notes indicate an alternate version for reduced orchestra.

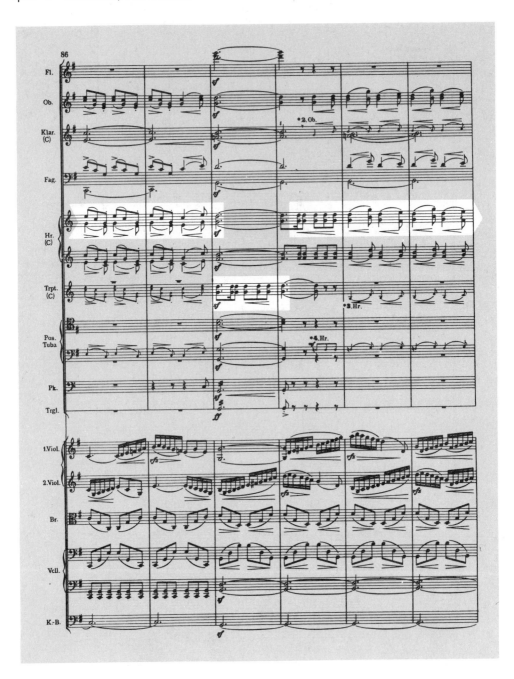

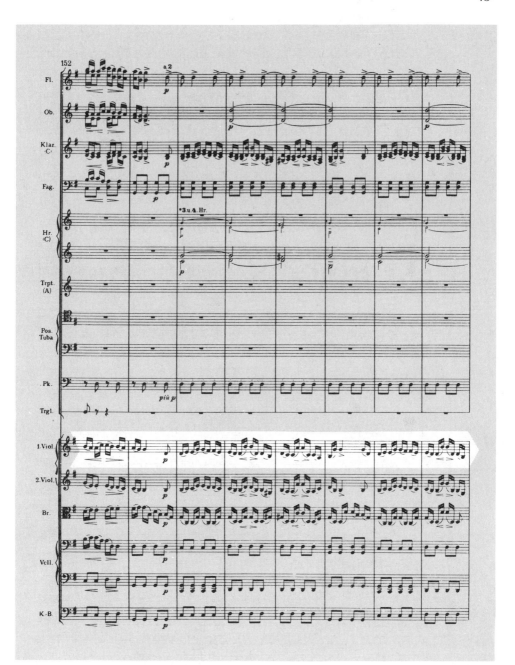

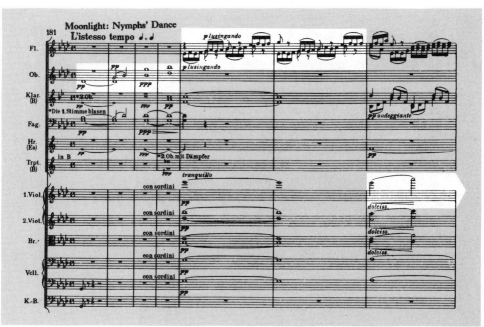

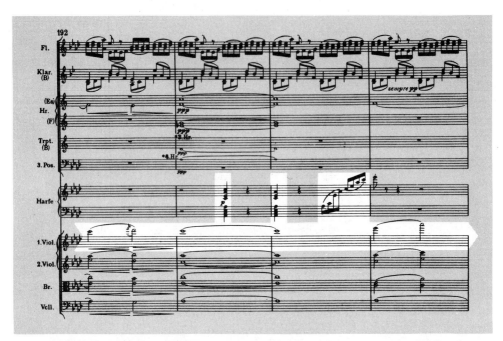

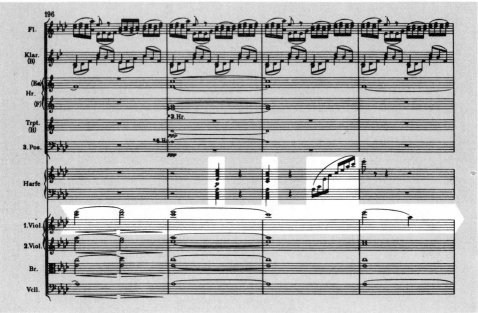

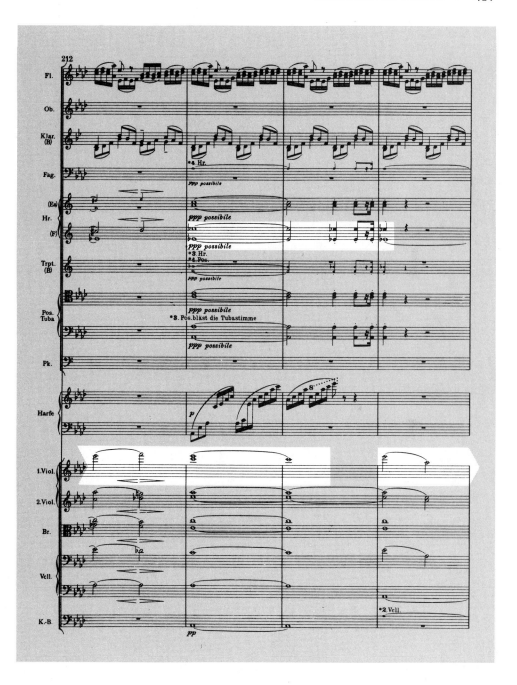

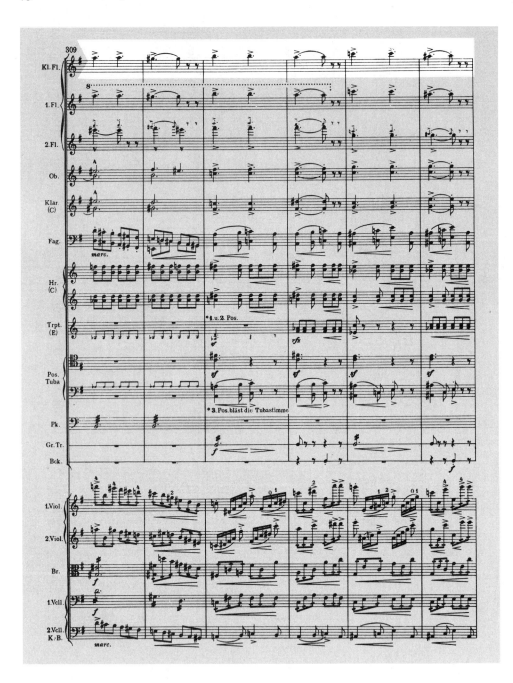

Vyšehrad Motive (Symphonic Poem No. 1)

17. Johannes Brahms (1833-1897),

A German Requiem, Third movement
(Fugue only) and fourth movement (1868)  7A/2 II/3/9

From Edition Peters No. 3672. Used by permission of C. F. Peters Corporation.

IV

TRANSLATION

End of Third movement:

Ich hoffe auf dich
Der Gerechten Seelen sind in Gottes hand,

und keine Qual rühret sie an.

My hope is in thee
But the righteous souls are in the hand of God,

nor pain nor grief shall touch them.

Fourth movement:

Wie lieblich sind deine
Wohnungen Herr Zebaoth!
Meine Seele verlanget und
sehnet sich nach den
Vorhöfen des Herrn: sein
Lieb und Seele freuen sich
in dem lebendigen Gott.
Wie lieblich . . .
Wohl denen, die in deinem
Hause wohnen, die loben
dich immerdar!
Wie lieblich . . .

How lovely is Thy dwelling
place, O Lord of hosts!
My soul longs and even
faints for the courts of the
Lord; my flesh and soul
rejoice in the living God.

How lovely . . .
Blessed are they that live in
Thy house, that praise Thee
evermore!
How lovely . . .

18. Brahms

Vergebliches Ständchen, Op. 84, No. 4
(1881?)

Translation

Guten Abend, mein Schatz,
Guten Abend, mein Kind!
Ich komm' aus Lieb' zu dir,
Ach, mach' mir auf die Tür!

"Meine Tür ist verschlossen,
Ich lass dich nicht ein;
Mutter die rät' mir klug,
Wär'st du herein mit Fug,
Wär's mit mir vorbei!"

So kalt ist die Nacht,
So eisig der Wind,
Dass mir das Herz erfriert,
Mein' Lieb' erlöschen wird;
Öffne mir, mein Kind!

"Löschet dein Lieb',
Lass sie löschen nur!
Löschet sie immer zu,
Geh' heim zu Bett zur Ruh',
Gute Nacht, mein Knab'!"

TRADITIONAL

Good evening, my dear
good evening, my child!
I come out of love for you,
ah, open the door for me!
Open the door for me!

"My door is locked,
I will not let you in.
Mother warned me
that if I let you in willingly
all would be over with me!"

The night is so cold,
the wind is so icy,
that my heart is freezing.
My love will be extinguished;
open up for me, child!

"If your love is extinguished,
just let it go out!
Just keep on extinguishing it;
go home to bed, to rest!
Good night, my boy!"

PHILIP L. MILLER

19. Brahms

Symphony No. 4 in E minor, Op. 98,
Fourth movement (1884–85)

  S3A/5  S3/12

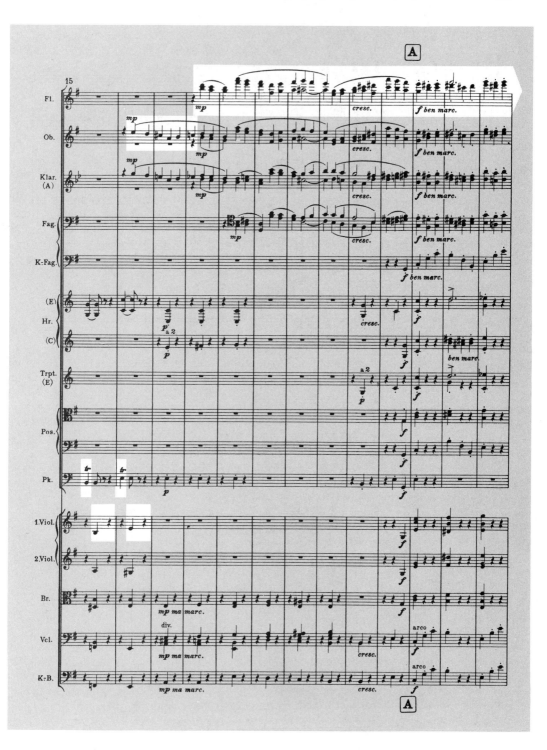

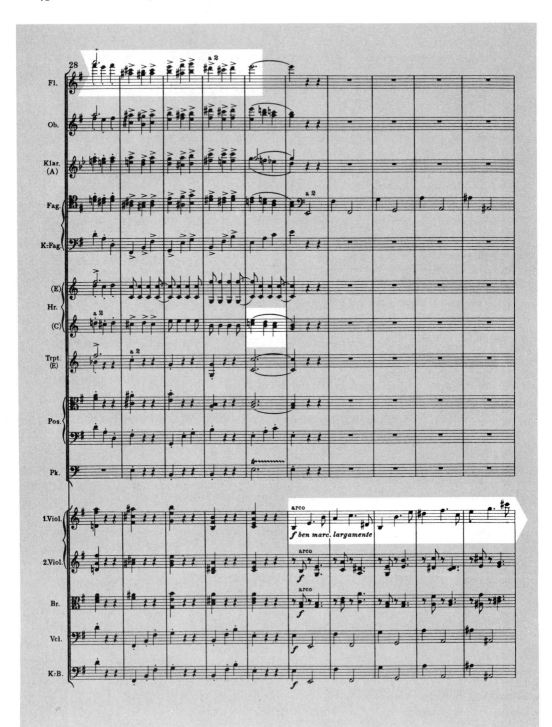

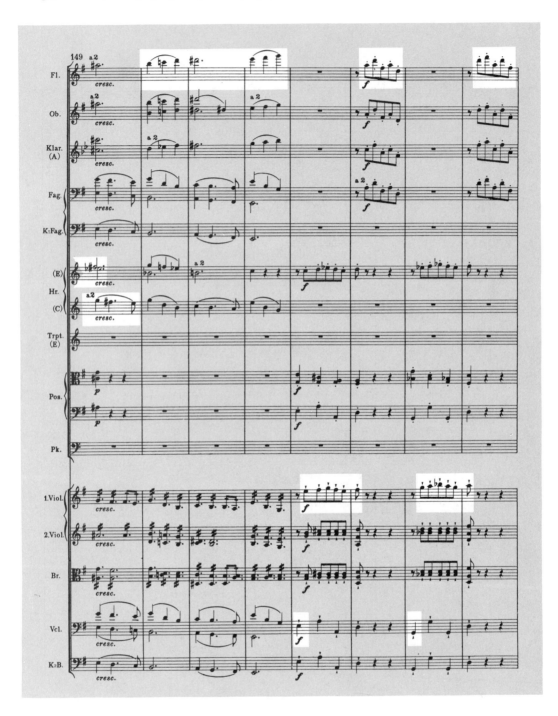

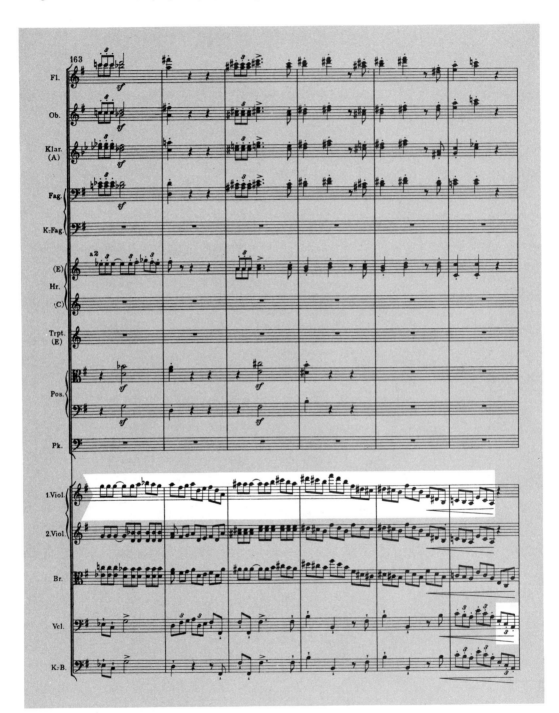

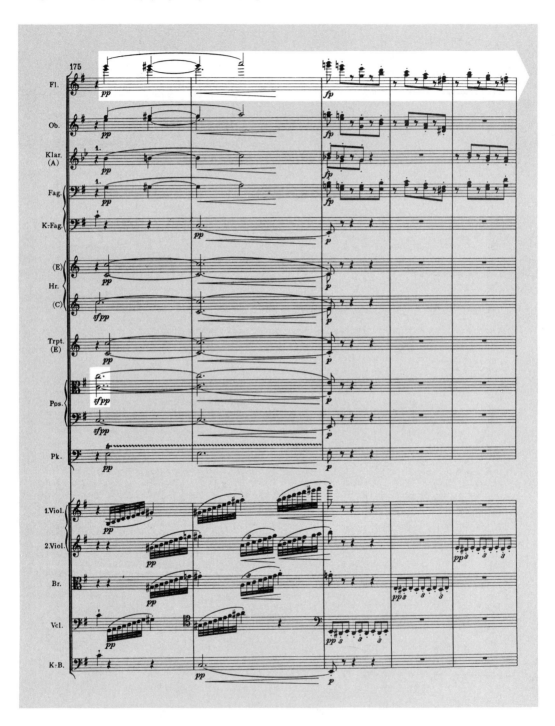

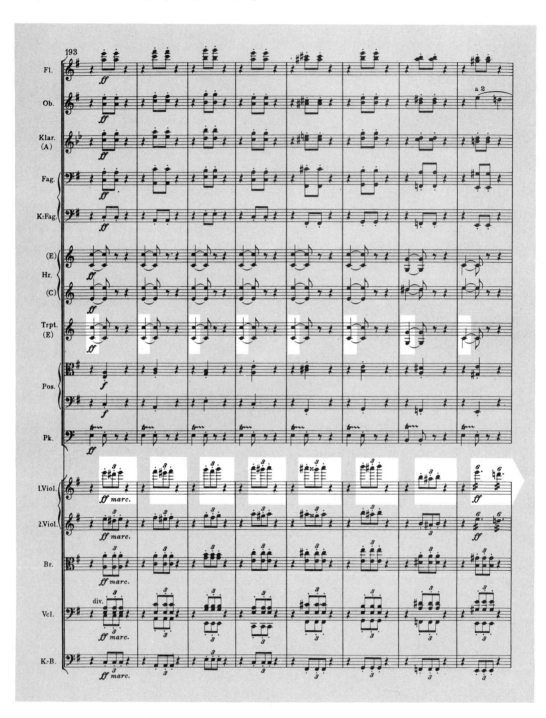

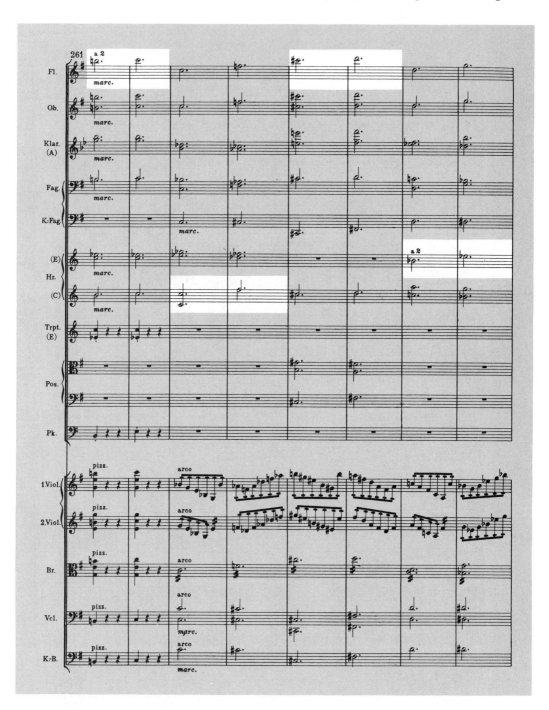

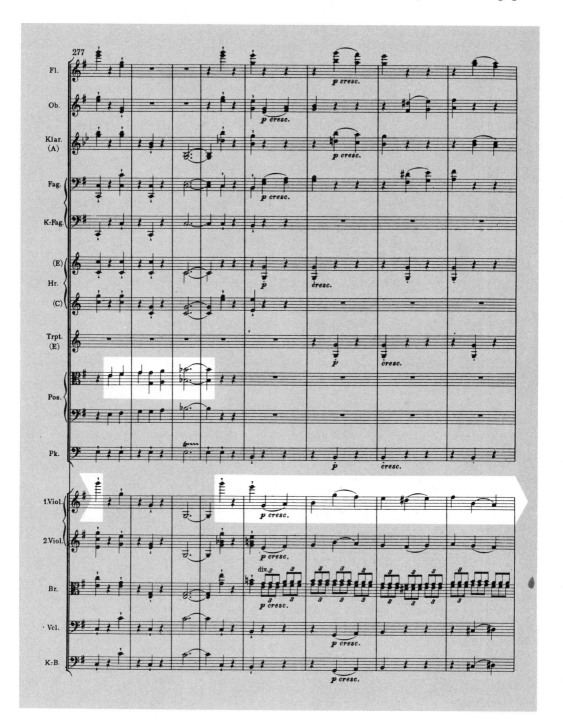

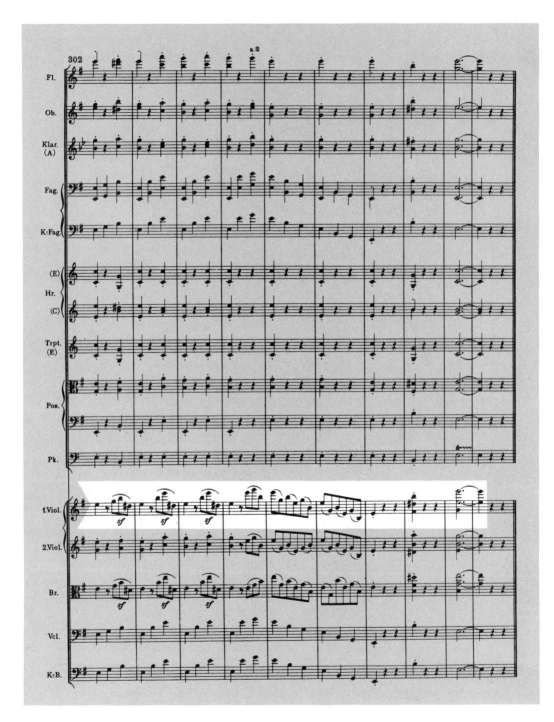

20. Georges Bizet (1838-1875),

Carmen, Scenes from Act I (1875)  S3B/2 S3/17

Scene No. 3

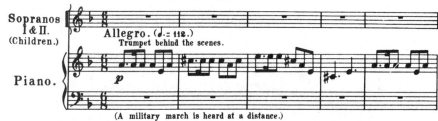

(The relief appears:

first a bugler and fifer, then a crowd of street-boys. — Following the latter, Lieutenant Zuniga and

Corporal Don José, then the dragoons. — During Street-boys' Chorus, the relief forms in front of the

guard going off duty.)

f ben ritmato, quasi staccato.

A - vec la gar - de mon-tan-te, Nous ar - ri-vons, nous voi - là! Son - ne, trom-
We are sol-diers marching proudly, Here we come to change the guard. Boys, blow your

petfe e -cla-tan- te! Ta ra ta ta ta ra ta ta. Nous mar-chons la tê- te hau - te
bu - gles _ loud-ly! See us march in per-fect man-ner,

Com - me de pe - tits sol - dats, Mar - quant sans fai - re de fau - te,
We are nev - er out of step. Fol - low the wav - ing _ ban - ner,

Recitative

Ju - pe bleue et nat - te tom - ban - te.
"Light blue skirt and ver - y long braids!"

Don José.

Tu ne ré - ponds rien __ à ce - la? Je ré - ponds que c'est
Well, am I right __ a - bout that? I ad - mit you are

vrai, je ré - ponds que je l'ai - - me!
right. I con - fess, she's the girl I love.

Recit.

Quant aux ou - vri - è - res d'i - ci, Quant __ à leur beau -
And as for the fac - to - ry girls, When __ you hear the

té, les voi - ci! Et vous pou - vez ju - ger vous - mê - me.
bell, they'll be here. Then you can judge their looks quite well.

attacca subito.

Scene No. 4

Scene No. 5

*) Imitated from a Spanish song.

t'ai - me, prends garde à ___ toi! ___
love you, you play with fire. ___

à ___ toi! ___
with ___ fire. ___

à ___ toi! ___
with ___ fire. ___

L'oiseau que tu croy - ais sur - prendre Battit de l'aile et_s'en - vo -
Wait for love and you wait for - ev - er, Don't wait at all,_ it_comes to

la; L'amour est loin, tu peux l'at - ten - dre; Tu·ne l'at - tends plus, il est
you. Try to grasp it, It's far too clev - er, It flies a - way_ in - to the

tu ne m'aimes pas, je___ t'ai - me; Mais si je

ev - er, ev - er try to___ spurn me. My friend, re -

Prends garde à toi!

You play with fire,

Prends garde à toi!

You play with fire,

t'ai - me, si je t'ai - me, prends garde à___ toi!___

mem-ber, if I love___ you, you play with___ fire!

à toi!

with fire!

à toi!

with fire!

attacca subito.

21. Peter Ilyich Tchaikovsky (1840-1893),

Violin Concerto in D major, Op. 35,
First movement (1878)    S3B/3   S3/22

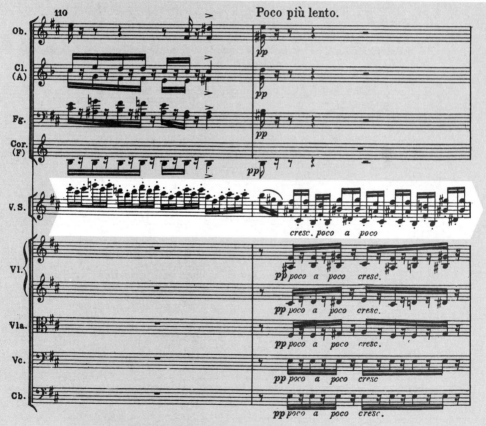

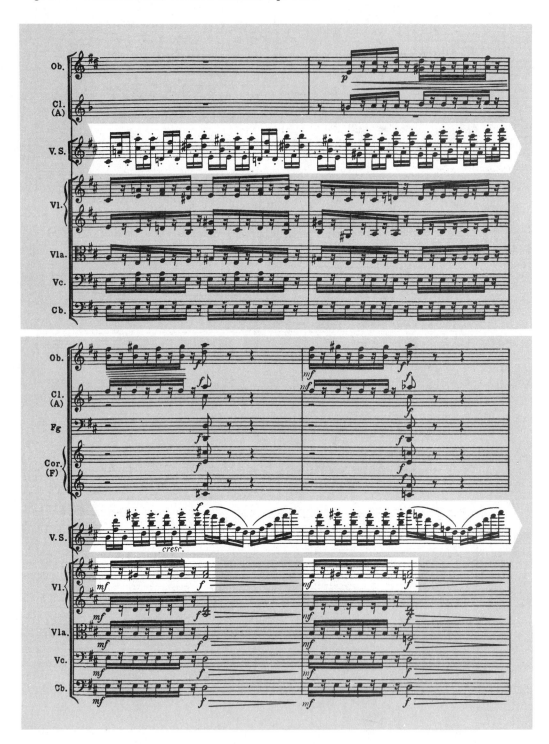

Moderato assai.

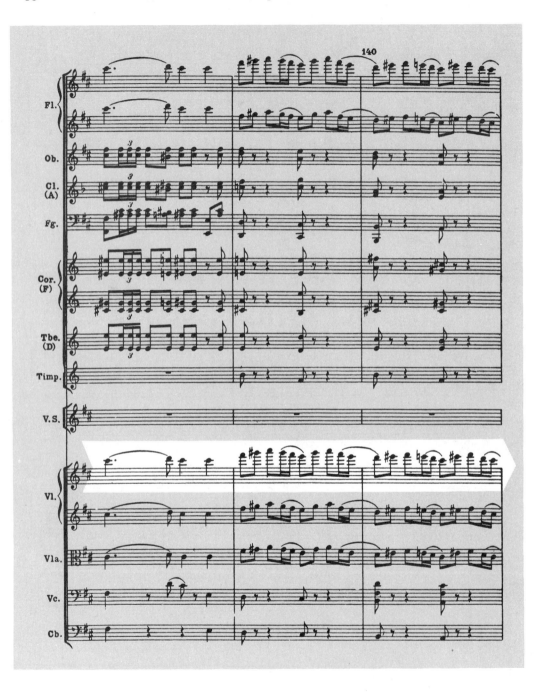

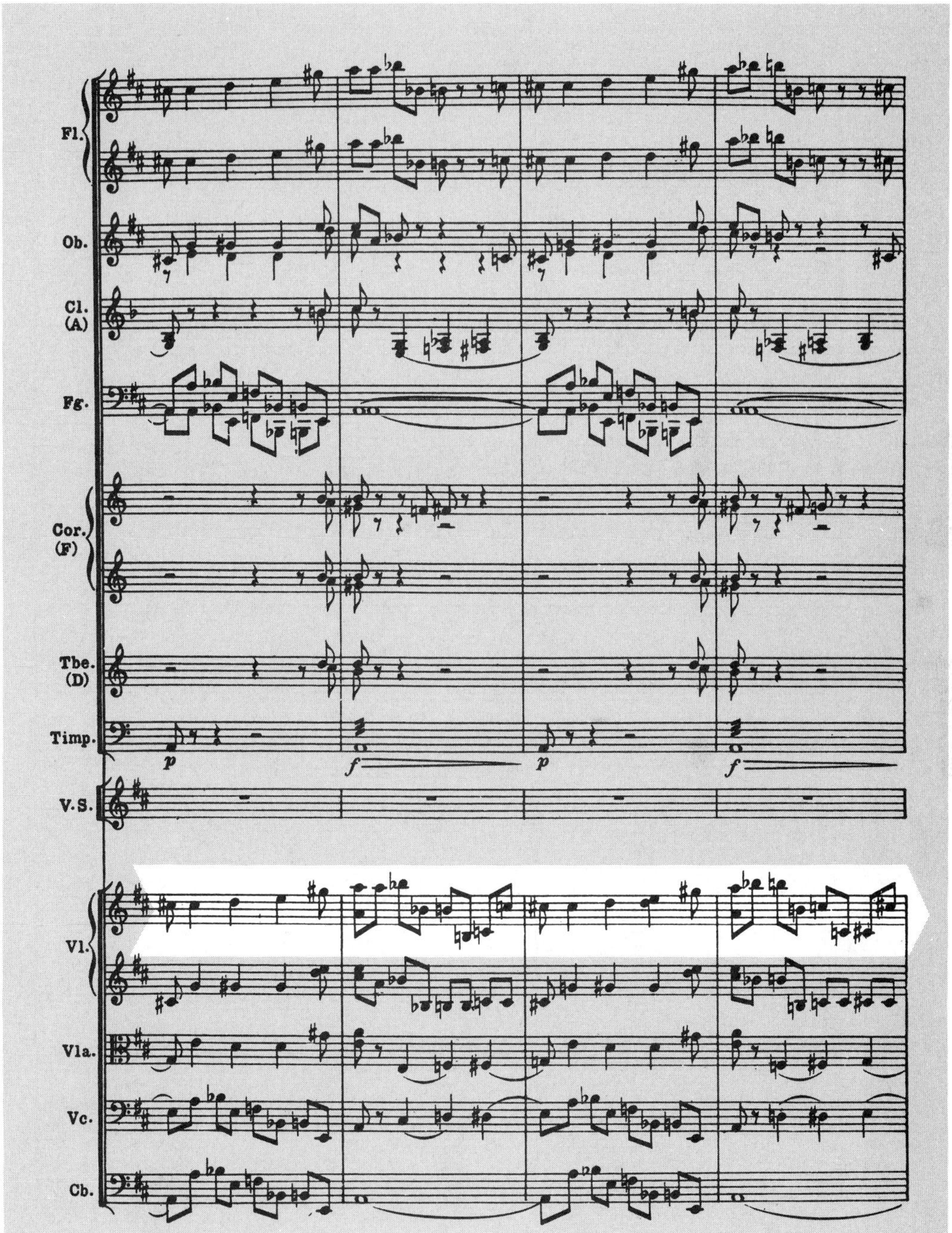
Fl.
Ob.
Cl. (A)
Fg.
Cor. (F)
Tbe. (D)
Timp.
p
f
p
f
V.S.
Vl.
Vla.
Vc.
Cb.

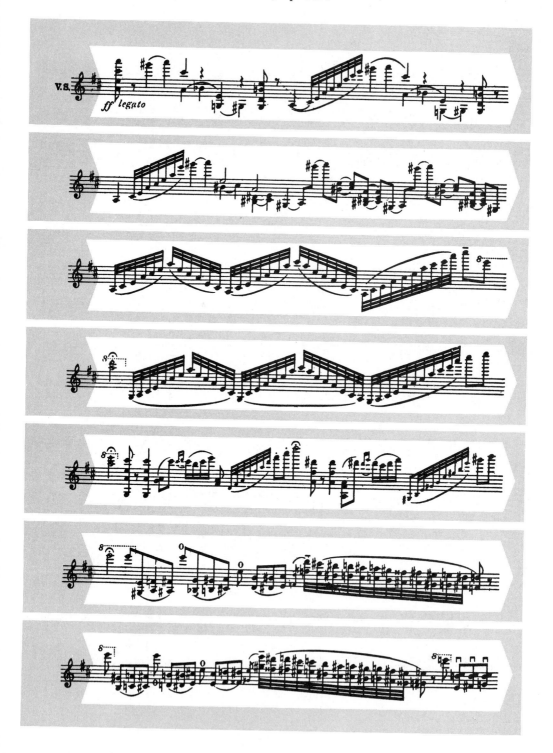

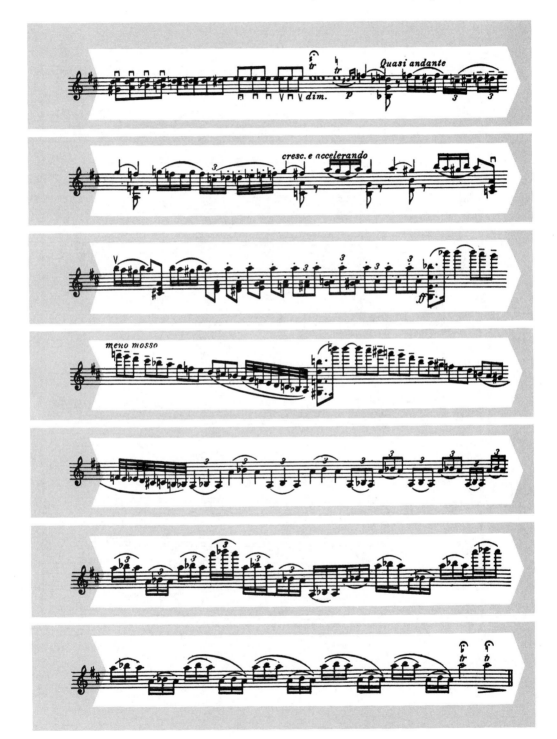

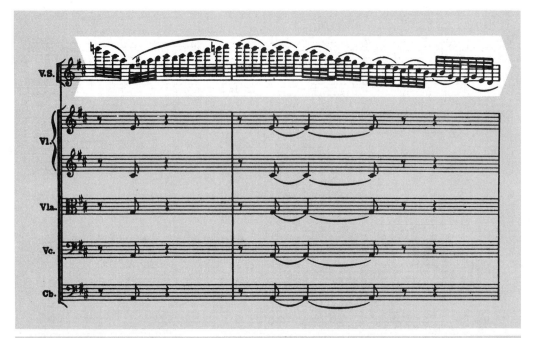

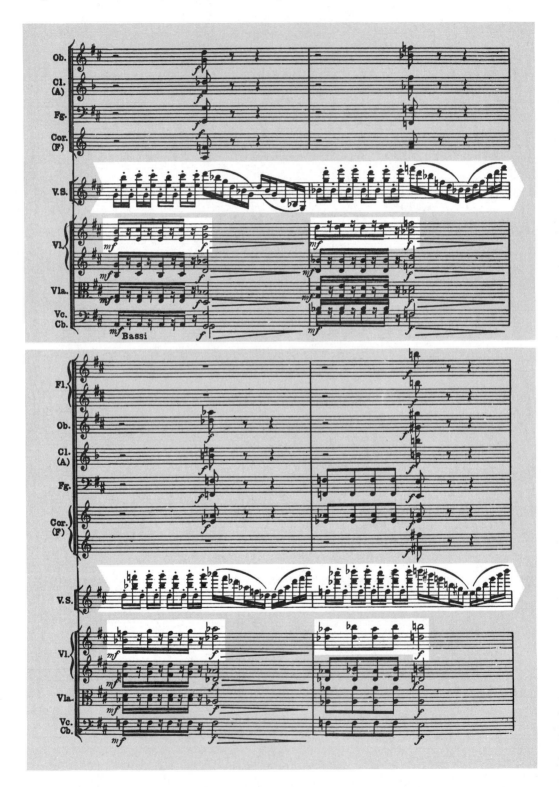

22. Giacomo Puccini (1858-1924),

La bohème, Finale of Act I (1896)   7B/1   II/3/11

(Mimi goes still nearer the window, The moonlight falls upon her.)

End of Act I

23. Gustav Mahler (1860-1911),

Symphony No. 4 in G major,
Fourth movement (1900)

S3A/6   S3/28

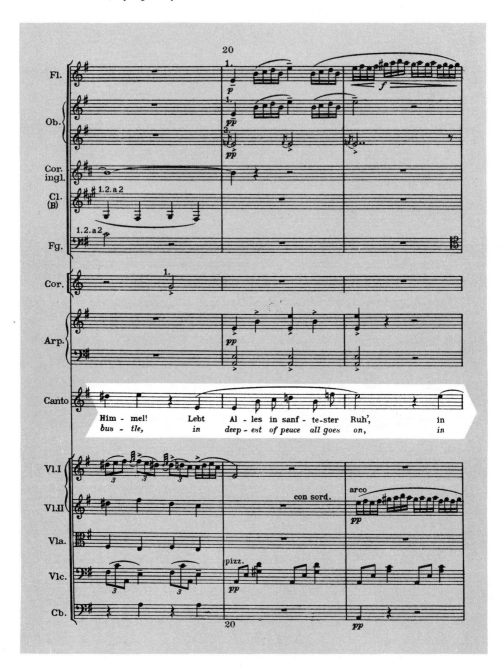

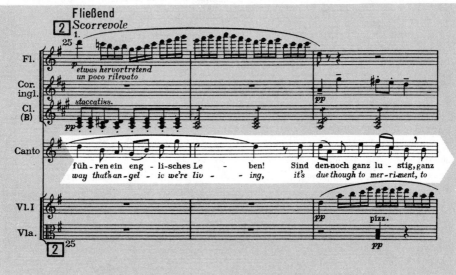

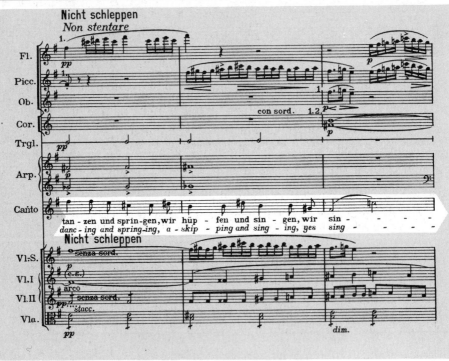

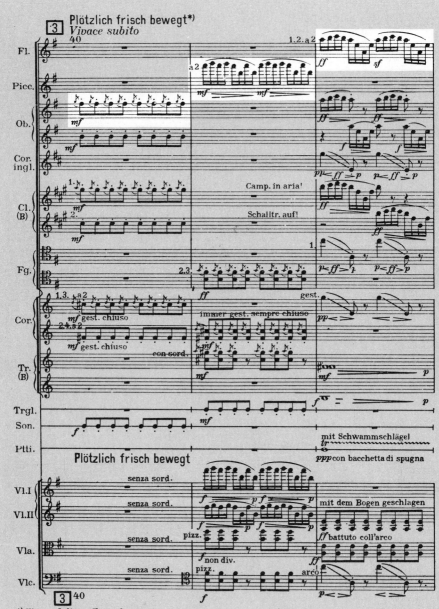

*) Hier muß dieses Tempo bewegter genommen werden, als an den korrespondierenden Stellen im ersten
*) Questo tempo deve essere portato più mosso che nel primo movimento
Satze

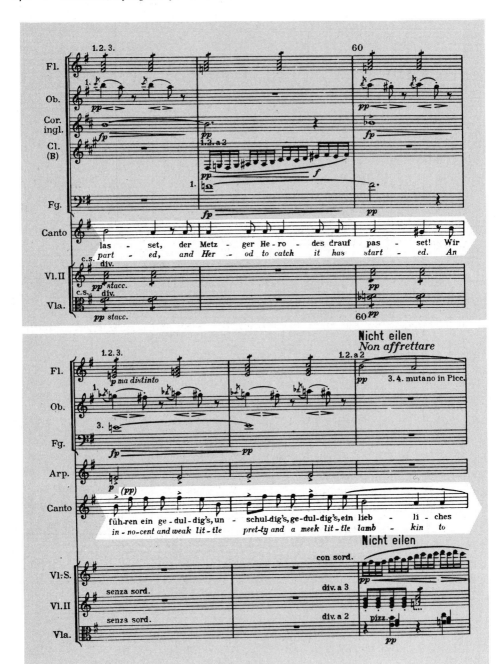

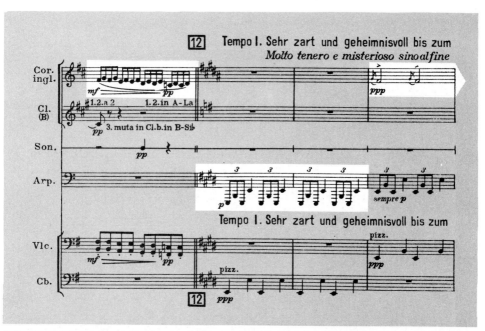

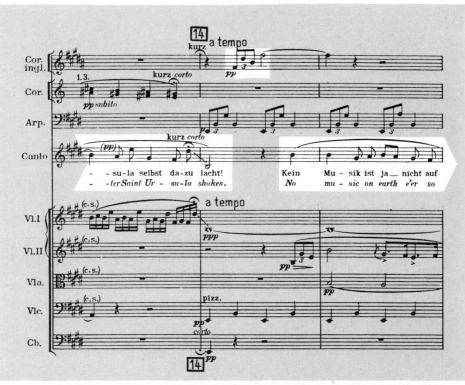

24. Claude Debussy (1862-1918),

Prelude to "The Afternoon of a Faun"
(1894)

  7A/4   II/3/14

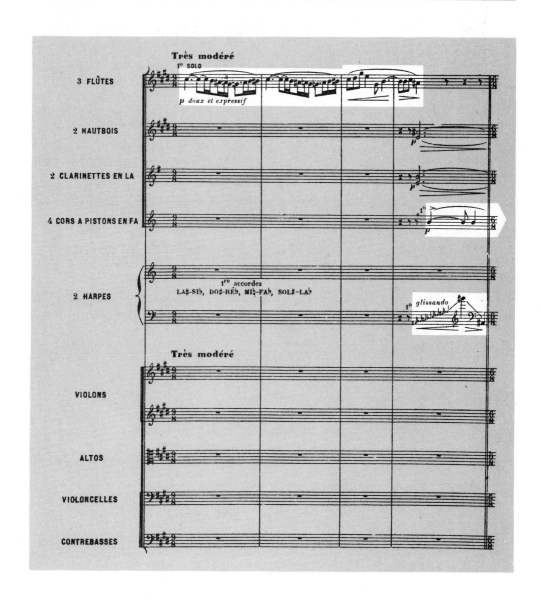

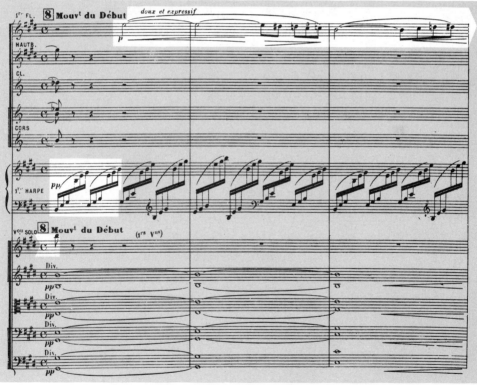

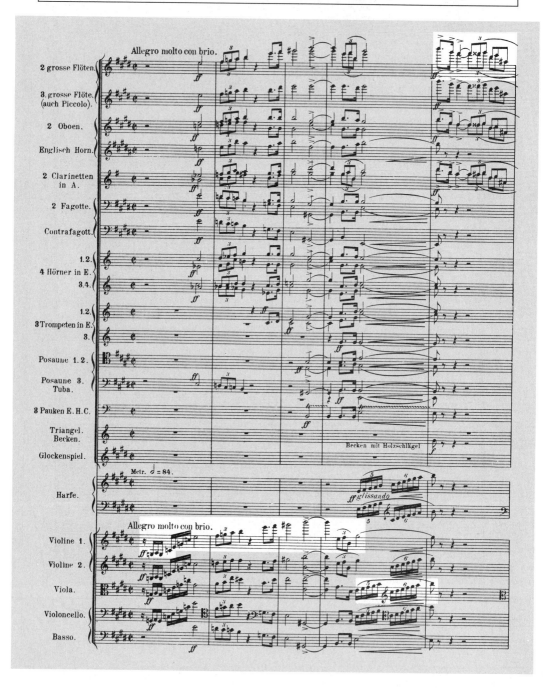

in E.
in E.
in E.
in E.
mit Holzschlägeln. Solo
pizz.
pizz.
pizz.
divisi

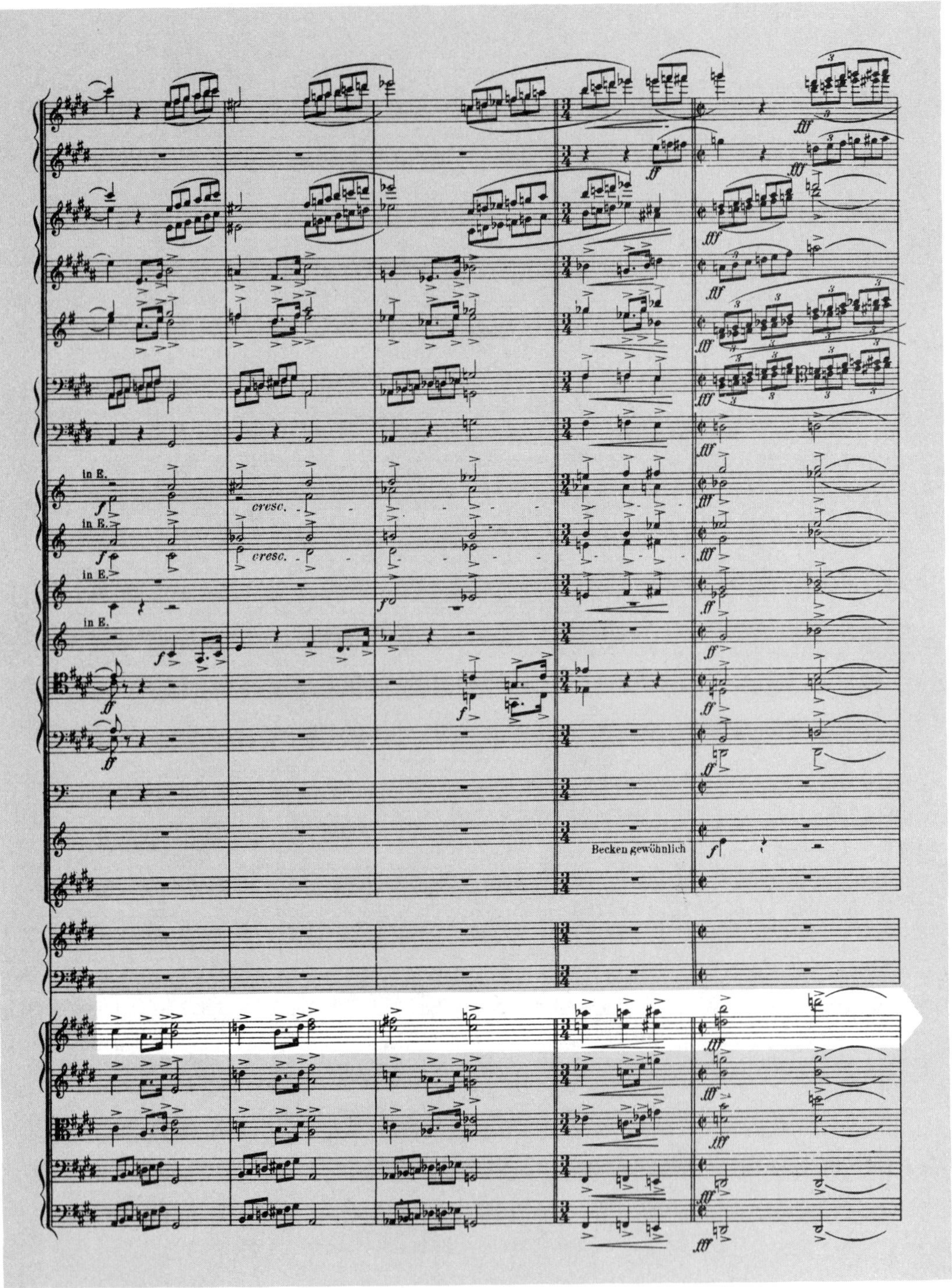
in E.
in E.
in E.
in E.
cresc.
cresc.
Becken gewöhnlich

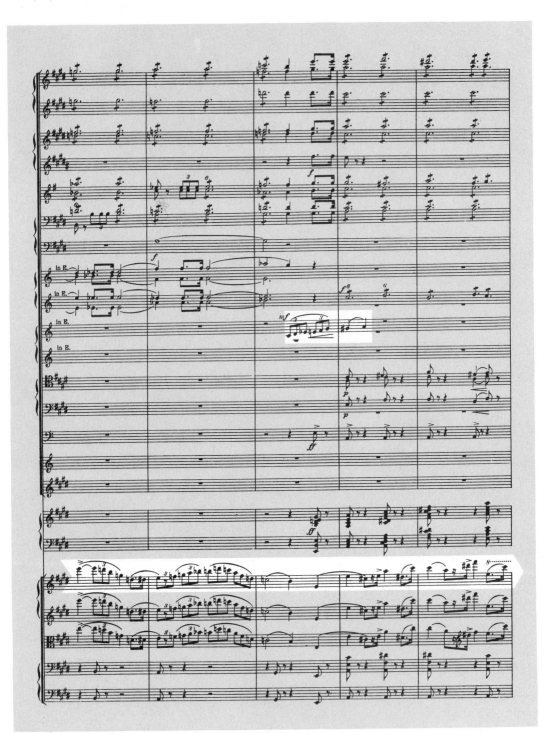

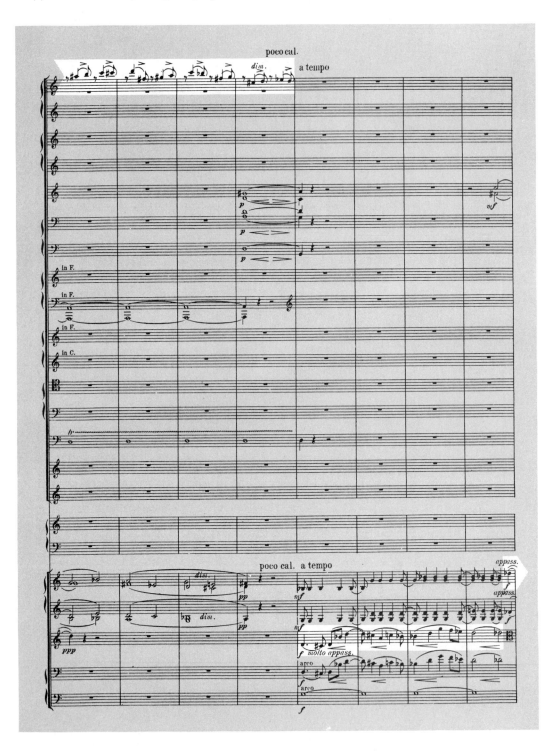

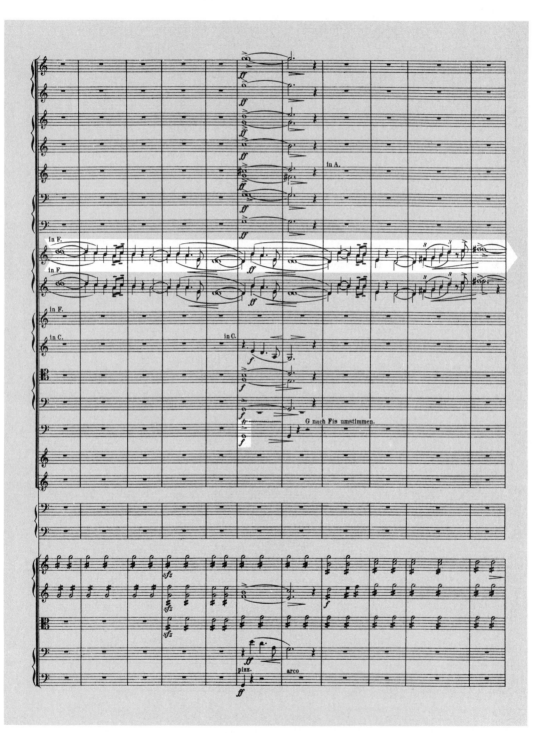

stringendo
a tempo, giocoso.
𝅗𝅥 = 92.
in F.
in F.
in F.
in C.
ffp
cresc.
Tr.
Solo.
con sord.
giocoso
stringendo
a tempo, giocoso.
pizz.
pizz.
pizz.
pizz.

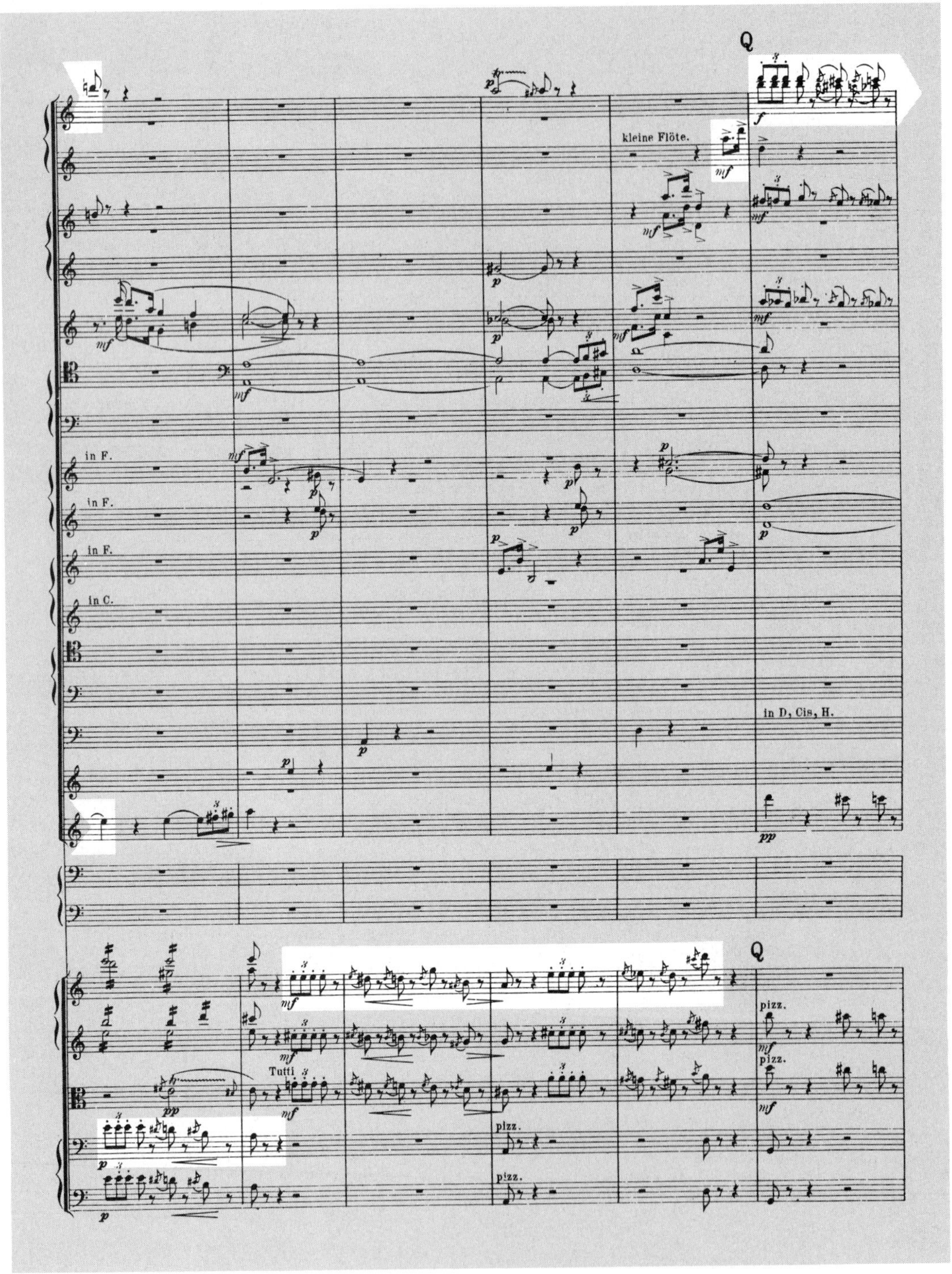
Q
kleine Flöte.
in F.
in F.
in F.
in C.
in D, Cis, H.
Tutti
pizz.
Q

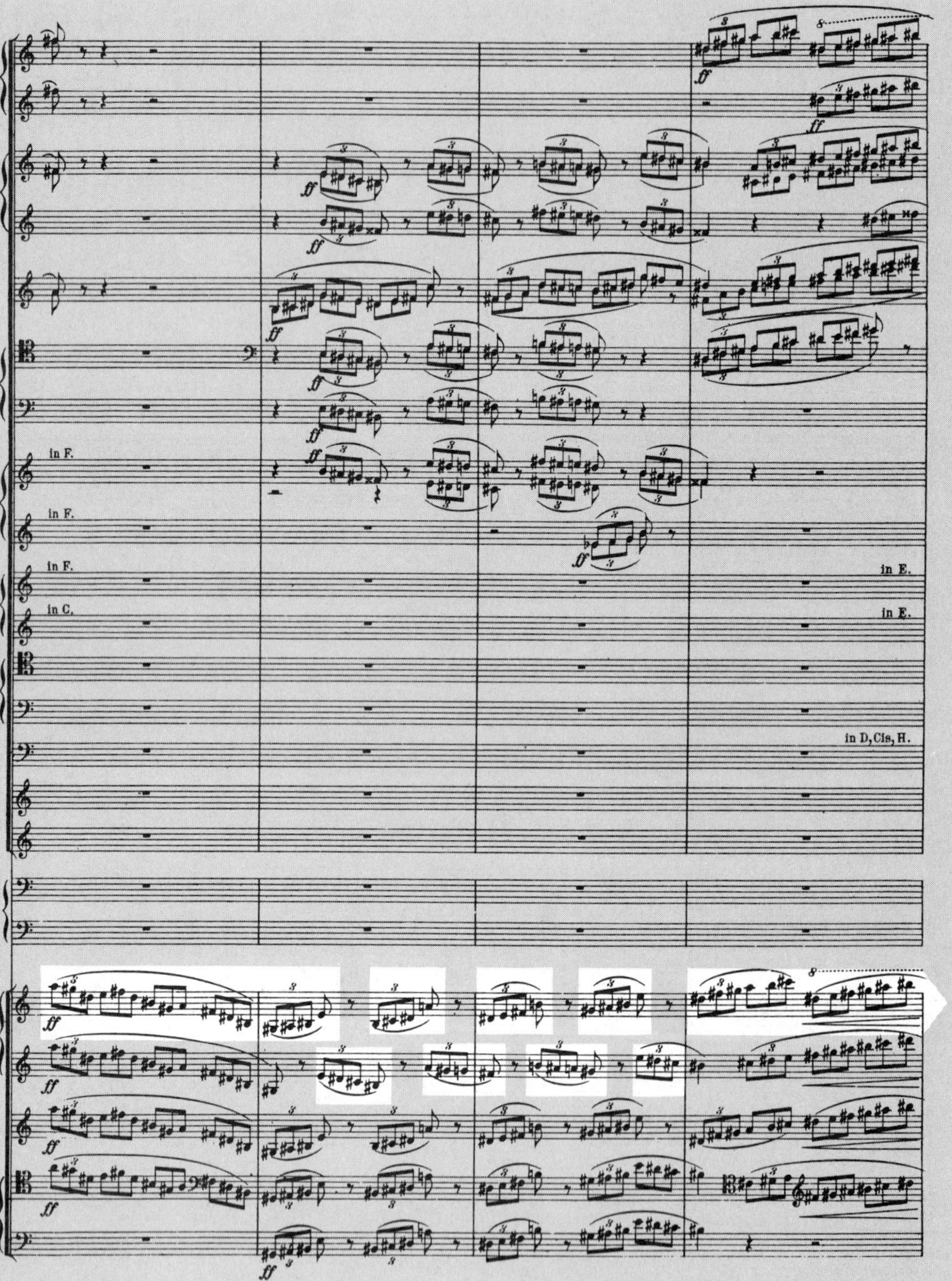
in F.
in F.
in F.
in C.
in E.
in E.
in D, Cis, H.
ff

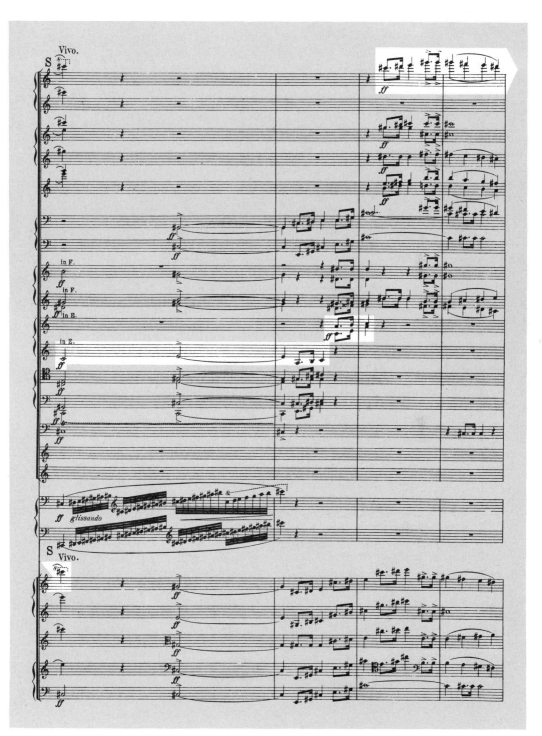

V molto tranquillo
pp tranquillo
tranquillo
pp
in E.
senza sord.
gestopft
sfz
IV.
p bispiglando
espr.
dreifach getheilt
sul ponticello
pp sul ponticello

W
in E.
in E.
in E.
in E.
mf molto cresc.
mf molto cresc.
in E, H, C
ff
mf
f
W
pizz.
pizz.

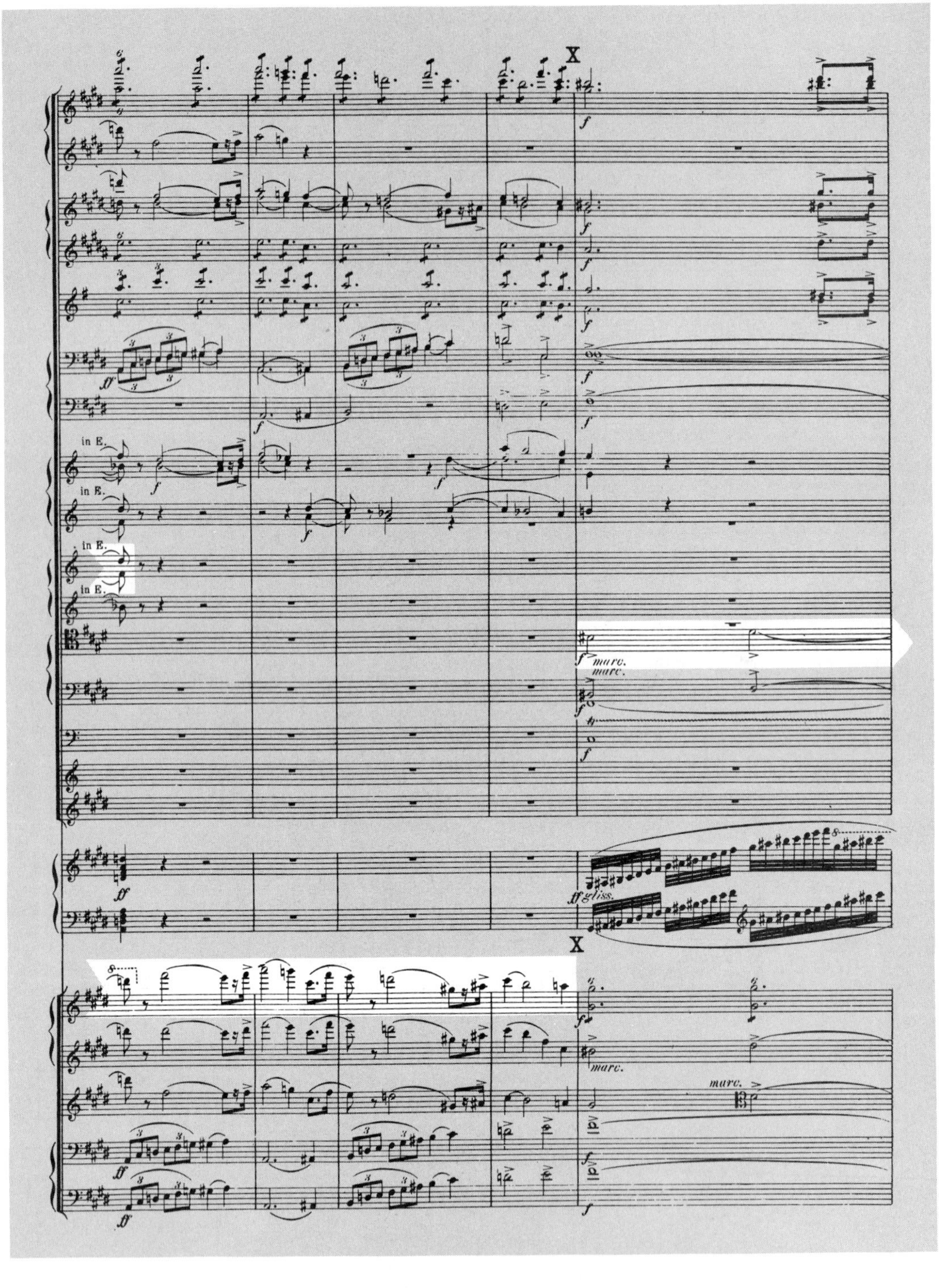
X
in E.
in E.
in E.
in E.
marc.
marc.
gliss.
X
marc.
marc.

*) ganze Takte schlagen.

26. Scott Joplin (1868-1917),

Treemonisha, Final scene (1911)  S4A/2   S4/7

late............ For ig - no-rance is crim - in - al In

this en-light-ened day,................ So let us all........ get....

bu - sy,............. When once........ we've found the way................

Directions for The Slow Drag.

1. The Slow Drag must begin on the first beat of each measure.
2. When moving forward, drag the left foot; when moving backward, drag the right foot.
3. When moving sideways to right, drag left foot; when moving sideways to left, drag right foot.
4. When prancing, your steps must come on each beat of the measure.
5. When marching and when sliding, your steps must come on the first and the third beat of each measure.
6. Hop and skip on second beat of measure. Double the Schottische step to fit the slow music.   SCOTT JOPLIN.

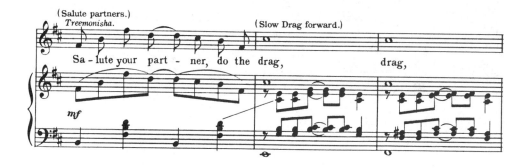

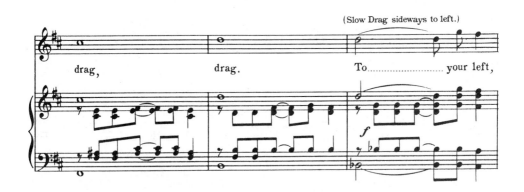

(All Slow Drag forward.)

do .... that slow, ... do .... that slow drag. ....

do .... that slow, ... do .... that slow drag. ....

do .... that slow, ... do .... that slow drag. ....

do .... that slow, ... do .... that slow drag. ....

do .... that slow, ... O do .... that slow drag. ....

now do the drag real slow, now do the real slow drag, slow drag.

27. Ralph Vaughan Williams (1872-1958),

Fantasia on "Greensleeves" (1934)

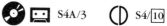 S4A/3 S4/10

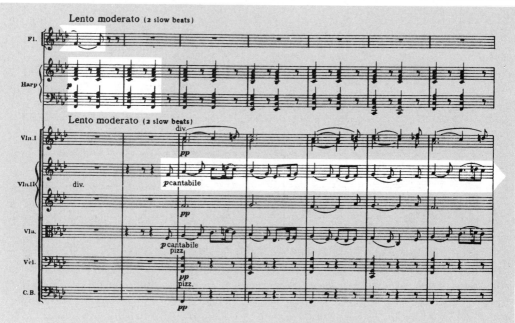

Fantasia on "Greensleeves" by Ralph Vaughan Williams, adapted from the opera "Sir John in Love" by Ralph Greaves. © 1934 by the Oxford University Press London; renewed in U.S.A. 1962. Reprinted by permission.

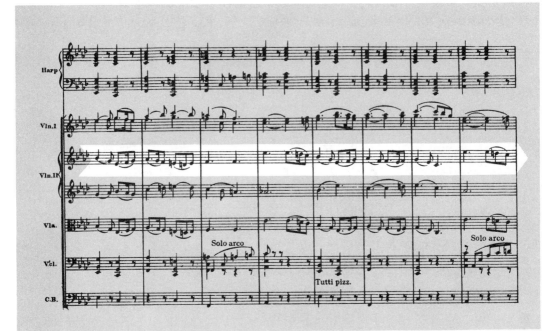

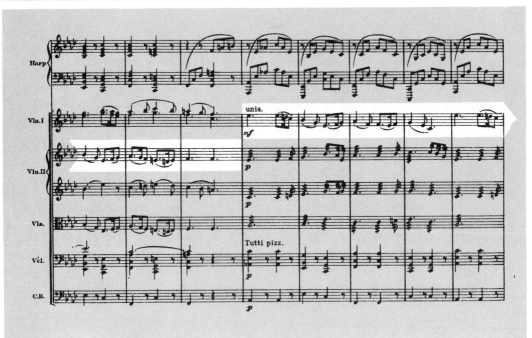

*Folk Tune 'Lovely Joan'

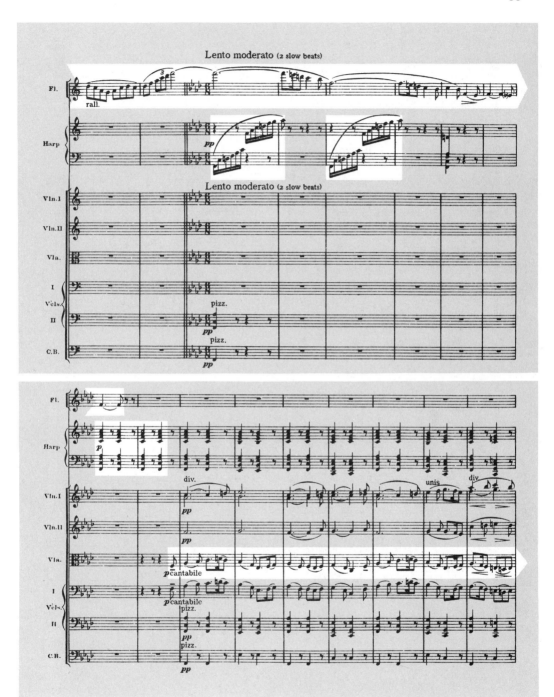

28. Arnold Schoenberg (1874-1951),

Pierrot lunaire, Op. 21,
Nos. 18 and 21 (1912)

 7A/5  II/3/18

No. 18 "Der Mondfleck"

gift _ geschwollen wei_ter, reibt und reibt bis an den frühen Morgen ei_nen

hervor

wei_ _ ßen Fleck des hel_len Mon_des.

ohne größere Pause, bloß ⌢
aushalten, folgt:

Serenade.
Klavier, Violoncell

Übergang zu Heimfahrt kommen dazu
Flöte, Klarinette in A, Geige.

TRANSLATION

Einen weissen Fleck des hellen Mondes

With a fleck of white—bright patch of moonlight—

Auf dem Rücken seines schwarzen Rockes,
So spaziert Pierrot im lauen Abend,
Aufzusuchen Glück und Abenteuer.

On the back of his black jacket,
Pierrot strolls about in the mild evening air
On his night-time hunt for fun and good
pickings.

Plötzlich stört ihn was an seinem Anzug,
Er beschaut sich rings und findet richtig—

Suddenly something strikes him as wrong,
He checks his clothes over and sure enough
finds

Einen weissen Fleck des hellen Mondes

A fleck of white—bright patch of moonlight—

Auf dem Rücken seines schwarzen Rockes.

On the back of his black jacket.

Warte! denkt er: das ist so ein Gipsfleck!

Damn! he thinks, There's a spot of white
plaster!

Wischt und wischt, doch—bringt ihn nicht
herunter!
Und so gent er, giftgeschwollen, weiter,
Reibt und reibt bis an den frühen Morgen—
Einen weissen Fleck des hellen Mondes.

Rubs and rubs, but can't get rid of it.

So goes on his way, his pleasure poisoned,
Rubbing and rubbing till dawn comes up—
*At a fleck of white, a bright patch of moon-
light!*

No. 21 "O alter Duft"

TRANSLATION

O alter Duft aus Märchenzeit.
Berauschest wieder meine Sinne:
Ein närrisch Heer von Scheimerein
Durchschwirrt die leichte Luft.

Ein glückhaft Wunschen macht mich froh
Nach Freuden, die ich lang verachtet:
O alter Duft aus Märchenzeit,
Berauschest wieder mich!

All meinen Unmut gab ich preis:
Aus meinem sonnumrahmten Fenster
Beschau ich frei die liebe Welt
Und träum hinaus in seige Weiten . . .
O alter Duft—aus Märchenzeit!

O scent of fabled yesteryear.
Befuddling my senses with bygone joys!
A silly swarm of idle fancies
Murmurs through the gentle air.

A happy ending so long yearned for
Recalls old pleasures long disdained:
O scent of fabled yesteryear,
Befuddling me again!

My bitter mood has turned to peace:
My sundrenched window opens wide
On daytime thoughts of world I love,
To daydreams of a world beyond . . .
O scent of fabled yesteryear!

29. Charles Ives (1874-1954),

Symphony No. 2, Fourth and fifth movements (1900–02)

 7B/2 II/3/20

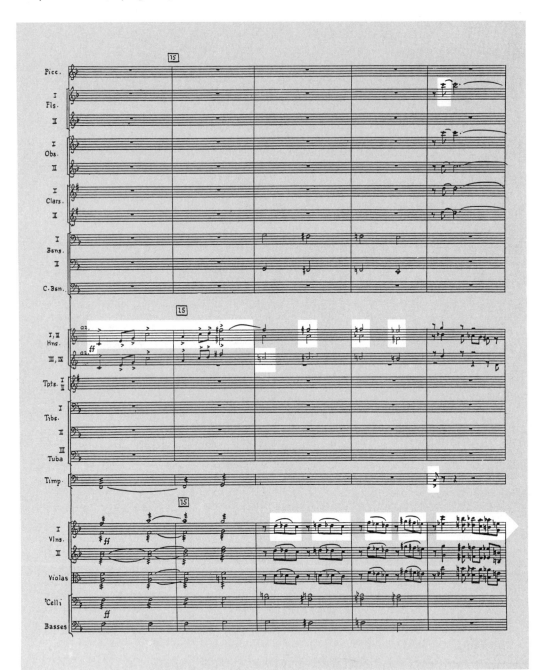

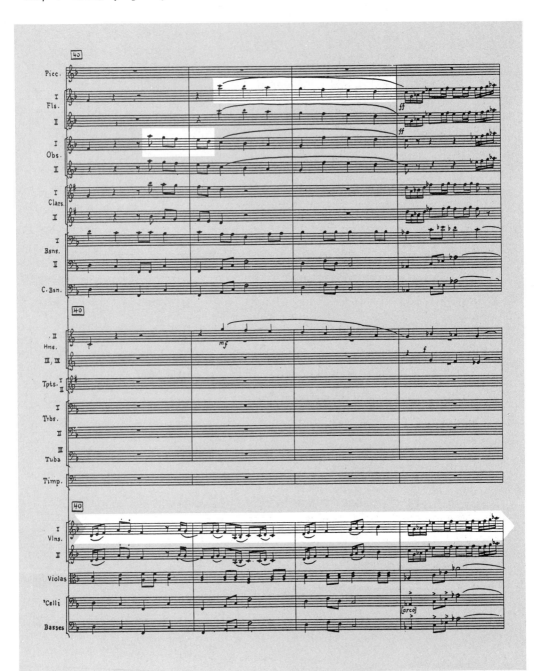

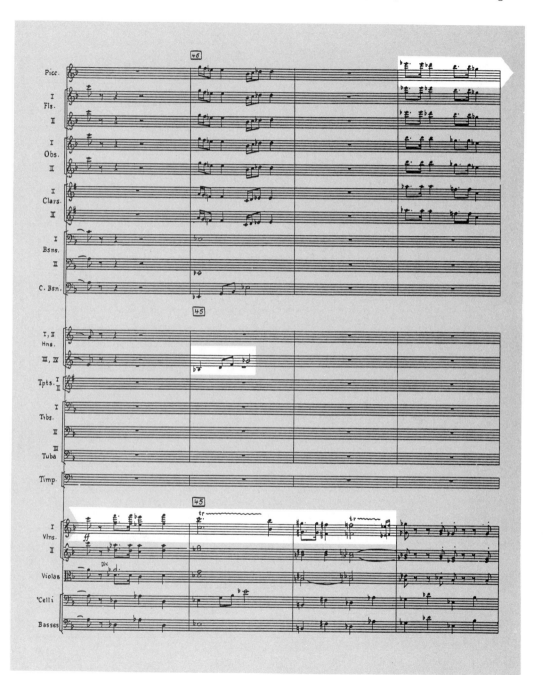

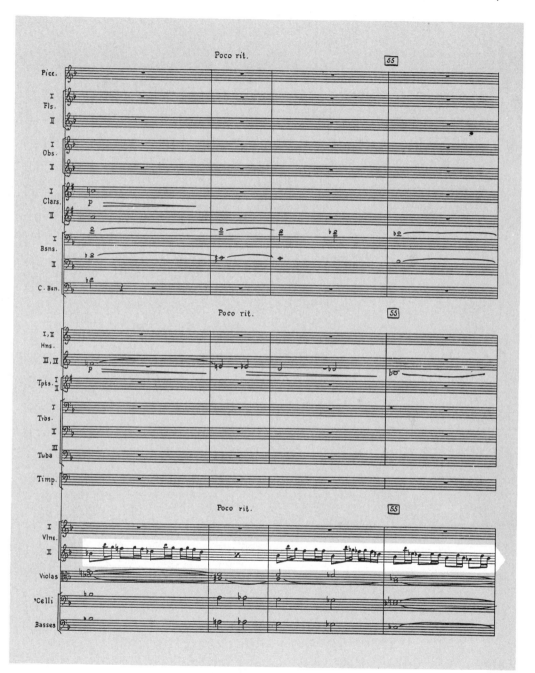

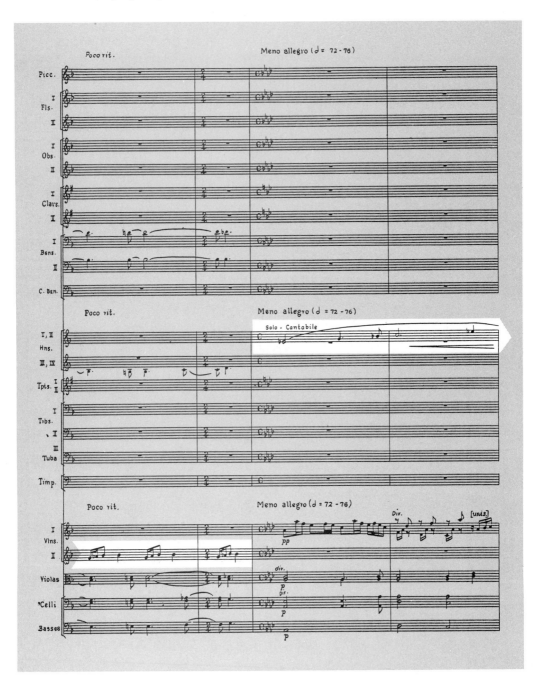

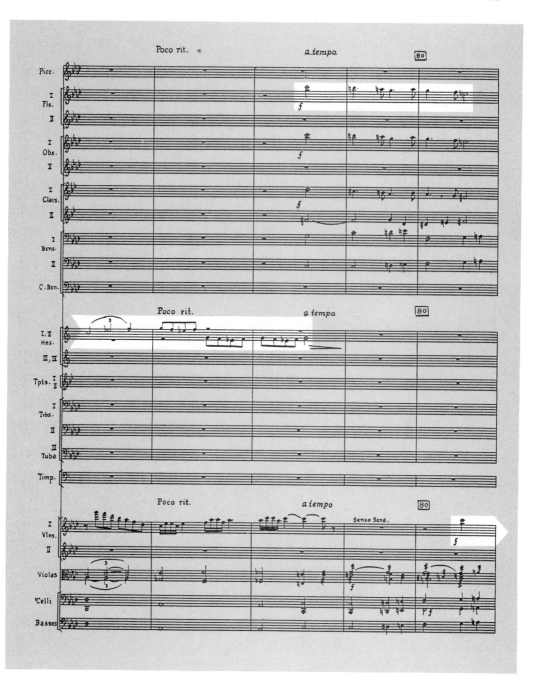

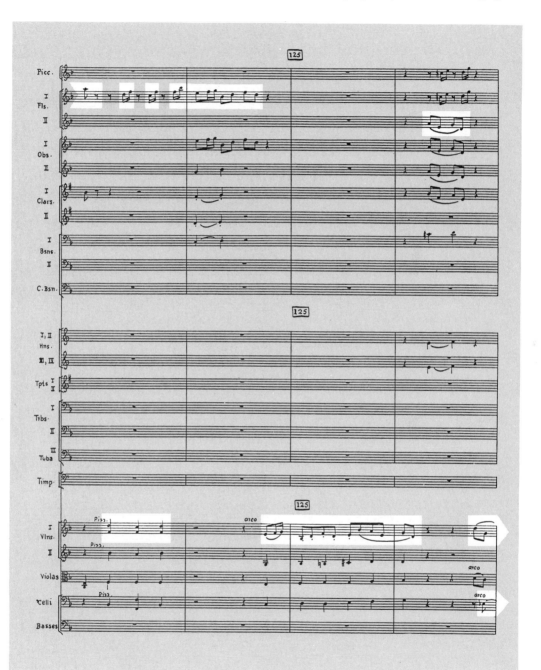

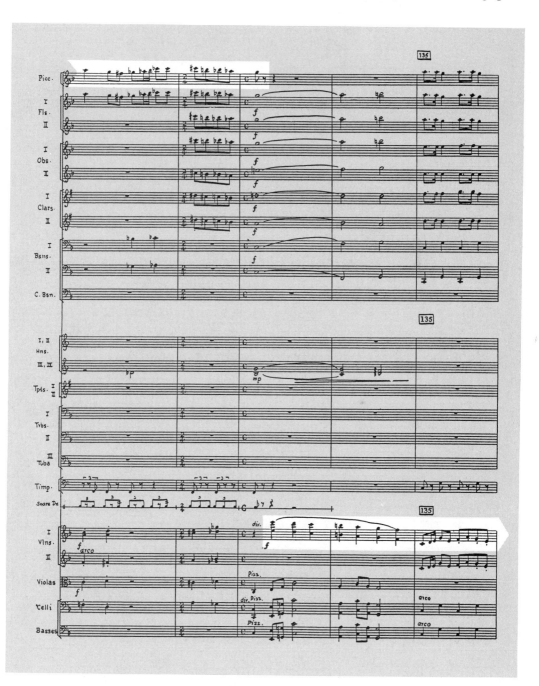

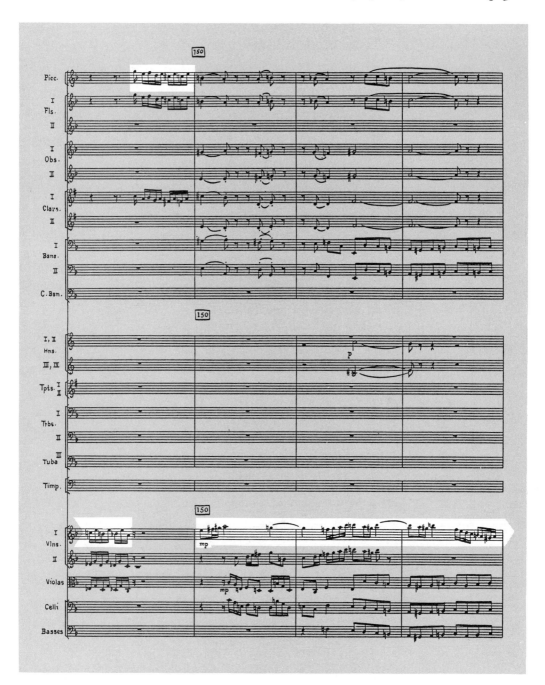

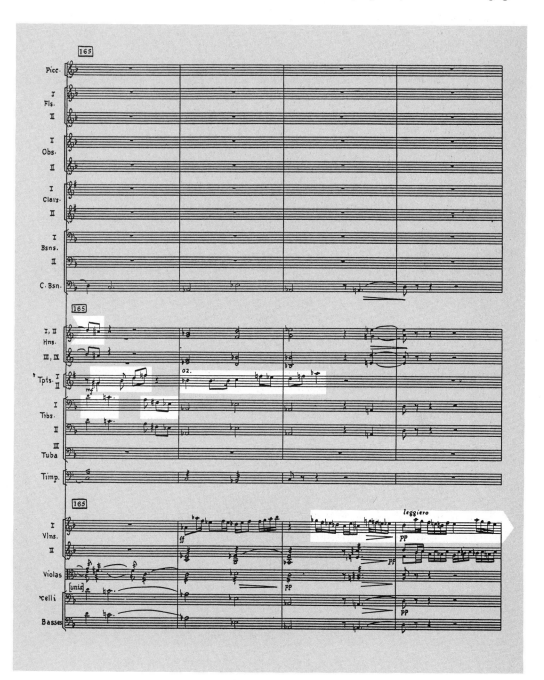

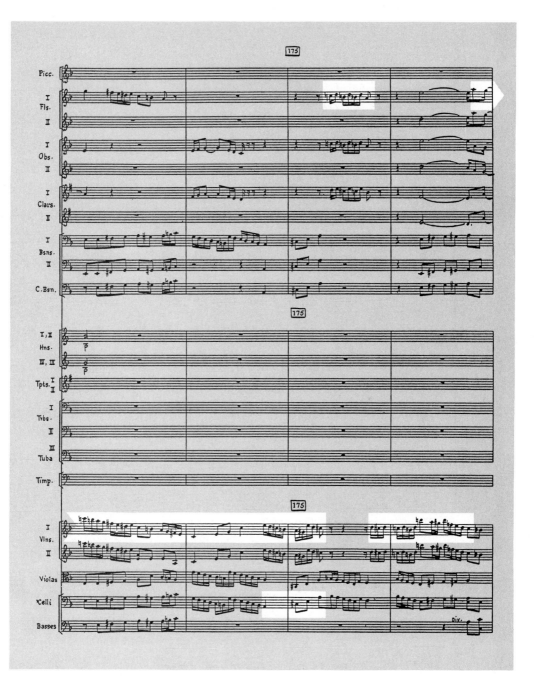

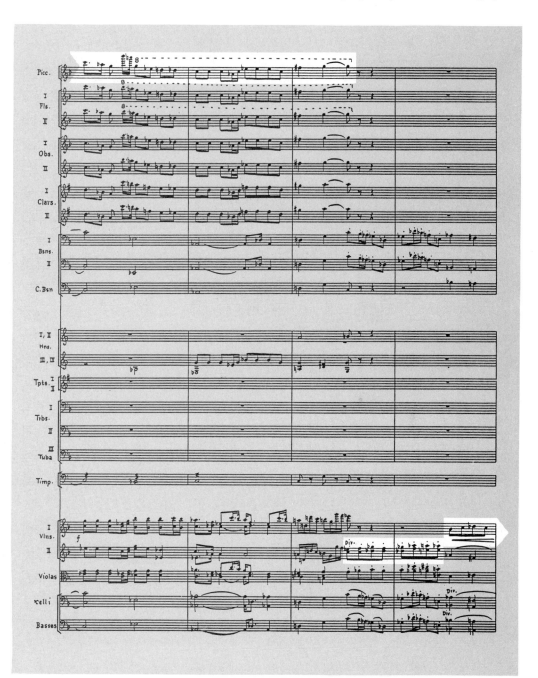

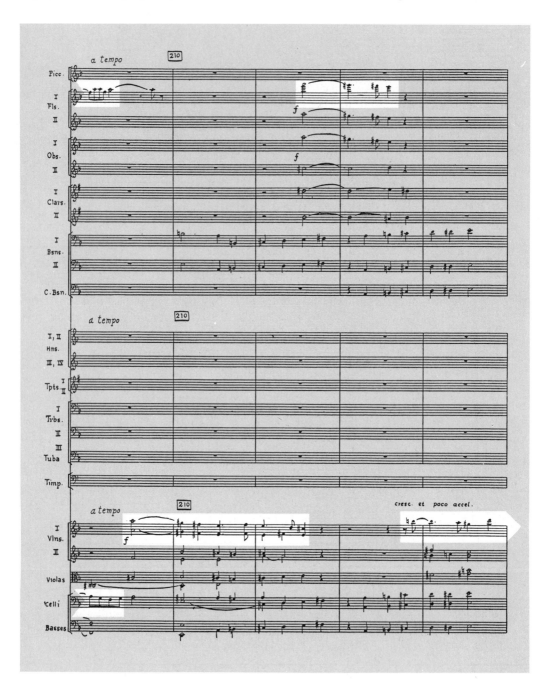

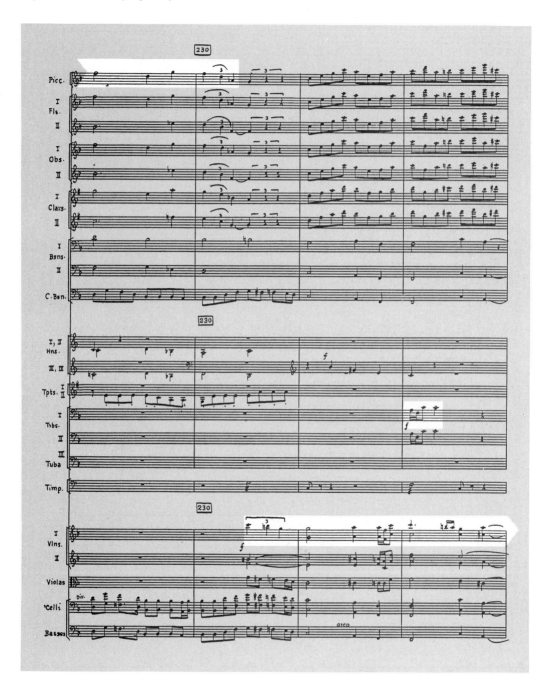

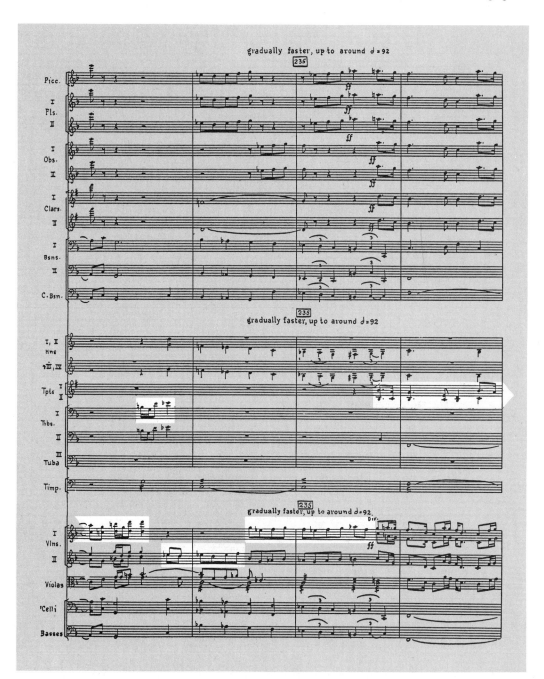

30. Maurice Ravel (1875-1937),

Le tombeau de Couperin, Rigaudon
(1919)

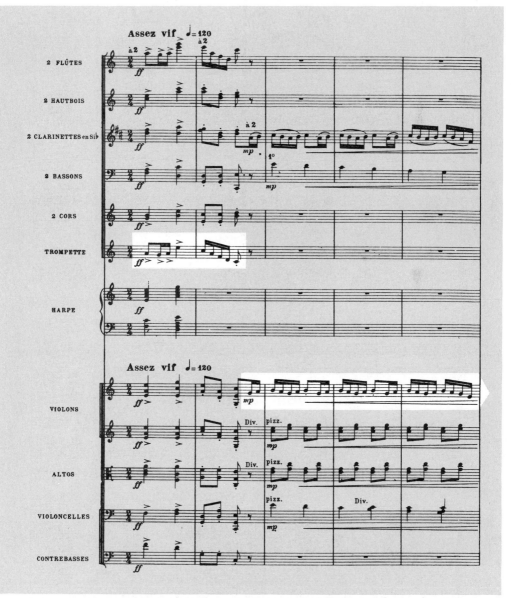

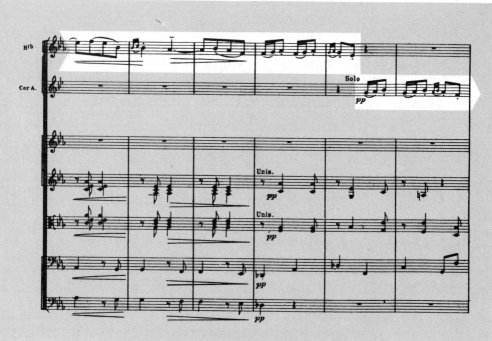

31. Béla Bartók (1881-1945),

Music for Strings, Percussion, and Celesta, Fourth movement (1936)

 7B/3 II/3/25

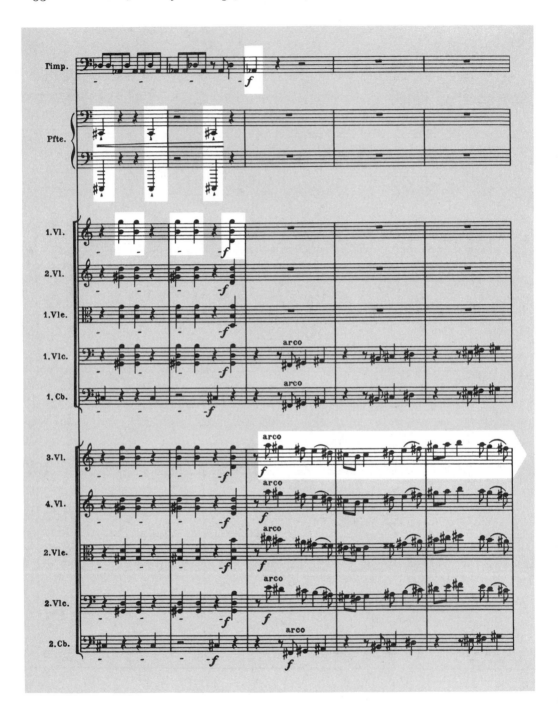

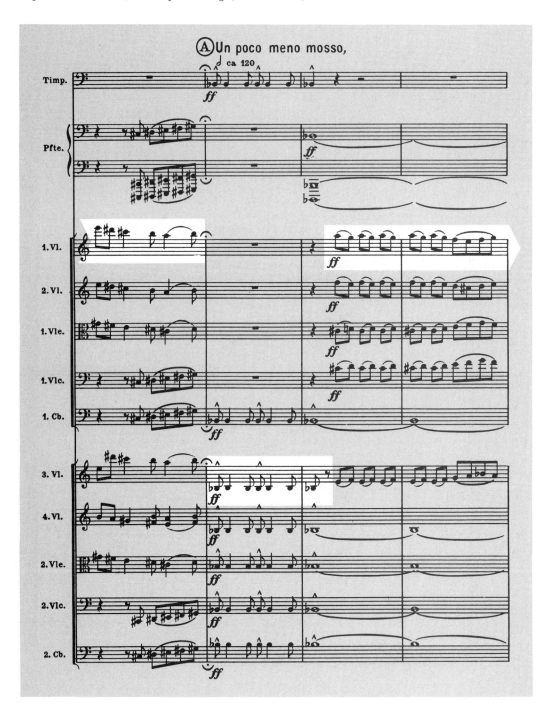

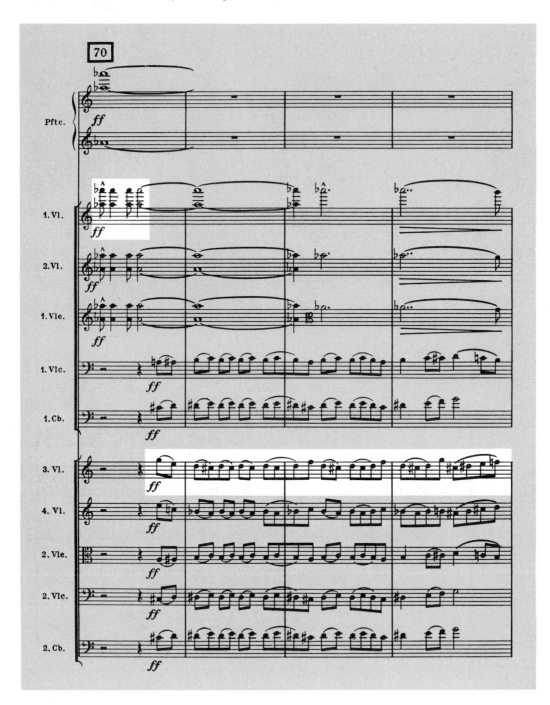

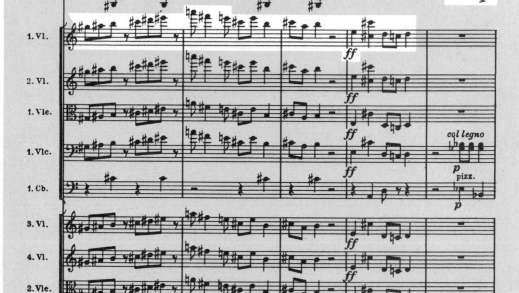

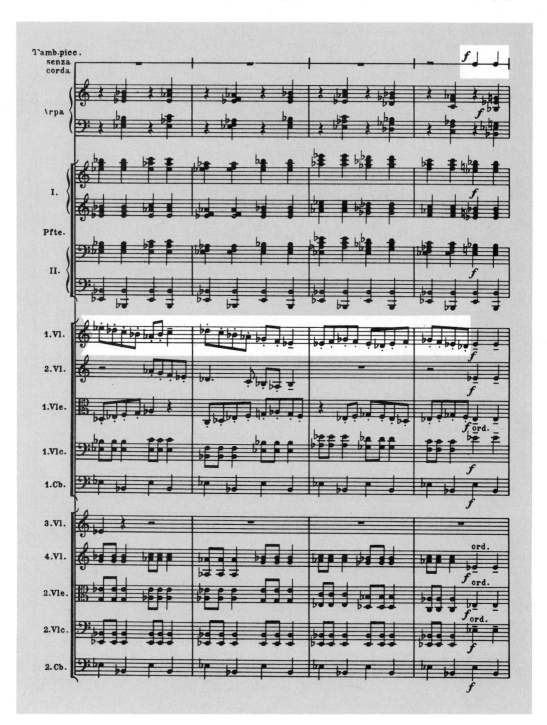

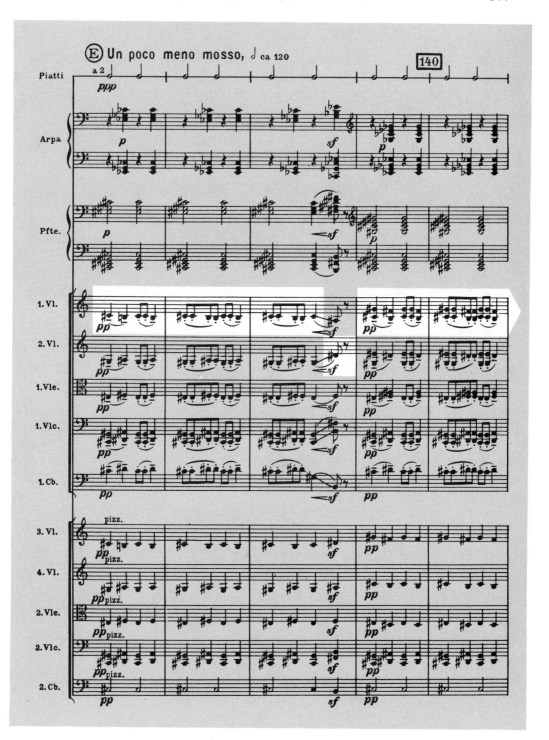

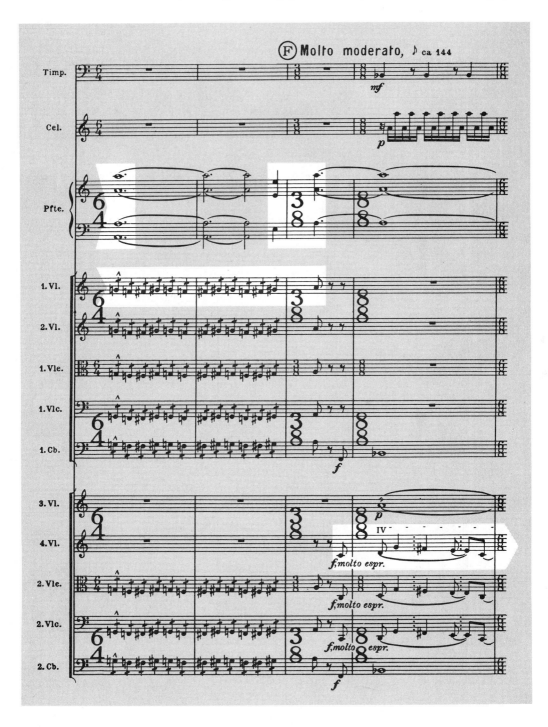

Durée d'exécution:			
- A = ca 50″	E - F = ca 55″	I. = ca 6′ 30″
A - B = ″ 21″	F - G = ″ 1′ 37″	II. = ″ 6′ 55″
B - C = ″ 9″	G - H = ″ 18″	III. = ″ 6′ 35″
C - D = ″ 29″	H - I = ″ 25″	IV. = ″ 5′ 40″
D - E = ″ 19″	I - = ″ 17″	ca 25′ 40″
	ca 5′ 40″	

32. Igor Stravinsky (1882-1971),

The Rite of Spring, Opening scene
(1913)

8A/1   II/4/1

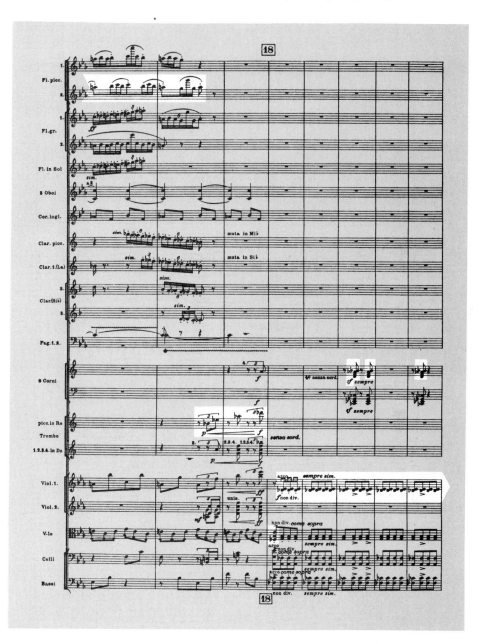

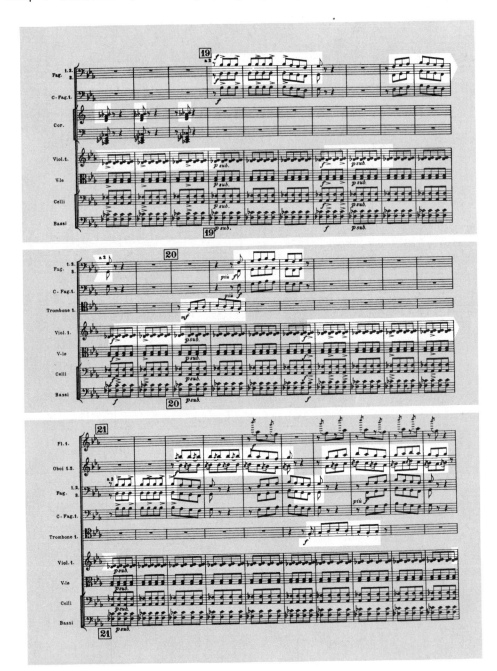

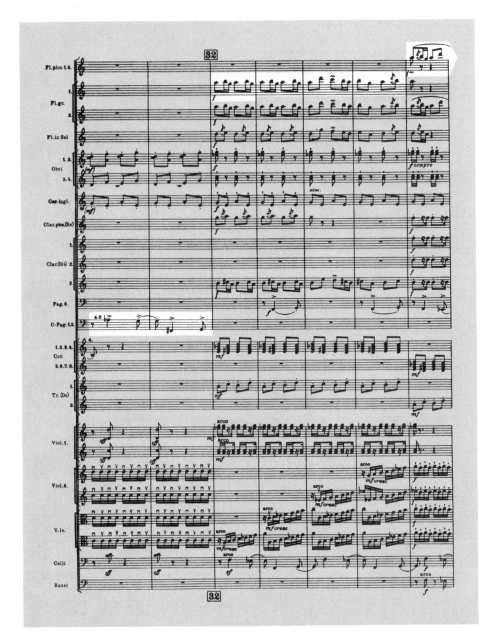

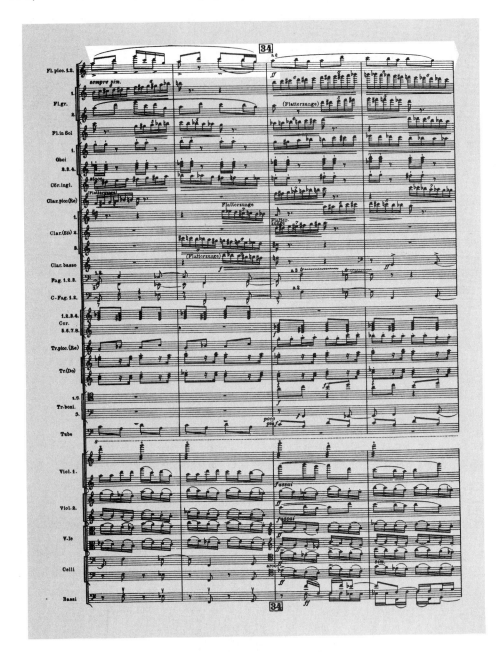

Ritual of Abduction

43
Fl. picc.
Fl. gr.
Fl. in Sol
Oboi
Cor. ingl.
Clar. picc. (Mi♭)
Clar. (Si♭)
Fag.
Cor.
Tr. picc. (Re)
Tr. (Do)
Tr. boni
4 Viol. Soli
Viol. 1.
Viol. 2.
V-le
Celli
a 2
unis.
arco
43

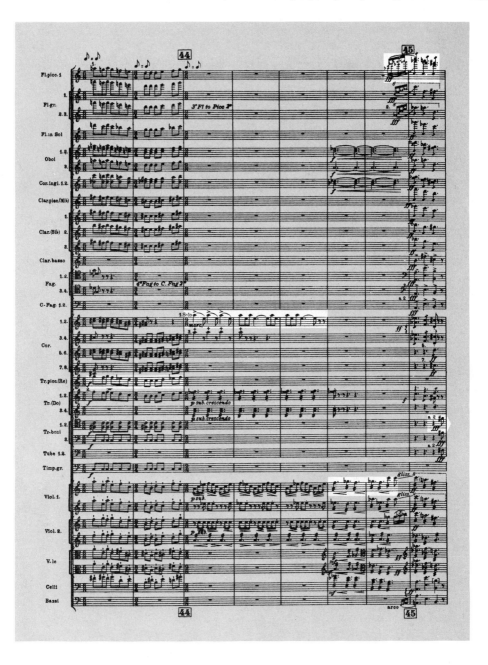

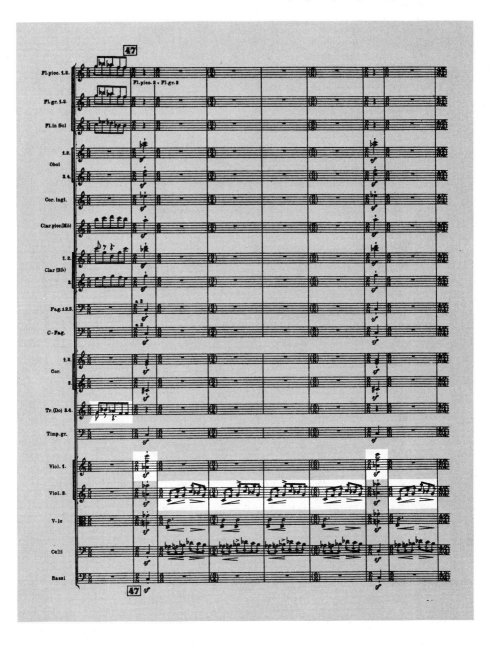

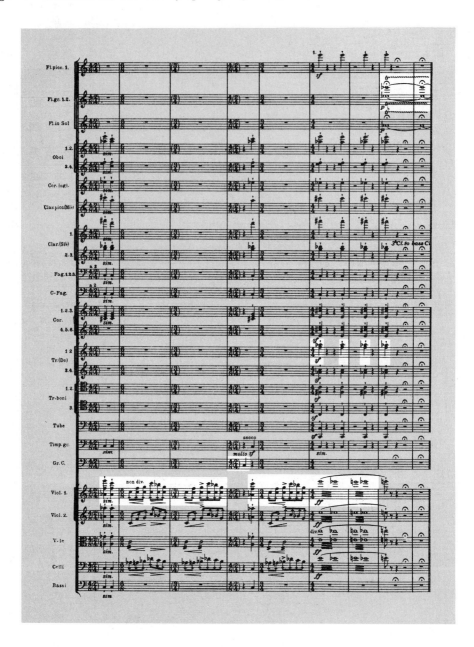

33. Anton Webern (1883-1945),

Symphony, Op. 21, Second movement
(1928)

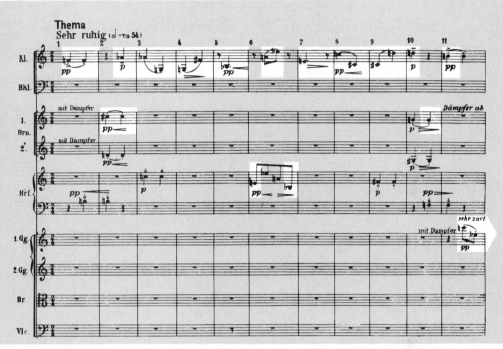

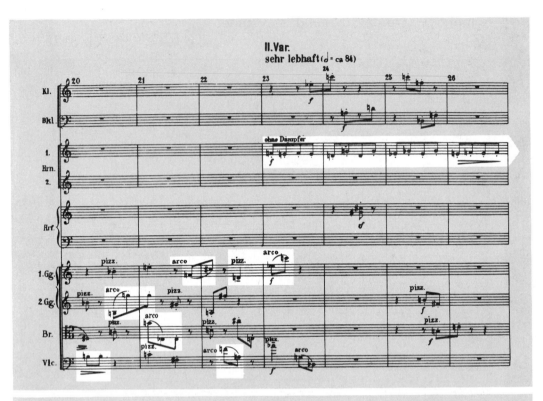

Wieder langsamer, aber nicht schleppend

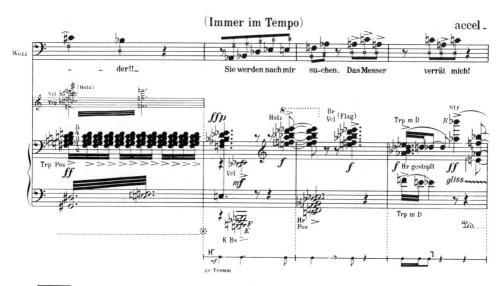

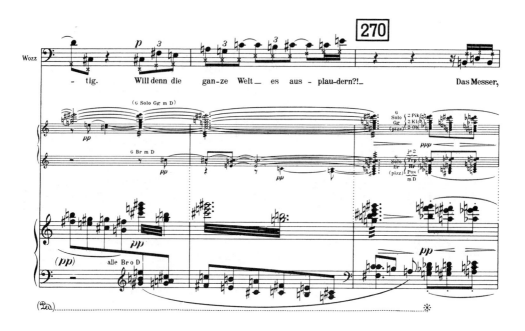

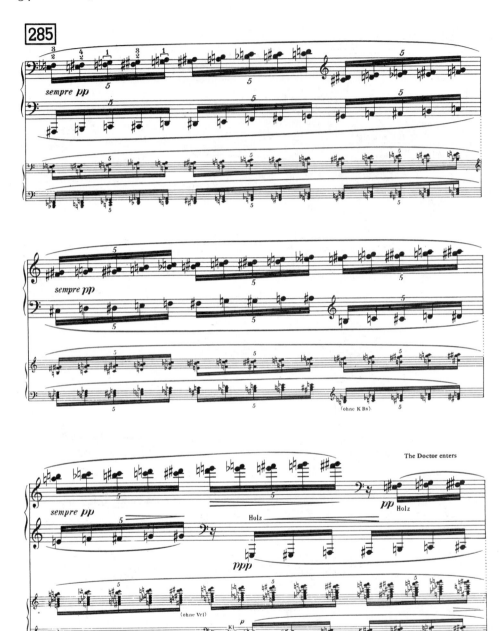

The **Captain** follows the Doctor (speaks)

sempre pp

The Doctor (stands still): *p* Hören Sie? Dort!

290 Hauptmann: *p* Jesus! Das war ein Ton. (also stands still)

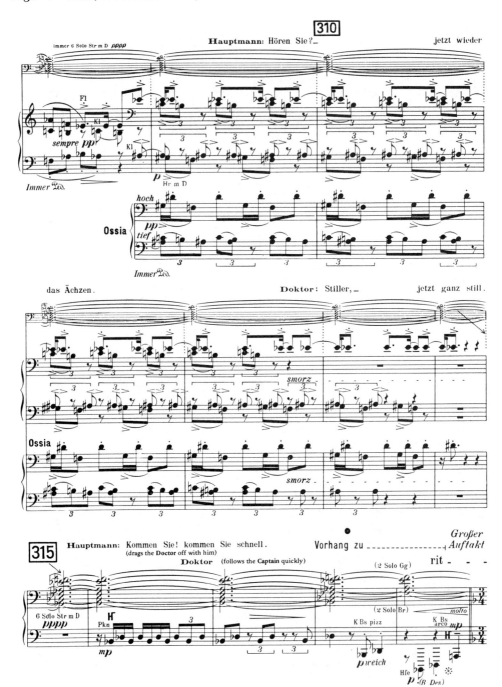

5th (last) Scene In front of Marie's house (bright morning, sunshine)

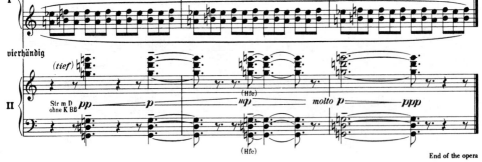

End of the opera

Translation

SCENE FOUR
Invention on a Chord of Six Notes
Path in the wood by the pond. Moonlight, as before.
(*Wozzeck stumbles hurriedly in, then stops, looking around for something.*)
WOZZECK

Das Messer? Wo ist das Messer? Ich hab's dagelassen. Näher, noch näher. Mir graut's... da regt sich was. Still! Alles still und tot.	The knife? Where is the knife? I left it there. Around here somewhere. I'm terrified . . . something's moving. Silence. Everything silent and dead.

(*shouting*)

Mörder! Mörder!	Murderer! Murderer!

(*whispering again*)

Ha! Da ruft's. Nein, ich selbst.	Ah! Someone called, No. it was only me.

(*still looking, he staggers a few steps further and stumbles against the corpse*)

Marie! Marie! Was hast Du für eine rote Schnur um den Hals? Hast Dir das rote Halsband verdient, wie die Ohrringlein, mit Deiner Sünde! Was hängen Dir die schwarzen Haare so wild? Mörder! Mörder! Sie werden nach mir suchen. Das Messer verrät mich!	Marie! Marie! What's that red cord around your neck! Was the red necklace payment for your sins, like the ear-rings? Why's your dark hair so wild about you? Murderer! Murderer! They will come and look for me. The knife will betray me!

(*looks for it in a frenzy*)

Da, da ist's!	Here! Here it is!

(*at the pond*)

So! Da hinunter!	There! Sink to the bottom!

(*throws the knife into the pond*)

Es taucht ins dunkle Wasser wie ein Stein.	It plunges into the dark water like a stone.

(*The moon appears, blood-red, from behind the clouds. Wozzeck looks up.*)

Aber der Mond verrät mich, der Mond is blutig. Will denn die ganze Welt es ausplaudern? Das Messer, es liegt zu weit vorn, sie finden's beim Baden oder wenn sie nach Muscheln tauchen.	But the moon will betray me: the moon is blood-stained. Is the whole world going to incriminate me. The knife is too near the edge: they'll find it when they're swimming or diving for snails.

(*wades into the pond*)

Ich find's nicht. Aber ich muss mich waschen. Ich bin blutig. Da ein Fleck—und noch einer. Weh! Weh! Ich wasche mich mit Blut—das Wasser ist Blut...Blut...	I can't find it. But I must wash myself. There's blood on me. There's a spot here—and there's another. Oh, God! I am washing myself in blood—the water is blood . . . blood . . .

(*drowns*)
(*The doctor appears, followed by the captain.*)
CAPTAIN

Halt!	Wait!

DOCTOR (*stops*)

Hören Sie? Dort!	Can you hear? There!

CAPTAIN

Jesus! Das war ein Ton!	Jesus! What a ghastly sound!

(*stops as well*)
DOCTOR (*pointing to the pond*)

Ja, dort!	Yes, there!

CAPTAIN

Es ist das Wasser im Teich. Das Wasser ruft.	It's the water in the pond. The water is calling.
Es ist schon lange Niemand ertrunken.	It's been a long time since anyone drowned.
Kommen Sie Doktor!	Come away, Doctor.
Es ist nicht gut zu hören.	It's not good for us to be hearing it.

(tries to drag the doctor away)

DOCTOR *(resisting, and continuing to listen)*

Das stöhnt, als stürbe ein Mensch.	There's a groan, as though someone were
Da ertrinkt Jemand!	dying. Somebody's drowning!

CAPTAIN

Unheimlich! Der mond rot, und die Nebel grau.	It's eerie! The moon is red, and the mist is grey.
Hören Sie?...	Can you hear? . . .
Jetzt wieder das Ächzen.	That moaning again.

DOCTOR

Stiller,...jetzt ganz still.	It's getting quieter . . . now it's stopped altogether.

CAPTAIN

Kommen Sie! Kommen Sie schnell!	Come! Come quickly!

(He rushes off, pulling the doctor along with him.)

SCENE CHANGE
INVENTION ON A KEY (D minor)
SCENE FIVE
Invention on a Quaver Rhythm
In front of Marie's door. Morning. Bright sunshine.
(Children are noisily at play. Marie's child is riding a hobby-horse.)

CHILDREN

Ringel, Ringel, Rosenkranz. Ringelreih'n,	Ring-a-ring-a-roses,
Ringel, Ringel, Rosenkranz, Ring...	A pocket full of . . .

(Their song and game is interrupted by other children bursting in.)

ONE OF THE NEWCOMERS

Du, Käthe! Die Marie!	Hey, Katie! Have you heard about Marie?

SECOND CHILD

Was ist?	What's happened?

FIRST CHILD

Weisst' es nit? Sie sind schon Alle'naus.	Don't you know? They've all gone out there.

THIRD CHILD *(to Marie's little boy)*

Du! Dein' Mutter ist tot!	Hey! Your mother's dead!

MARIE'S SON *(still riding)*

Hopp, hopp! Hopp, hopp! Hopp, hopp!	Hop hop! Hop hop! Hop hop!

SECOND CHILD

Wo ist sie denn?	Where is she then?

FIRST CHILD

Drauss' liegt sie, am Weg, neben dem Teich.	She's lying out there, on the path near the pond.

THIRD CHILD

Kommt, anschaun!	Come and have a look!

(*All the children run off.*)
MARIE'S SON (*continuing to ride*)
Hopp, hopp! Hopp, hopp! Hopp, hopp!   Hop hop! Hop hop! Hop hop!
(*He hesitates for a moment and then rides after the other children.*)
END OF THE OPERA
LIBRETTO BY ALBAN BERG AFTER GEORG BÜCHNER'S PLAY *Woyzeck*

SARAH E. SOULSBY

35. Sergei Prokofiev (1891-1953),

Alexander Nevsky, No. 7, Alexander's
Entry into Pskov (1939)

36. Louis Armstrong (c. 1898-1971),

West End Blues, Excerpt (1928)   8A/5   II/4/14

37. Duke Ellington (1899-1974),

Ko-Ko (1940)

38. Aaron Copland (b. 1900),

Rodeo, "Hoe-Down" (1942)

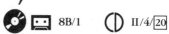 8B/1   II/4/[20]

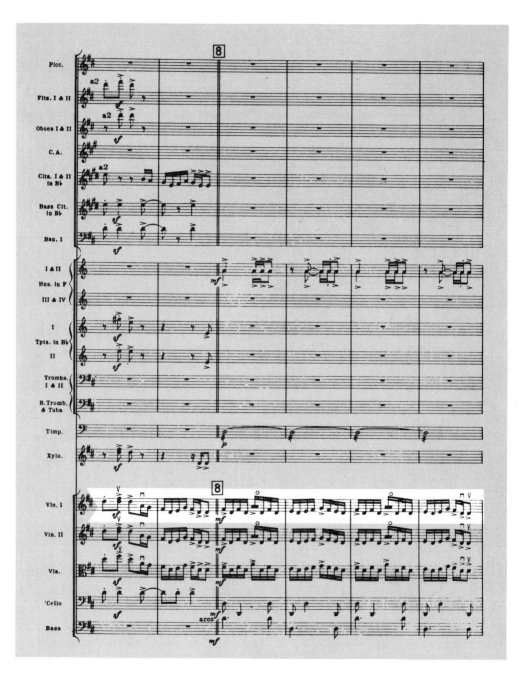

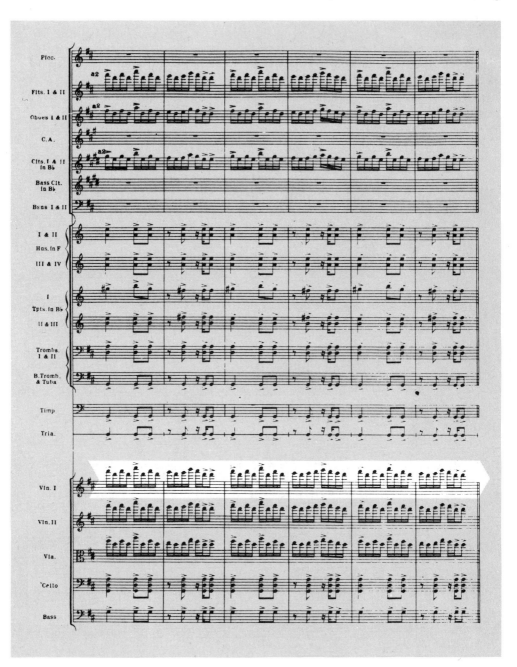

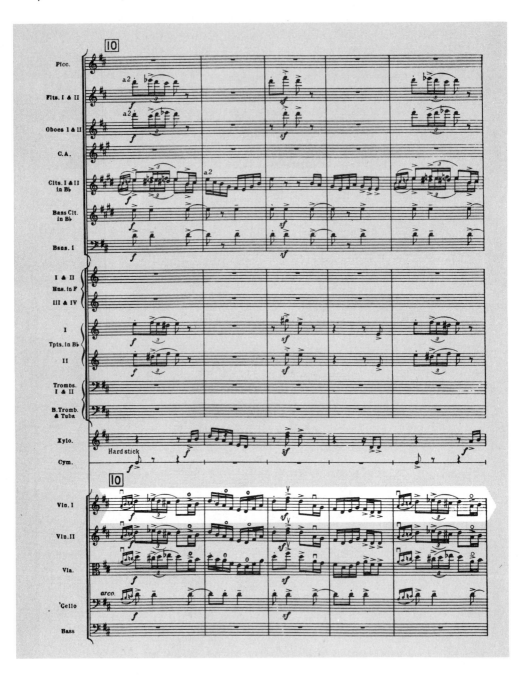

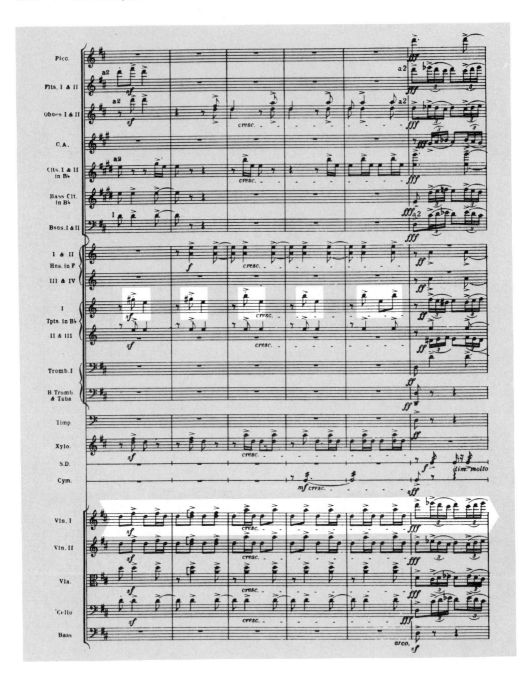

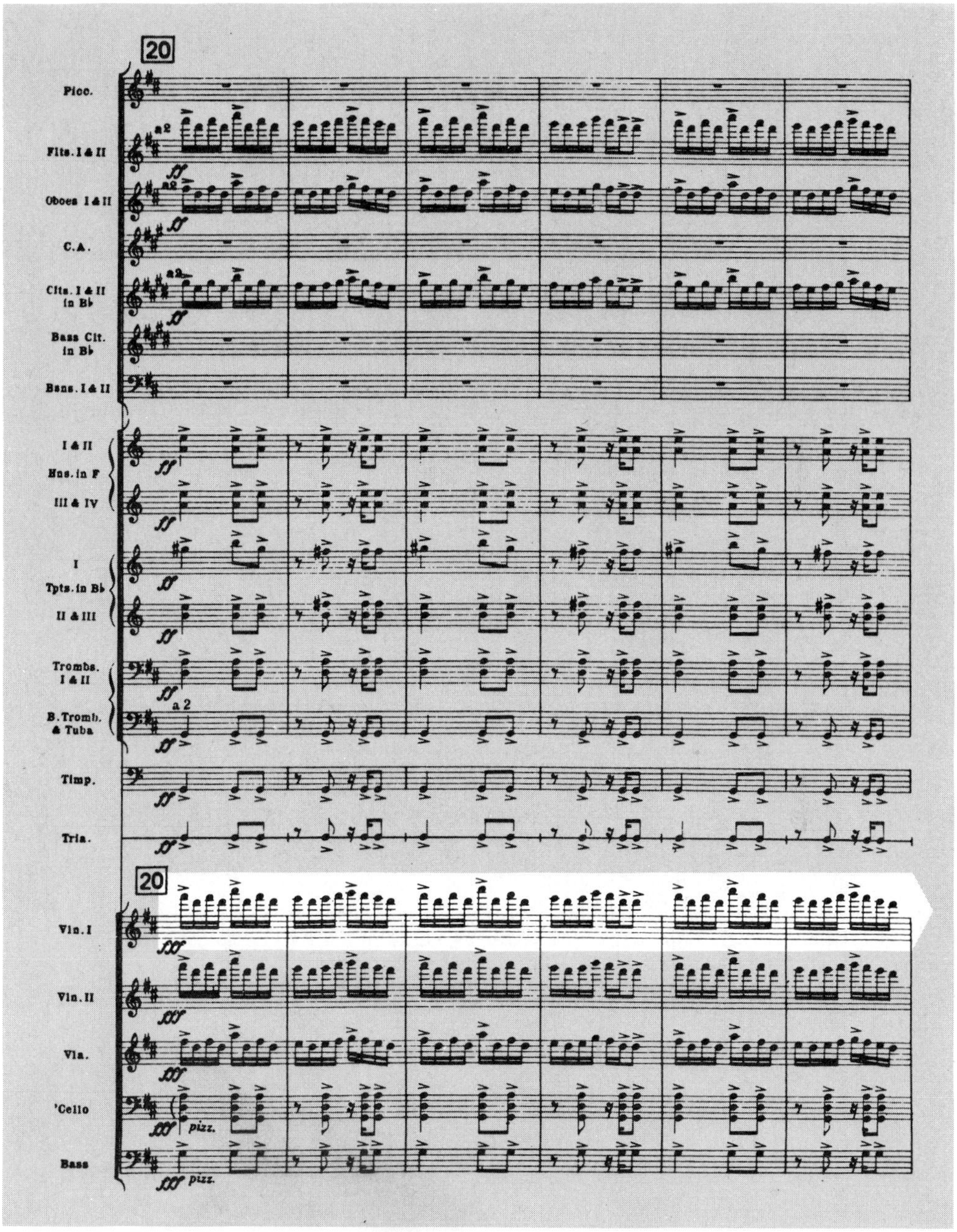
20
Picc.
Flts. I & II
Oboes I & II
C.A.
Clts. I & II in B♭
Bass Clt. in B♭
Bsns. I & II
I & II
Hns. in F
III & IV
I
Tpts. in B♭
II & III
Trombs. I & II
B. Tromb. & Tuba
a 2
Timp.
Tria.
20
Vln. I
Vln. II
Vla.
'Cello
Bass
pizz.
pizz.

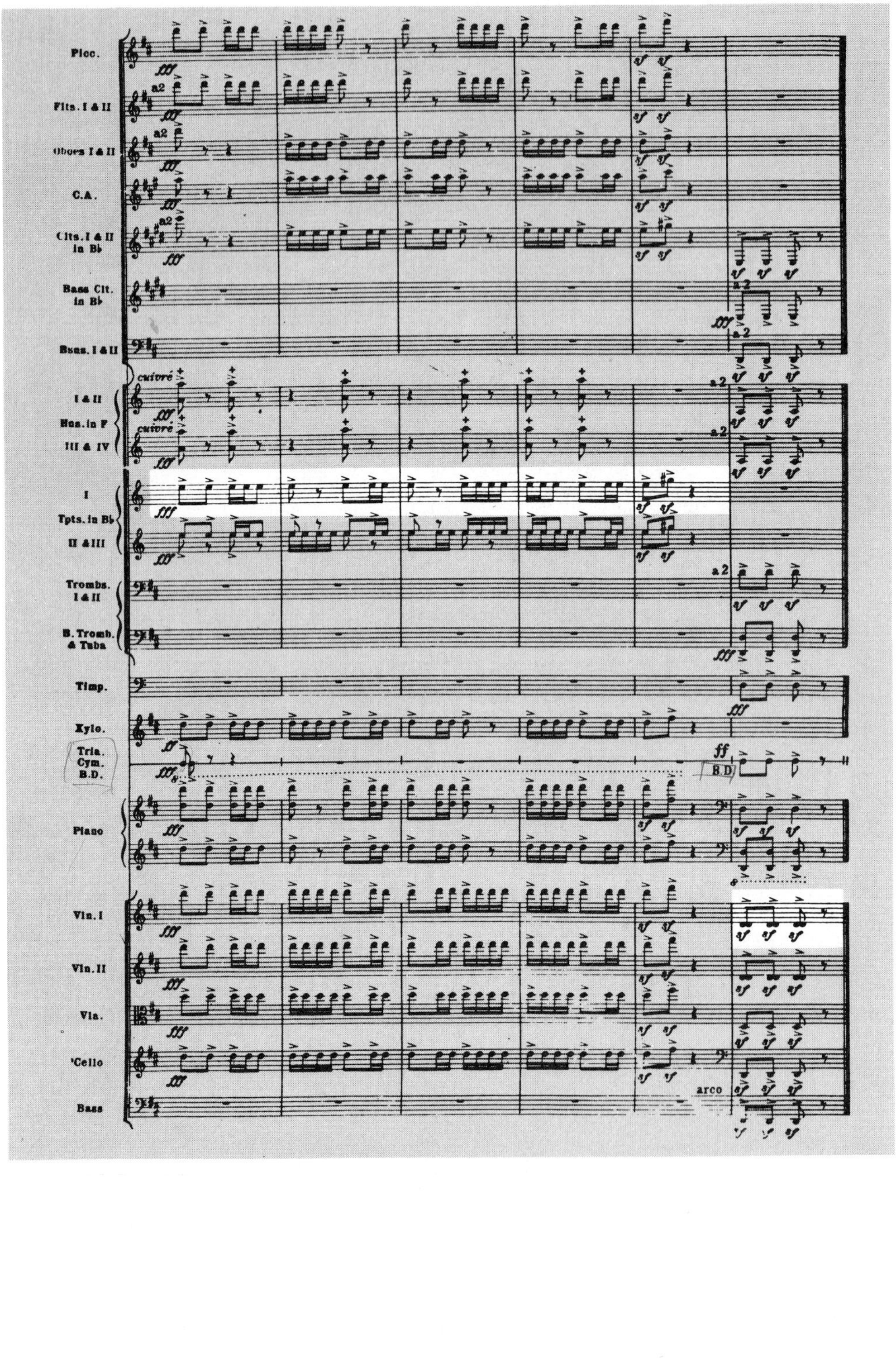
Picc.
Fls. I & II
Oboes I & II
C.A.
Clts. I & II in B♭
Bass Clt. in B♭
Bsns. I & II
I & II
Hns. in F
III & IV
I
Tpts. in B♭
II & III
Trombs. I & II
B. Tromb. & Tuba
Timp.
Xylo.
Tria.
Cym.
B.D.
Piano
Vln. I
Vln. II
Vla.
'Cello
Bass
a2
cuivré
B.D.
arco

39. Olivier Messiaen (b. 1908),

Vingt Régards sur L'enfant Jésus,
No. 2, "Regard de l'étoile" (1944)

 S4B/3 S4/26

40. Elliott Carter (b. 1908),

Eight Etudes and a Fantasy for Woodwind Quartet, Etudes 5 and 8 (1950) S4B/4 S4/28

V

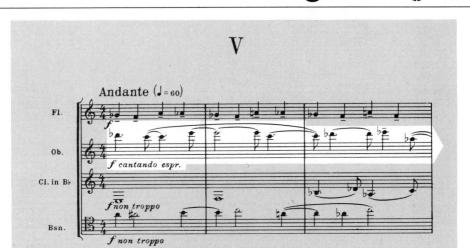

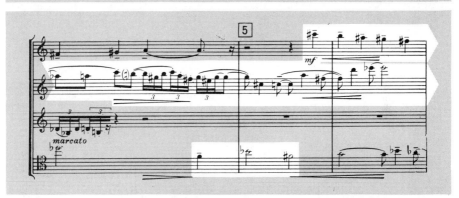

VIII

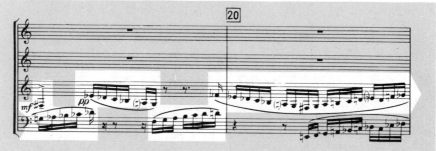

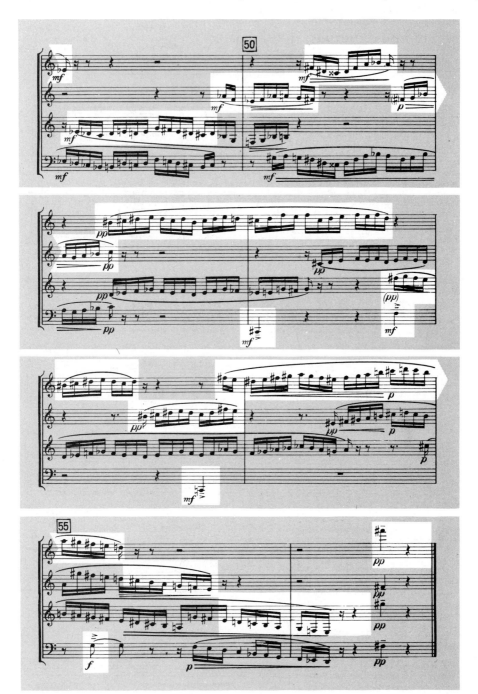

41. John Cage (b. 1912),

Sonatas and Interludes for Prepared Piano, Sonata V (1946–48)

 S4B/5 S4/30

—— = PEDAL   ---- = UNA CORDA

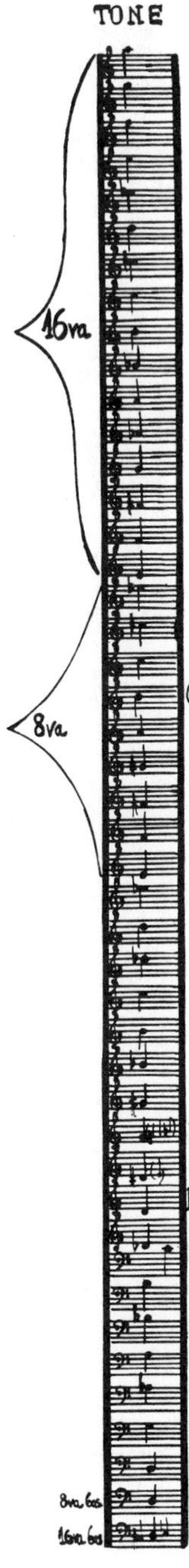

MATERIAL	STRINGS LEFT TO RIGHT	DISTANCE FROM DAMPER (INCHES)	MATERIAL	STRINGS LEFT TO RIGHT	DISTANCE FROM DAMPER (INCHES)	MATERIAL	STRINGS LEFT TO RIGHT	DISTANCE FROM DAMPER (INCHES)	TONE
			SCREW	2-3	1¼*				A
			MED. BOLT	2-3	1⅜*				G
			SCREW	2-3	1⅝*				F
			SCREW	2-3	1 13/16*				E
			SCREW	2-3	1¾*				E♭
			SM. BOLT	2-3	2*				D
			SCREW	2-3	1 1/16*				C♯
			FURNITURE BOLT	2-3	2 3/16*				C
			SCREW	2-3	2½*				B
			SCREW	2-3	1⅞*				B♭
			MED. BOLT	2-3	2⅞*				A
			SCREW	2-3	2¼*				A♭
			SCREW	2-3	3¾*				G
			SCREW	2-3	2 15/16*				F♯
SCREW	1-2	¾*	FURN. BOLT + 2 NUTS	2-3	2⅛*	SCREW + 2 NUTS	2-3	3¼*	F
			SCREW	2-3	1 13/16*				E
			FURNITURE BOLT	2-3	1⅞				E♭
			SCREW	2-3	1 15/16				C♯
			SCREW	2-3	1 1/16				C
(DAMPER TO BRIDGE = 4 5/16; ADJUST ACCORDINGLY)			MED. BOLT	2-3	3¾				B
			SCREW	2-3	4 7/16				A
RUBBER	1-2-3	4½	FURNITURE BOLT	2-3	1¼				G♯
			SCREW	2-3	1¾				F♯
			SCREW	2-3	2 5/16				F
RUBBER	1-2-3	5¾							E
RUBBER	1-2-3	6½	FURN. BOLT + NUT	2-3	6⅞				E♭
			FURNITURE BOLT	2-3	2 9/16				D
RUBBER	1-2-3	3⅝							D♭
			BOLT	2-3	7⅛				C
			BOLT	2-3	2				B
SCREW	1-2	10	SCREW	2-3	1	RUBBER	1-2-3	8¼	B♭
(PLASTIC (See G))	1-2-3	2 5/16				RUBBER	1-2-3	4½	G♯
PLASTIC (OVER 1: UNDER 2-3)	1-2-3	2⅞				RUBBER	1-2-3	10⅛	G
(PLASTIC (See D))	1-2-3	4¼				RUBBER	1-2-3	5 7/16	D♯
PLASTIC (OVER 1 - UNDER 2-3)	1-2-3	4⅛				RUBBER	1-2-3	9¾	D
BOLT	1-2	15½	BOLT	2-3	11/16	RUBBER	1-2-3	14⅛	D♭
BOLT	1-2	14½	BOLT	2-3	⅞	RUBBER	1-2-3	6½	C
BOLT	1-2	14¾	BOLT	2-3	9/16	RUBBER	1-2-3	14	B
RUBBER	1-2-3	9½	MED. BOLT	2-3	10⅛				B♭
SCREW	1-2	5⅞	LG. BOLT	2-3	5⅞	SCREW + NUTS	1-2	1	A
BOLT	1-2	7⅛	MED. BOLT	2-3	2¼	RUBBER	1-2-3	4⅛	A♭
LONG BOLT	1-2	8¾	LG BOLT	2-3	3¼				G
			BOLT	2-3	11/16				D
SCREW + RUBBER	1-2	4 7/16							D
ERASER (OVER D UNDER C♯ + E♭) AM. PENCIL CO. #346	1	6¾							D

*MEASURE FROM BRIDGE.

42. Witold Lutosławski (b. 1913),

Jeux vénitiens, First movement
(1961)

  8B/2 II/4/22

STRUMENTI DELL'ORCHESTRA

2 flauti (II anche flauto piccolo)
1 oboe
3 clarinetti in sib (III anche clarinetto basso in sib)
1 fagotto

1 tromba in do
1 corno in fa
1 trombone

percussione (4 esecutori)
     I 3 timpani scordati (3 dimensioni)
     II 3 tamburi (soprano, alto, tenore), tamburo rullante
     III xilofono, 3 piatti sospesi (soprano, alto, tenore), tam-tam, 5 tom-tom
     IV claves, vibrafono senza motore

arpa
pianoforte (2 esecutori; II anche celesta)

4 violini
3 viole
3 violoncelli
2 contrabbassi

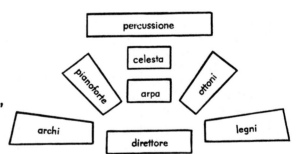

DURATA ca 13'

The piccolo, xylophone, and celesta are notated an octave lower, and the double-basses an octave higher, than they sound. All the other instruments are notated at their actual pitch. In this score the signs ♯ and ♭ apply only to the notes they precede. Notes without accidentals should always be read as naturals.

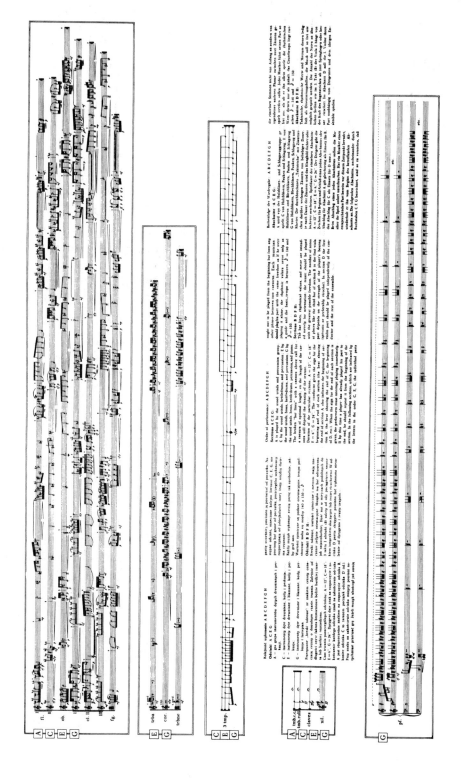

Edition Moeck - 5012

43. Milton Babbitt (b. 1916),

Phonemena, Excerpt (1969–70)   S4B/6   S4/32

44. Leonard Bernstein (b. 1918),

Symphonic Dances from "West Side Story,"
"Cool" (Fugue) and "Rumble"
(1957/61)

 8B/3   II/4/23

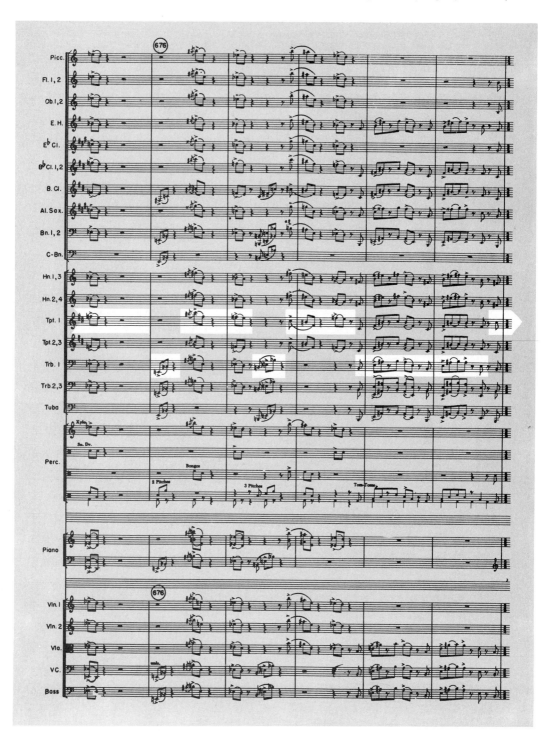

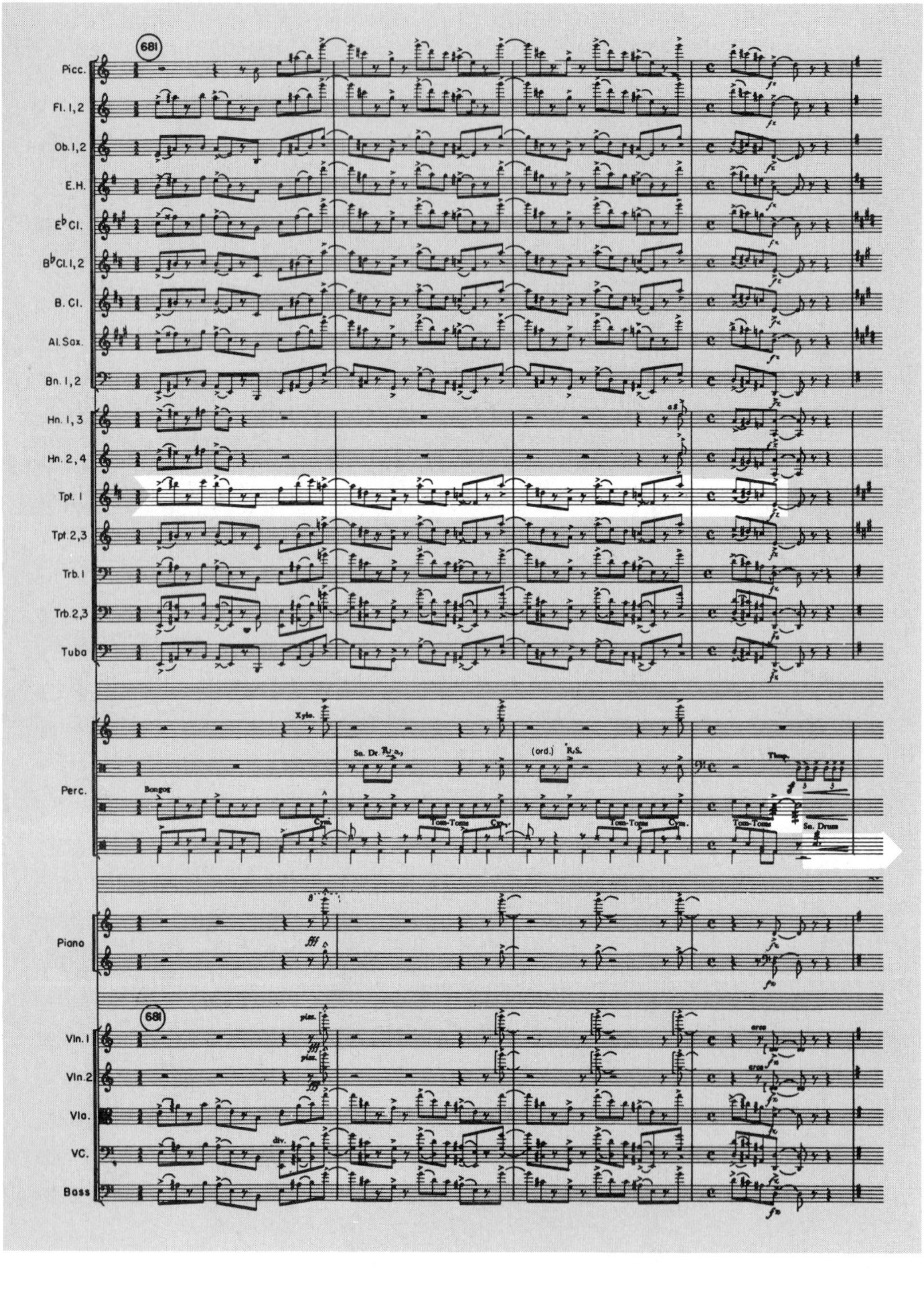
681
Picc.
Fl. 1, 2
Ob. 1, 2
E.H.
E♭ Cl.
B♭ Cl. 1, 2
B. Cl.
Al. Sax.
Bn. 1, 2
Hn. 1, 3
Hn. 2, 4
Tpt. 1
Tpt. 2, 3
Trb. 1
Trb. 2, 3
Tuba
Perc.
Xylo.
Sn. Dr.
(ord.)
R.S.
Bongos
Tom-Toms
Cym.
Timp.
Sn. Drum
Piano
Vln. 1
Vln. 2
Vla.
VC.
Bass
pizz.
arco
div.

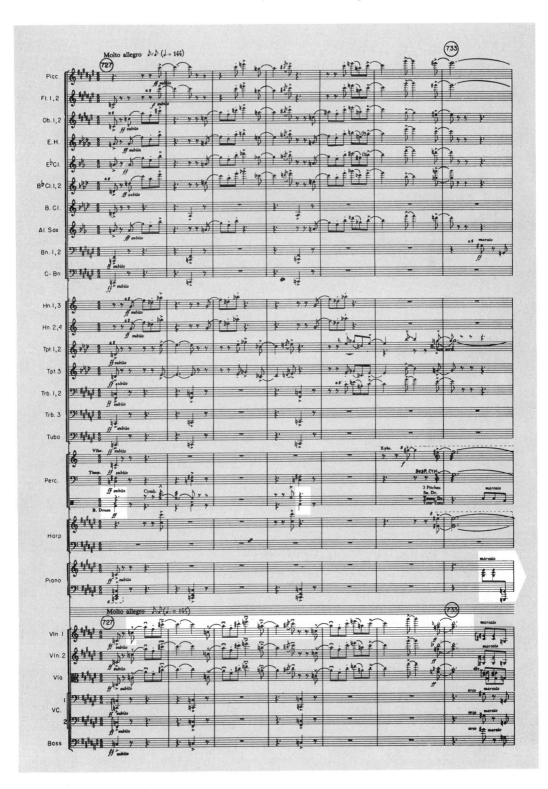

737
Picc.
Fl. 1, 2
Ob. 1, 2
E.H.
E♭ Cl.
B♭ Cl. 1, 2
B. Cl.
Al. Sax.
Bn. 1, 2
C-Bn.
Hn. 1, 3
Hn. 2, 4
Tpt. 1, 2
Tpt. 3
Trb. 1, 2
Trb. 3
Tuba
Perc.
Harp.
Piano
Vln. I
Vln. 2
Vla.
VC. 1
VC. 2
Bass
Xylo.
Cymb.
3 Pitches
Timp.
Bass Dr.
II.
I.
a2
II. senza sord.

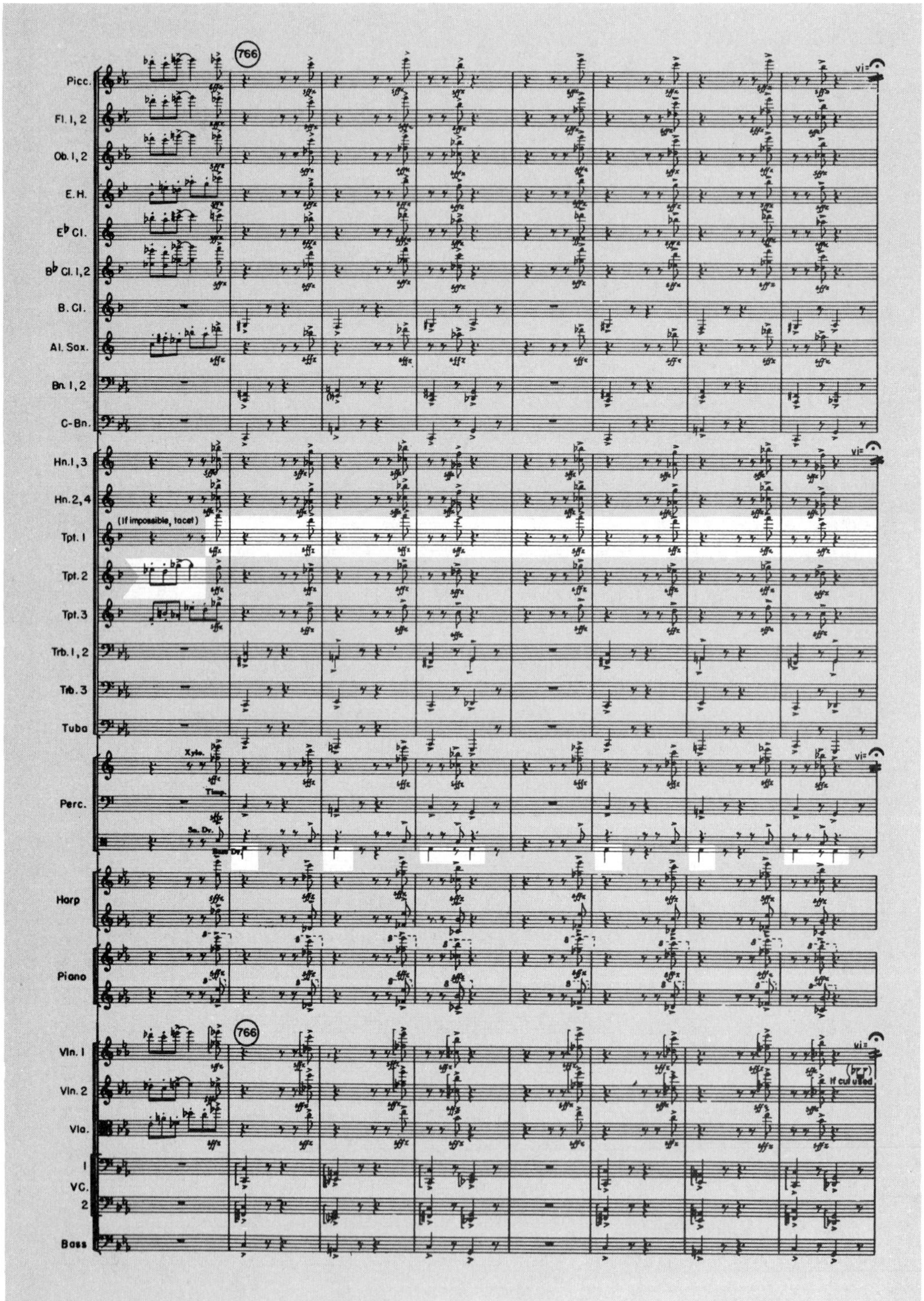
766
Picc.
Fl. 1, 2
Ob. 1, 2
E. H.
E♭ Cl.
B♭ Cl. 1, 2
B. Cl.
Al. Sax.
Bn. 1, 2
C-Bn.
Hn. 1, 3
Hn. 2, 4
(If impossible, tacet)
Tpt. 1
Tpt. 2
Tpt. 3
Trb. 1, 2
Trb. 3
Tuba
Xylo.
Timp.
Sn. Dr.
Bass Dr.
Perc.
Harp
Piano
766
Vln. I
Vln. 2
Vla.
VC.
Bass

793
Picc.
Fl. 1
Fl. 2
Ob. 1
Ob. 2
E.H.
E♭ Cl.
B♭ Cl. 1
B♭ Cl. 2
B. Cl.
Al. Sax.
Bn. 1, 2
Hn. 1, 3
Hn. 2, 4
Tpt. 1
Tpt. 2, 3
Trb. 1
Trb. 2
Xylo.
Perc.
Sn. Drum
Harp
Piano
Vln. 1
Vln. 2
Vla.
VC.
stacc.
f
dim.

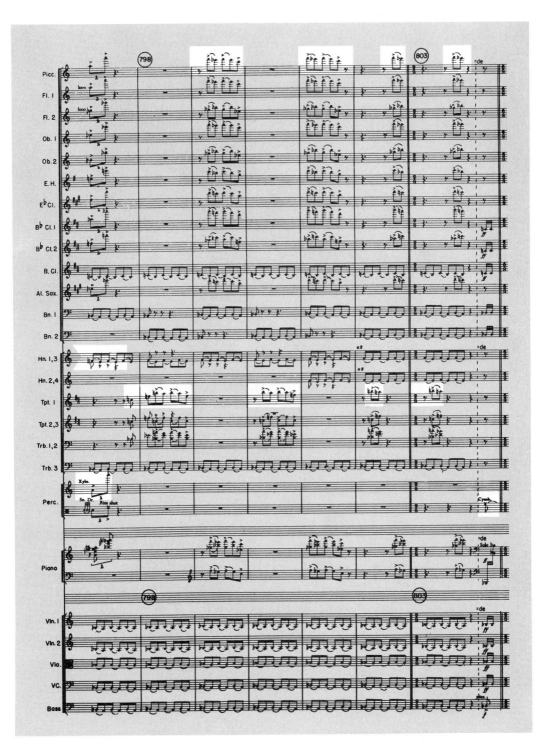

45. John Lewis (b. 1920),

Sketch (1959)   S4B/7   S4/33

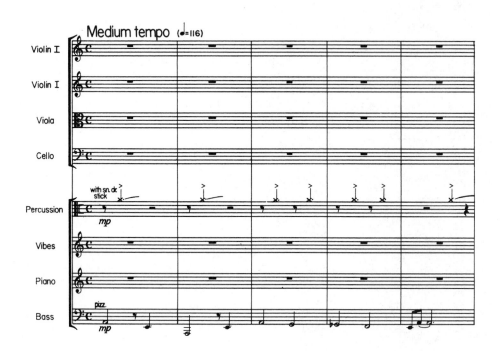

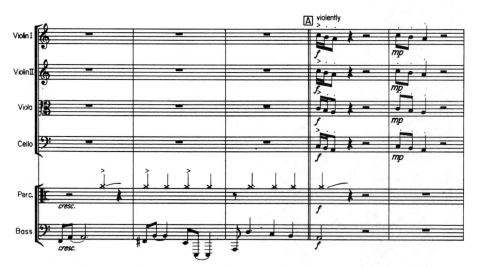

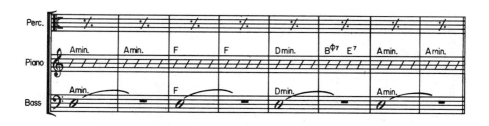

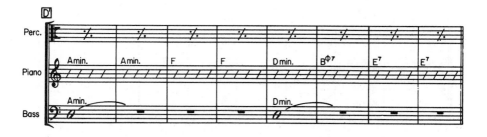

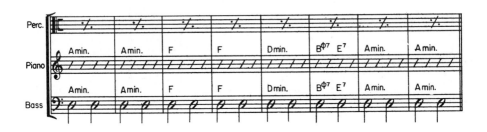

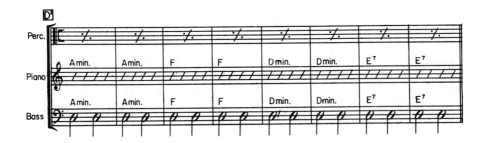

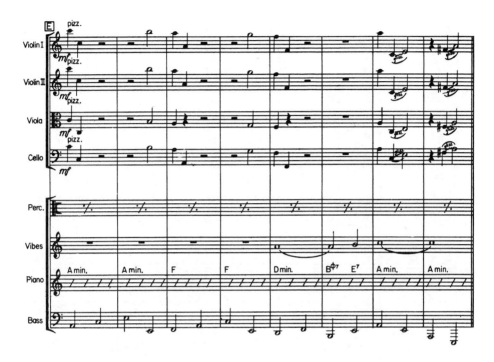

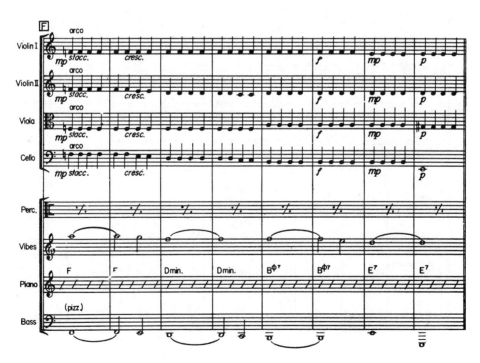

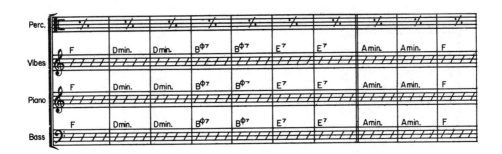

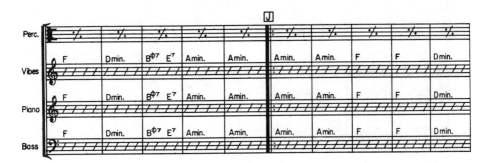

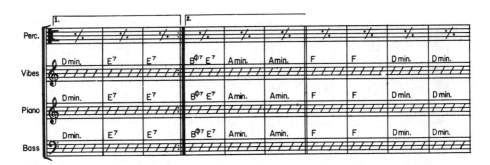

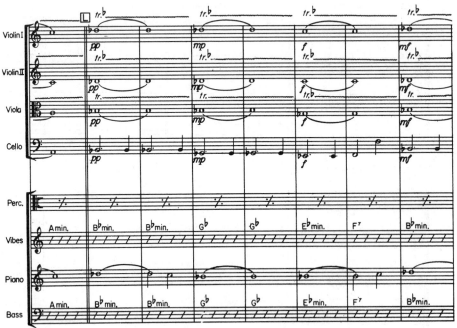

Twice as slow (♩ = ♩.)(♩. = 116)

46. György Ligeti (b. 1923),

Atmosphères, Excerpt (1961)

 S4B/8   S4/37

* Den Ton halten, falls möglich, aber keinesfalls noch einmal anblasen. (Wenn die Luft nicht ausreicht, lieber etwas früher aufhören.) Eventuell Aerophon verwenden.   Hold the tone if possible, but in no event attack again. (If the breath does not suffice, it is better to stop a bit early.) Aerophone can also be used.

** Bogenwechsel unauffällig, selten und alternierend (möglichst nicht nach dem Taktstrich). / Change of bow inconspicuously, seldom and alternating (as much as possible not with the bar-line).

1) or slower

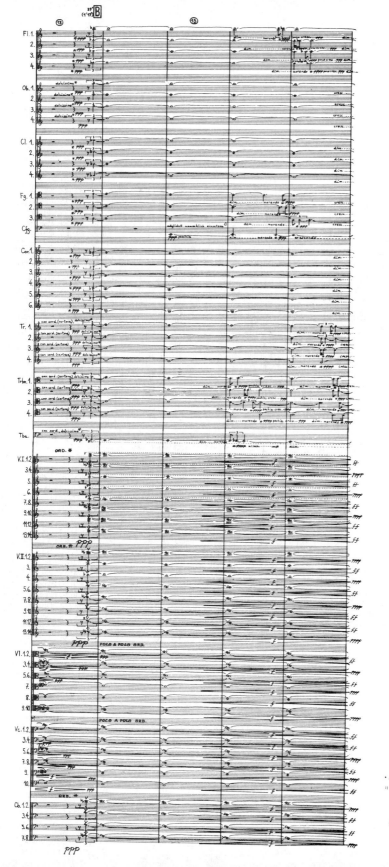

* unmerklich einsetzen / imperceptible attack
1) attack as imperceptibly as possible

continued on p. 1208

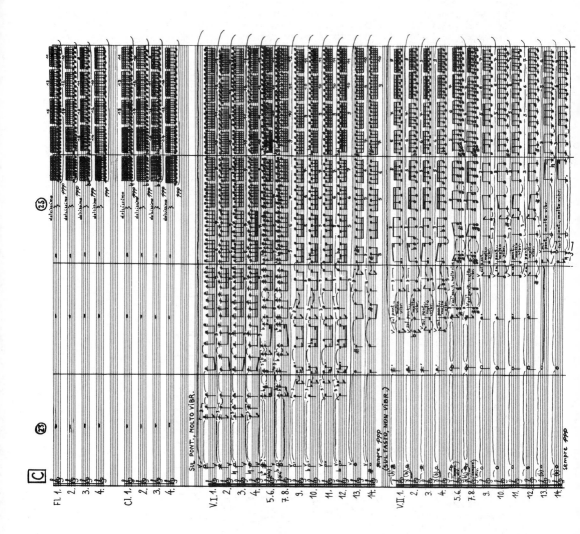

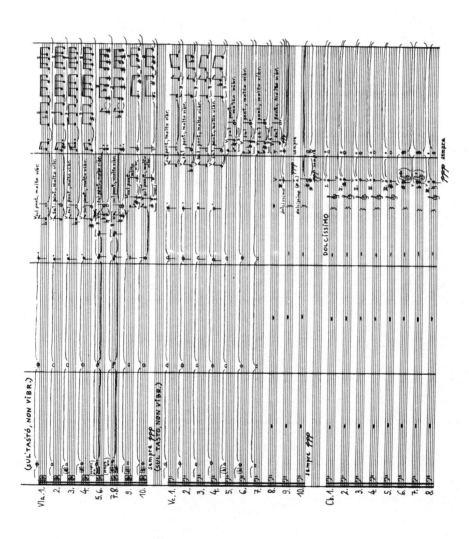

continued on p. 1206

47. Thea Musgrave (b. 1929),

Mary, Queen of Scots, Act III,
Scene 1 (1977)

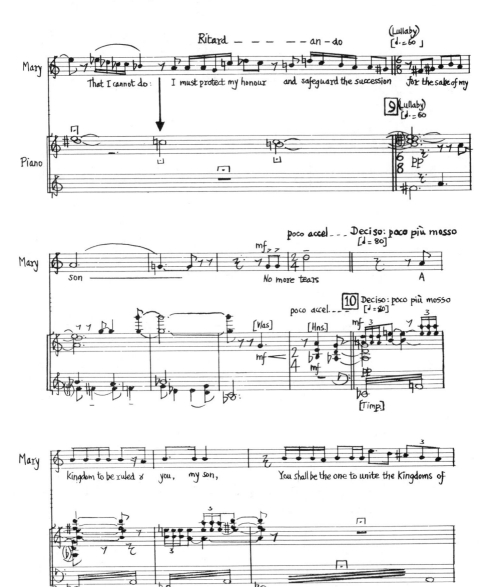

Mary: Mary, go & see if Lord Bothwell has come----

16

Mary: Yes! He is loyal and

Mary Seton: [alarmed] Bothwell! You have sent for Bothwell?

Mary: will protect me and my son. I fear----

17

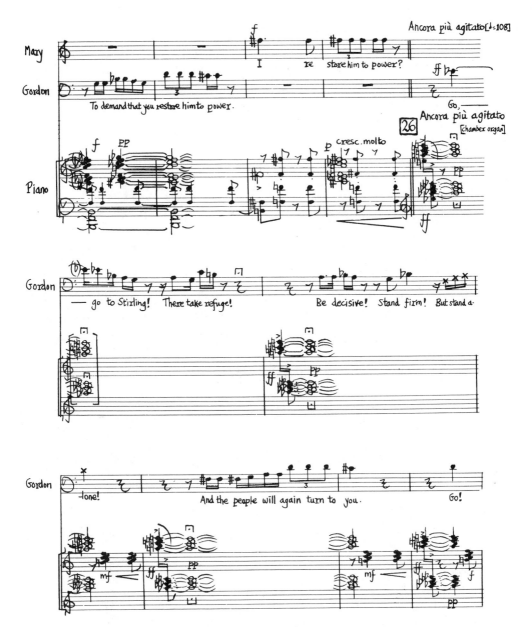

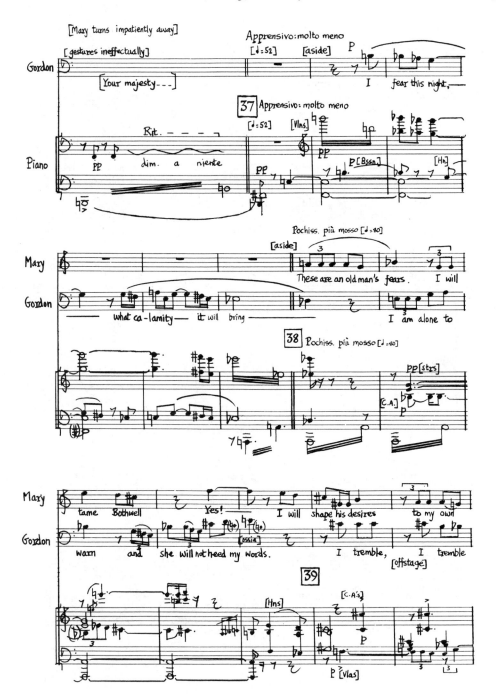

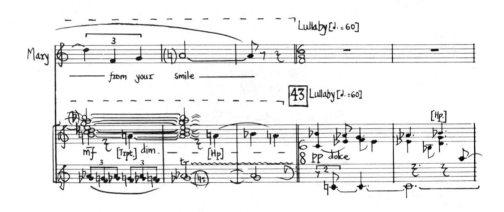

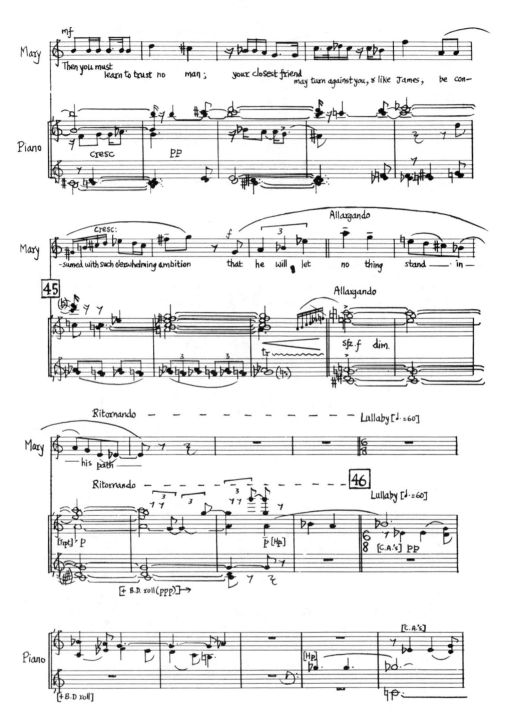

[Mary gives her child into Mary Seton's care . . . they exeunt]

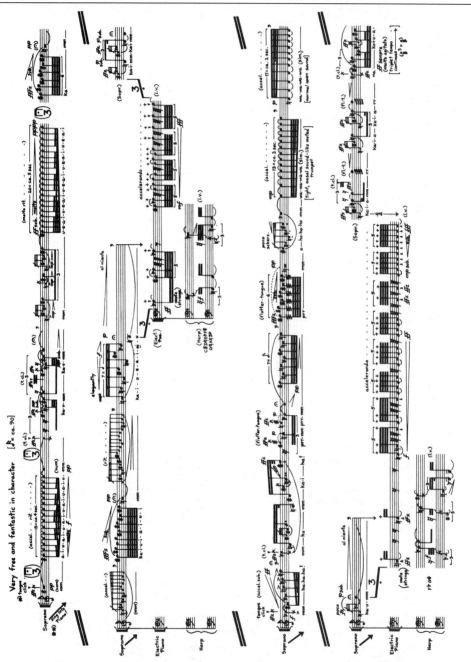

El niño busca su voz *from* Ancient Voices of Children *by George Crumb. Copyright © 1970 by C. F. Peters Corporation, 373 Park Avenue South, New York 10016. Reprinted with permission of the publishers who published the score of the complete work under Peters Edition No. 66303.

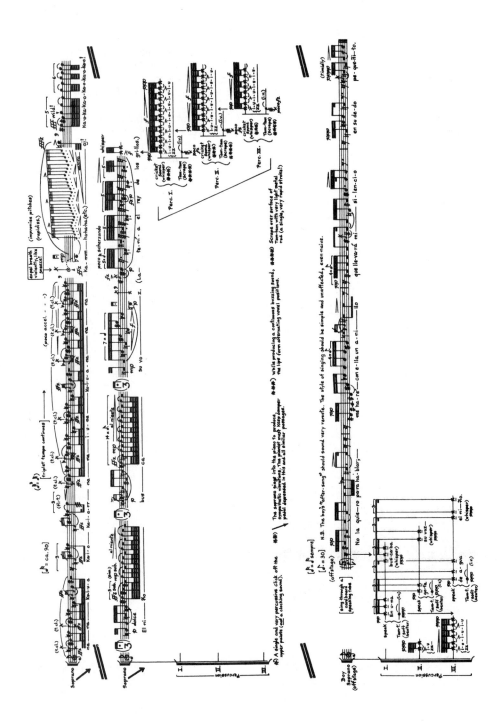

Translation

El niño busca su voz.
(La tenía el rey de los grillos.)
En una gota de agua
buscaba su voz el niño.

No la quiero para hablar;
me haré con ella un anillo
que llevará mi silencio
en su dedo pequeñito.

FEDERICO GARCÍA LORCA

The little boy was looking for his voice.
(The king of the crickets had it.)
In a drop of water
the little boy was looking for his voice.

I do not want it for speaking with;
I will make a ring of it
so that he may wear my silence
on his little finger.

W. S. MERWIN

49. Tobias Picker (b. 1954),

Old and Lost Rivers (1986)

 S4B/9   S4/40

* Optional parts, only in the absence of Horns 5, 6

APPENDIX A

Reading an Orchestral Score

CLEFS

The music for some instruments is written in clefs other than the familiar treble and bass. In the following example, middle C is shown in the four clefs used in orchestral scores:

The *alto clef* is primarily used in viola parts. The *tenor clef* is employed for cello, bassoon, and trombone parts when these instruments play in a high register.

TRANSPOSING INSTRUMENTS

The music for some instruments is customarily written at a pitch different from their actual sound. The following list, with examples, shows the main transposing instruments and the degree of transposition. (In some modern works—such as the Stravinsky example included in this anthology—all instruments are written at their sounding pitch.)

Instrument	*Transposition*	*Written Note*	*Actual Sound*
Piccolo Celesta	sound an octave higher than written		
Trumpet in F	sound a fourth higher than written		
Trumpet in E	sound a major third higher than written		

Instrument	Transposition	Written Note	Actual Sound

Clarinet in E♭
  Trumpet in E♭
	sound a minor third
	  higher than written		

Trumpet in D
  Clarinet in D
	sound a major second
	  higher than written		

Clarinet in B♭
  Trumpet in B♭
  Cornet in B♭
  Horn in B♭ alto
	sound a major second
	  lower than written		

Clarinet in A
  Trumpet in A
  Cornet in A
	sound a minor third
	  lower than written		

Horn in G
  Alto flute
	sound a fourth
	  lower than written		

English horn
  Horn in F
	sound a fifth
	  lower than written		

Horn in E	sound a minor sixth lower than written		
Horn in E♭	sound a major sixth lower than written		
Horn in D	sound a minor seventh lower than written		

Contrabassoon
  Horn in C
  Double bass
	sound an octave
	  lower than written		

Bass clarinet in B♭
  (written in treble
  clef)
	sound a major ninth
	  lower than written		

(written in bass
  clef)
	sound a major second
	  lower than written		

Bass clarinet in A
  (written in treble
  clef)
	sound a minor tenth
	  lower than written		

(written in bass
  clef)
	sound a minor third
	  lower than written		

APPENDIX B

Instrumental Names and Abbreviations

The following tables set forth the English, Italian, German, and French names used for the various musical instruments in these scores, and their respective abbreviations. A table of the foreign-language names for scale degrees and modes is also provided.

WOODWINDS

English	Italian	German	French
Piccolo (Picc.)	Flauto piccolo (Fl. Picc.)	Kleine Flöte (Kl. Fl.)	Petite flûte
Flute (Fl.)	Flauto (Fl.); Flauto grande (Fl. gr.)	Grosse Flöte (Fl. gr.)	Flûte (Fl.)
Alto flute	Flauto contralto fl.c-alto)	Altflöte	Flûte en sol
Oboe (Ob.)	Oboe (Ob.)	Hoboe (Hb.); Oboe (Ob.)	Hautbois (Hb.)
English horn (E. H.)	Corno inglese (C. or Cor. ingl., C.i.)	Englisches Horn (E. H.)	Cor anglais (C. A.)
Sopranino clarinet	Clarinetto piccolo (clar. picc.)		
Clarinet (C., Cl., Clt., Clar.)	Clarinetto (Cl. Clar.)	Klarinette (Kl.)	Clarinette (Cl.)
Bass clarinet (B. Cl.)	Clarinetto basso (Cl. b., Cl. basso, Clar. basso)	Bass Klarinette (Bkl.)	Clarinette basse Cl. bs.)
Bassoon (Bsn., Bssn.)	Fagotto (Fag., Fg.)	Fagott (Fag., Fg.)	Basson (Bssn.)
Contrabassoon (C. Bsn.)	Contrafagotto (Cfg., C. Fag., Cont. F.)	Kontrafagott (Kfg.)	Contrebasson (C. bssn.)

BRASS

English	Italian	German	French
French horn (Hr., Hn.)	Corno (Cor., C.)	Horn (Hr.) [*pl.* Hörner (Hrn.)]	Cor; Cor à pistons
Trumpet (Tpt., Trpt., Trp., Tr.)	Tromba (Tr.)	Trompete (Tr., Trp.)	Trompette (Tr.)
Trumpet in D	Tromba piccola (Tr. picc.)		
Cornet	Cornetta	Kornett	Cornet à pistons (C. à p., Pist.)
Trombone (Tr., Tbe., Trb., Trm., Trbe.)	Trombone [*pl.* Tromboni (Tbni., Trni.)]	Posaune. (Ps., Pos.)	Trombone (Tr.)
Tuba (Tb.)	Tuba (Tb, Tba.)	Tuba (Tb.) [*also* Basstuba (Btb.)]	Tuba (Tb.)

PERCUSSION

English	Italian	German	French
Percussion (Perc.)	Percussione	Schlagzeug (Schlag.)	Batterie (Batt.)
Kettledrums (K. D.)	Timpani (Timp., Tp.)	Pauken (Pk.)	Timbales (Timb.)
Snare drum (S. D.)	Tamburo piccolo (Tamb. picc.)	Kleine Trommel (Kl. Tr.)	Caisse claire (C. cl.), Caisse roulante
	Tamburo militare (Tamb. milit.)		Tambour militaire (Tamb. milit.)
Bass drum (B. drum)	Gran cassa (Gr. Cassa, Gr. C., G. C.)	Grosse Trommel (Gr. Tr.)	Grosse caisse (Gr. c.)
Cymbals (Cym., Cymb.)	Piatti (P., Ptti., Piat.)	Becken (Beck.)	Cymbales (Cym.)
Tam-Tam (Tam.-T.)			
Tambourine (Tamb.)	Tamburino (Tamb.)	Schellentrommel, Tamburin	Tambour de Basque (T. de B., Tamb. de Basque)
Triangle (Trgl., Tri.)	Triangolo (Trgl.)	Triangel	Triangle (Triang.)
Glockenspiel (Glocken.)	Campanelli (Cmp.)	Glockenspiel	Carillon
Bells (Chimes)	Campane (Cmp.)	Glocken	Cloches

Antique Cymbals	Crotali Piatti antichi	Antiken Zimbeln	Cymbales antiques
Sleigh Bells	Sonagli (Son.)	Schellen	Grelots
Xylophone (Xyl.)	Xilofono	Xylophon	Xylophone
Cowbells		Herdenglocken	
Crash cymbal			Grande cymbale chinoise
Siren			Sirène
Lion's roar			Tambour à corde
Slapstick			Fouet
Wood blocks			Blocs chinois

STRINGS

English	Italian	German	French
Violin (V., Vl., Vln, Vi.)	Violino (V., Vl., Vln.)	Violine (V., Vl., Vln.) Geige (Gg.)	Violon (V., Vl., (Vln.)
Viola (Va., Vl., *pl.* Vas.)	Viola (Va., Vla.) *pl.* Viole (Vle.)	Bratsche (Br.)	Alto (A.)
Violoncello, Cello (Vcl., Vc.)	Violoncello (Vc., Vlc., Vcllo.)	Violoncell (Vc., Vlc.)	Violoncelle (Vc.)
Double bass (D. Bs.)	Contrabasso (Cb., C. B.) *pl.* Contrabassi or Bassi (C. Bassi, Bi.)	Kontrabass (Kb.)	Contrebasse (C. B.)

OTHER INSTRUMENTS

English	Italian	German	French
Harp (Hp., Hrp.)	Arpa (A., Arp.)	Harfe (Hrf.)	Harpe (Hp.)
Piano	Pianoforte (P.-f., Pft.)	Klavier	Piano
Celesta (Cel.)			
Harpsichord	Cembalo	Cembalo	Clavecin
Harmonium (Harmon.)			
Organ (Org.)	Organo	Orgel	Orgue
Guitar		Gitarre (Git.)	
Mandoline (Mand.)			

Names of Scale Degrees and Modes

SCALE DEGREES

English	Italian	German	French
C	do	C	ut
C-sharp	do diesis	Cis	ut dièse
D-flat	re bemolle	Des	ré bémol
D	re	D	ré
D-sharp	re diesis	Dis	ré dièse
E-flat	mi bemolle	Es	mi bémol
E	mi	E	mi
E-sharp	mi diesis	Eis	mi dièse
F-flat	fa bemolle	Fes	fa bémol
F	fa	F	fa
F-sharp	fa diesis	Fis	fa dièse
G-flat	sol bemolle	Ges	sol bémol
G	sol	G	sol
G-sharp	sol diesis	Gis	sol dièse
A-flat	la bemolle	As	la bémol
A	la	A	la
A-sharp	la diesis	Ais	la dièse
B-flat	si bemolle	B	si bémol
B	si	H	si
B-sharp	si diesis	His	si dièse
C-flat	do bemolle	Ces	ut bémol

MODES

major	maggiore	dur	majeur
minor	minore	moll	mineur

APPENDIX C

Glossary of Musical Terms Used in the Scores

The following glossary is not intended to be a complete dictionary of musical terms, nor is knowledge of all these terms necessary to follow the scores in this book. However, as listeners gain experience in following scores, they will find it useful and interesting to understand the composer's directions with regard to tempo, dynamics, and methods of performance.

In most cases, compound terms have been broken down in the glossary and defined separately, as they often recur in varying combinations. A few common foreign-language particles are included in addition to the musical terms. Note that names and abbreviations for instruments and for scale degree will be found in Appendix B.

a   The phrases *a 2, a 3* (etc.) indicate the number of parts to be played by 2, 3 (etc.) players; when a simple number (1., 2., etc.) is placed over a part, it indicates that only the first (second, etc.) player in that group should play.

aber   But.

accelerando (accel.)   Growing faster.

accordato, accordez   Tune the instrument as specified.

adagio   Slow, leisurely.

affettuoso   With emotion.

affrettare (affrett.)   Hastening a little.

agitando, agitato   Agitated, excited.

al fine   "The end"; an indication to return to the start of a piece and to repeat it only to the point marked "fine."

alla breve   Indicates two beats to a measure, at a rather quick tempo.

allargando (allarg.)   Growing broader.

alle, alles   All, every, each.

allegretto   A moderately fast tempo (between allegro and andante).

allegro   A rapid tempo (between allegretto and presto).

allein   Alone, solo.

allmählich   Gradually (*allmählich wieder gleich mässig fliessend werden*, gradually becoming even-flowing again).

alta, alto, altus (A.)   The deeper of the two main divisions of women's (or boys') voices.

am steg   On the bridge (of a string instrument).

ancora   Again.

andante   A moderately slow tempo (between adagio and allegretto).

andantino   A moderately slow tempo.

anfang   Beginning, initial.

anima   Spirit, animation.

animando   With increasing animation.

animant, animato, animé, animez   Animated.

aperto   Indicates open notes on the horn, open strings, and undamped piano notes.

a piacere   The execution of the passage is left to the performer's discretion.

appassionato   Impassioned.

appena   Scarcely, hardly.

apprensivo   Apprehensive.

archet   Bow.

archi, arco   Played with the bow.

arditamente   Boldly.

arpeggiando, arpeggiato (arpegg.)   Played in harp style, i.e. the notes of the chord played in quick succession rather than simultaneously.

assai   Very.

assez Fairly, rather.

attacca Begin what follows without pausing.

a tempo At the original tempo.

auf dem On the (as in *auf dem G*, on the G string).

ausdruck Expression.

ausdrucksvoll With expression.

äusserst Extreme, utmost.

avec With.

bachetta, bachetti Drumsticks (*bachetti di spugna*, sponge-headed drumsticks).

baguettes Drumsticks (*baguettes de bois*, wooden drumsticks; *baguettes d'éponge*, spong-headed drumsticks).

bass, bassi, basso, bassus (B.) The lowest male voice.

battere, battuta, battuto (batt.) To beat.

becken Cymbals.

bedeutend bewegter With significantly more movement.

beider Hände With both hands.

ben Very.

bewegt Agitated.

bewegter More agitated.

bisbigliando, bispiglando (bis.) Whispering.

bis zum schluss dieser szene To the end of this scene.

blasen Blow.

blech Brass instruments.

bogen (bog.) Played with the bow.

bois Woodwind.

bouché Muted.

breit Broadly.

breiter More broadly.

brio Spirit, vivacity.

burden Refrain.

cadenza (cad., cadenz.) An extended passage for solo instrument in free, improvisatory style.

calando (cal.) Diminishing in volume and speed.

calma, calmo Calm, calmly.

cantabile (cant.) In a singing style.

cantando In a singing manner.

canto Voice (as in *col canto*, a direction for the accompaniment to follow the solo part in tempo and expression).

cantus An older designation for the highest part in a vocal work.

capriccio Capriciously, whimsically.

changez Change (usually an instruction to re-tune a string or an instrument).

chiuso See *gestopft*.

chromatisch Chromatic.

circa (ca.) About, approximately.

coda The last part of a piece.

col, colla, coll' With the.

colore Colored.

come prima, come sopra As at first, as previously.

commodo Comfortable, easy.

con With.

corda String; for example, *seconda (2a) corda* is the second string (the A string on the violin).

corto Short, brief.

crescendo (cresc.) An increase in volume.

cuivré Played with a harsh, blaring tone.

da capo (D.C.) Repeat from the beginning.

dal segno (D.S.) Repeat from the sign.

dämpfer (dpf.) Mutes.

dazu In addition to that, for that purpose.

de, des, die Of, from.

début Beginning.

deciso Determined, resolute.

decrescendo (decresc., decr.) A decreasing of volume.

dehors Outside.

dem To the.

détaché With a broad, vigorous bow stroke, each note bowed singly.

deutlich Distinctly.

d'exécution Performance.

diminuendo, diminuer (dim., dimin.) A decreasing of volume.

distinto Distinct, clear.

divisés, divisi (div.) Divided; indicates that the instrumental group should be divided into two parts to play the passage in question.

dolce Sweetly and softly.

dolcemente Sweetly.

dolcissimo (dolciss.) Very sweetly.

doppelgriff Double stop.

doux Sweetly.

drängend Pressing on.

dreifach Triple.

dreitaktig Three beats to a measure.

dur Major, as in *G dur* (G major).

durée Duration.

e, et And.

eilen To hurry.

ein One, a.

elegante Elegant, graceful.

energico Energetically.

espansione Expansion, broadening.

espressione With expression.

espressivo (espr., espress.) Expressively.

etwas Somewhat, rather.

expressif Expressively.

facile Simple.

fin, fine End, close.

flatterzunge, flutter-tongue A special tonguing technique for wind instruments, producing a rapid trill-like sound.

flebile Feeble, plaintive, mournful.

fliessend Flowing.

forte (f) Loud.

fortissimo (ff) Very loud (*fff* indicates a still louder dynamic).

forza Force.

fou Frantic.

frappez To strike.

frei Freely.

freihäng, freihängendes Hanging freely. An indication to the percussionist to let the cymbals vibrate freely.

frisch Fresh, lively.

furioso Furiously.

ganz Entirely, altogether.

ganzton Whole tone.

gedämpft (ged.) Muted.

geheimnisvoll Mysteriously.

geschlagen Pulsating.

gestopft (gest.) Stopping the notes of a horn; that is, the hand is placed in the bell of the horn, to produce a muffled sound. Also *chiuso*.

geteilt (get.) Divided; indicates that the instrumental group should be divided into two parts to play the passage in question.

getragen Sustained.

gewöhnlich As usual.

giocoso Humorous.

giusto Moderately.

glissando (gliss.) Rapid scales produced by running the fingers over all the strings.

gradamente Gradually.

grande Large, great.

grandioso Grandiose.

grave Slow, solemn; deep, low.

grazioso Gracefully.

grosser auftakt Big upbeat.

gut Good, well.

hälfte Half.

hauptzeitmass Original tempo.

hervortreten Prominent.

hoch High, nobly.

holz Woodwinds.

holzschlägel Wooden drumstick.

im gleichen rhythmus In the same rhythm.

immer Always.

in Oktaven In octaves.

insensibilmente Slightly, imperceptibly.

intensa Intensely.

istesso tempo .Duration of beat remains unaltered despite meter change.

jeu Playful.

jusqu'à Until.

kadenzieren To cadence.

klagend Lamenting.

kleine Little.

klingen To sound.

komisch bedeutsam Very humorously.

kurz Short.

langsam Slow.

langsamer Slower.

languendo, langueur Languor.

l'archet See *archet*.

largamente Broadly.

larghetto Slightly faster than largo.

largo A very slow tempo.

lasci, lassen To abandon.

lebhaft Lively.

lebhafter Livelier.

legatissimo A more forceful indication of *legato*.

legato Performed without any perceptible interruption between notes.

légèrement, leggieramente Lightly.

leggiero (legg.) Light and graceful.

legno The wood of the bow (*col legno gestrich*, played with the wood).

lent Slow.

lentamente Slowly.

lento A slow tempo (between andante and largo).

l.h. Abbreviation for "left hand."

liricamente Lyrically.

loco Indicates a return to the written pitch, following a passage played an octave higher or lower than written.

luftpause Pause for breath.

lunga Long, sustained.

lusingando Caressing.

ma, mais But.

maestoso Majestic.

marcatissimo (marcatiss.) With very marked emphasis.

marcato (marc.) Marked, with emphasis.

marschmässig, nicht eilen Moderate-paced march, not rushed.

marziale Military, martial, march-like.

mässig Moderately.

mässiger More moderately.

même Same.

meno Less.

mezzo forte (mf) Moderately loud.

mezzo piano (mp) Moderately soft.

mindestens At least.

misterioso Mysterious.

misura Measured.

mit With.

moderatissimo A more forceful indication of *moderato*.

moderato, modéré   At a moderate tempo.
moins   Less.
molto   Very, much.
mordenti   Biting, pungent.
morendo   Dying away.
mormorato   Murmured.
mosso   Rapid.
moto   Motion.
mouvement (mouv., mouvt.)   Tempo.
muta, mutano   Change the tuning of the instrument as specified.

nach   More.
naturalezza   A natural, unaffected manner.
neuen   New.
nicht   Not.
niente   Nothing.
nimmt   To take; to seize.
noch   Still.
non   Not.
nuovo   New.

obere, oberer (ob.)   Upper, leading.
oder langsamer   Or slower.
offen   Open.
ohne   Without.
ondeggiante   Undulating movement of the bow, which produces a tremolo effect.
ordinario (ord., ordin.)   In the usual way (generally cancelling an instruction to play using some special technique).
ossia   An alternative (usually easier) version of a passage.
ôtez vite les sourdines   Remove the mutes quickly.
ottoni   Brass.
ouvert   Open.

parte   Part (*colla parte,* the accompaniment is to follow the soloist in tempo).
passionato   Passionately.
paukenschlägel   Timpani stick.
pavillons en l'air   An indication to the player of a wind instrument to raise the bell of the instrument upward.
pedal, pedale (ped., P.)   (1) In piano music, indicates that the damper pedal should be depressed; an asterisk indicates the point of release (brackets below the music are also used to indicate pedaling); (2) on an organ, the pedals are a keyboard played with the feet.
per   During.
perdendosi   Gradually dying away.
pesante   Heavily.
peu   Little, a little.
piacevole   Agreeable, pleasant.
pianissimo (pp)   Very soft (*ppp* indicates a still softer dynamic).
piano (p)   Soft.

più   More.
pizzicato (pizz.)   The string plucked with the finger.
plötzlich   Suddenly, immediately.
plus   More.
pochissimo (pochiss.)   Very little, a very little.
poco   Little, a little.
ponticello (pont.)   The bridge (of a string instrument).
portamento   Continuous smooth and rapid sliding between two pitches.
position naturel (pos. nat.)   In the normal position (usually cancelling an instruction to play using some special technique).
possibile   Possible.
premier mouvement (1er mouvt.)   At the original tempo.
prenez   Take up.
préparez   Prepare.
presque   Almost, nearly.
presser   To press.
prestissimo   A more forceful indication of presto.
presto   A very quick tempo (faster than allegro).
prima, primo   First, principal.

quarta   Fourth.
quasi   Almost, as if.
quinto   Fifth.

rallentando (rall., rallent.)   Growing slower.
rapidamente   Quickly.
rapidissimo (rapidiss.)   Very quickly.
rasch   Quickly.
rascher   More quickly.
rauschend   Rustling, roaring.
recitative (recit.)   A vocal style designed to imitate and emphasize the natural inflections of speech.
rein   Perfect interval.
respiro   Pause for breath.
retenu   Held back.
r.h.   Abbreviation for "right hand."
richtig   Correct (*richtige lage,* correct pitch).
rien   Nothing.
rigore di tempo   Strictness of tempo.
rinforzando (rf., rfz., rinf.)   A sudden accent on a single note or chord.
ritardando (rit., ritard.)   Gradually slackening in speed.
ritenuto (riten.)   Immediate reduction of speed.
ritmato   Rhythmic.
ritornando, ritornello (ritor.)   Refrain.
rubato   A certain elasticity and flexibility of tempo, consisting of slight accelerandos and ritardandos according to the

requirements of the musical expression.
ruhig Quietly.

sans Without.
schalltrichter Horn.
scherzando (scherz.) Playful.
schlagen To strike in a usual manner.
schlagwerk Striking mechanism.
schleppen, schleppend Dragging.
schluss Cadence, conclusion.
schnell Fast.
schneller Faster.
schon Already.
schwammschlagëln Sponge-headed drumstick.
scorrevole Flowing, gliding.
sec, secco Dry, simple.
secunda Second.
sehr Very.
semplicita Simplicity.
sempre Always, continually.
senza Without.
sforzando (sf., sfz.) With sudden emphasis.
simile (sim.) In a similar manner.
sin Without.
singstimme Singing voice.
sino al Up to the . . . (usually followed by a new tempo marking, or by a dotted line indicating a terminal point).
si piace Especially pleasing.
smorzando (smorz.) Dying away.
sofort Immediately.
soli, solo (s.) Executed by one performer.
sopra Above; in piano music, used to indicate that one hand must pass above the other.
soprano (S.) The voice classification with the highest range.
sordini, sordino (sord.) Mute.
sostenendo, sostenuto (sost.) Sustained.
sotto voce In an undertone, subdued, under the breath.
sourdine (sourd.) Mute.
soutenu Sustained.
spiel, spielen Play (an instrument).
spieler Player, performer.
spirito Spirit, soul.
spiritoso In a spirited manner.
spugna Sponge
staccato (stacc.) Detached, separated, abruptly, disconnected.
stentando, stentare, stentato (stent.) Delaying, retarding.
stesso The same.
stimme Voice.
stimmen To tune.
strascinare To drag.
streichinstrumente (streichinstr.) Bowed string instruments.
strepitoso Noisy, loud.

stretto In a non-fugal composition, indicates a concluding section at an increased speed.
stringendo (string.) Quickening.
subito (sub.) Suddenly, immediately.
sul On the (as in *sul G*, on the G string).
superius In older music, the uppermost part.
sur On.

tacet The instrument or vocal part so marked is silent.
tasto solo In a continuo part, this indicates that only the string instrument plays; the chord-playing instrument is silent.
tempo primo (tempo I) At the original tempo.
teneramente, tenero Tenderly, gently.
tenor, tenore (T.) The highest male voice.
tenuto (ten., tenu.) Held, sustained.
tertia Third.
tief Deep, low.
touche Key; note.
toujours Always, continually.
tranquillo Quietly, calmly.
tre corde (t.c.) Release the soft (or *una corda*) pedal of the piano.
tremolo (trem.) On string instruments, a quick reiteration of the same tone, produced by a rapid up-and-down movement of the bow; also a rapid alternation between two different notes.
très Very.
trill (tr.) The rapid alternation of a given note with the diatonic second above it. In a drum part it indicates rapid alternating strokes with two drumsticks.
trommschlag (tromm.) Drumbeat.
troppo Too much.
tutta la forza Very emphatically.
tutti Literally, "all"; usually means all the instruments in a given category as distinct from a solo part.

übergreifen To overlap.
übertonend Drowning out.
umstimmen To change the tuning.
un One, a.
una corda (u.c.) With the "soft" pedal of the piano depressed.
und And.
unison (unis.) The same notes or melody played by several instruments at the same pitch. Often used to emphasize that a phrase is not to be divided among several players.
unmerklich Imperceptible.

velocissimo Very swiftly.
verklingen lassen To let die away.

vibrare To sound.

vibrato (vibr.) To fluctuate the pitch on a single note.

vierfach Quadruple.

vierhändig Four-hand piano music.

vif Lively.

vigoroso Vigorous, strong.

vivace Quick, lively.

vivacissimo A more forceful indication of *vivace*.

vivente, vivo Lively.

voce Voice (as in *colla voce*, a direction for the accompaniment to follow the solo part in tempo and expression).

volles orch. Entire orchestra.

vorhang auf Curtain up.

vorhang zu Curtain down.

vorher Beforehand, previously.

voriges Preceding.

waltzertempo In the tempo of a waltz.

weg Away, beyond.

weich Mellow, smooth, soft.

wie aus der fern As if from afar.

wieder Again.

wie zu anfang dieser szene As at the beginning of this scene.

zart Tenderly, delicately.

zeit Time; duration.

zögernd Slower.

zu The phrases *zu 2, zu 3* (etc.) indicate the number of parts to be played by 2, 3 (etc.) players.

zum In addition.

zurückhaltend Slackening in speed.

zurücktreten To withdraw.

zweihändig With two hands.

Index of Forms and Genres

A roman numeral following a title indicates a movement within the work named.